W9-DHF-752

FREE PRESS
AND
FAIR TRIAL

FREE PRESS
AND
FAIR TRIAL

Donald M. Gillmor

School of Journalism, University of Minnesota

Public Affairs Press, Washington, D.C.

To J. Edward Gerald, *un esprit seminal*

ACKNOWLEDGMENTS

I am indebted to J. Edward Gerald, Professor of Journalism at the University of Minnesota, for stimulating my interest in the law as it relates to mass communications and for giving me the vision of excellence; and to Robert L. Jones, Director of the School of Journalism and Mass Communication, University of Minnesota, for helping to make the writing task so much easier that it might have been.

To Justice Bernard S. Meyer of the Supreme Court of the State of New York I am grateful for a marvelously detailed criticism of an earlier draft, for his generosity in providing research material from his personal files, and for his continuing encouragement and advice. To my friends and colleagues, Gerald Kline and Paul Jess, my sincere thank for yeoman service in researching, updating and rewriting Chapter 14. I am in debt also to colleagues James Barden, Larry Day, Jerry Nelson, William Shaffer and Robert Simmons for applying their professional editing skills to segments of the manuscript.

Donald Brod, Wisconsin State College, is largely responsible for the research and rewriting of Chapter 6, an assignment which he completed with uncommon proficiency.

I wish also to acknowledge the patient assistance of two law school librarians, Mrs Fern O. Day of the University of North Dakota and Miss Arlette M. Soderberg of the University of Minnesota, without whom I could not have undertaken this work. My thanks also to Profs. John Crabb and Paul Matthews of the University of North Dakota Law School—the former for the use of his office, the latter for bringing current legal periodical articles to my attention and for elucidating many points of trial procedure.

I must not forget Prof. Leo. H. Whinery of the University of Oklahoma Law School for his initial suggestions; and Dr. Robert B. Campbell, Professor of Sociology at Southern Illinois University, for his initial help with Chapter 14. To my friend and former colleague

Paul Schmidt, Professor of Journalism and Manager of the North Dakota Press Association, I will always be grateful for wise counsel; and to Prof. William McReynolds of the University of Texas for bibliographic and editorial assistance.

There are others, of course, but foremost among them is my wife, Sophie, to whom I owe so much for her unfailing confidence in my modest abilities and for her unwillingness to complain.

DONALD M. GILLMOR

Minneapolis, Minn.

CONTENTS

"But to wear out our lives in the pursuit of worthy though imperfectly attainable ideals is the essence of human dignity."

Morris Cohen, *Reason and Nature*

CHAPTER 1

RIGHTS IN COLLISION

"For free speech and fair trials are two of the most cherished policies of our civilization, and it would be a trying task to choose between them."—Justice Hugo Black in *Bridges* v. *California*.

In the early morning hours of July 4, 1954, the battered body of Mrs. Samuel Sheppard was found in her comfortable suburban Cleveland home. Her skull had been crushed almost beyond recognition by a heavy instrument.

Although his story was confused and somewhat disconnected, the victim's husband, a prominent young osteopathic surgeon, told of grappling with a burly intruder just before dawn, of being knocked unconscious, and of recovering to find his wife brutally murdered.

There were discrepancies in Dr. Sheppard's story. The intruder, if there had been one, had left no fingerprints; neither the couple's son, Chip, nor the family dog, in a nearby room, had been awakened.

And so began one of the most celebrated murder cases in the annals of American crime. Although his guilt or innocence was not at issue, Sheppard's subsequent conviction was reversed June 6, 1966, by the United States Supreme Court on the grounds that virulent publicity had denied him a fair trial (see Appendix, pages 239-247). Four days later Ohio ordered a new trial, and Dr. Sheppard welcomed the opportunity for vindication.

Sheppard had frantically called for assistance from a friend, the mayor of Bay Village, two hours after detectives estimated the young matron had died. When Mayor Spence Houk and his wife arrived at Sheppard's home, they found him in a dazed condition, apparently suffering from face and neck injuries.

The young physician's story, from which he has not deviated throughout the years, is that he had fallen asleep in his living room after entertaining neighbors the night before, and that while he slept Marilyn had been beaten to death by a "bushy-haired" assailant.

1

Awakened by her cries and loud moans, Sheppard said he grappled with the man and twice had been knocked out.

"As I went up the stairs and into the room," he declared in his trial testimony, "I felt that I could visualize a form of some type . . . I was intercepted or grappled. As I tried to shake loose or strike, I felt I was struck from behind, and my recollection was cut off. I felt that it was a large, relatively large form. The clothing was dark from behind. There was evidence of a good-sized head with a bushy appearance to the top of the head, the hair."

Possibly for lack of tangible evidence, the investigation at first moved slowly. Cleveland newspapers called impatiently for a solution to the crime, and hinted at Sheppard's guilt. Bay Village police were criticized for the way they were handling the case. Sheppard was questioned by police along with other suspects; and his decision to refuse to answer questions except in the presence of his attorney only served to cast further suspicion on him. So did neighborhood gossip that he had wanted to divorce his wife, and that he had had an affair with a pretty hospital technician—an affair that he first denied, but later admitted on the witness stand.

Soon Cleveland newspapers were demanding an inquest. When an inquest was held, it attracted so many newsmen and spectators that it had to be moved to a school auditorium.

In early August the *Cleveland Press* suggested in a prominent headline that "Somebody is Getting Away With Murder" and demanded the arrest of Dr. Sheppard. Subsequent headlines were even more pointed: "Why Isn't Sam Sheppard in Jail?" and "Quit Stalling—Bring Him In."

With 30 of its reporters busily searching for clues, the *Press* became engaged in what it called a sustained effort to see justice done. Hitting hard with headlines and front-page editorials, the newspaper declared that Bay Village officials had balked at arresting their friend and prominent fellow townsman and hinted that it was for this reason that five separate investigations had petered out. The protective ring thrown around the suspect by family, friends, and a five-attorney defense battery was also condemned.

At one point in this newspaper crusade, Louis B. Seltzer, editor of the *Press,* was moved to write in a front-page editorial:

"If ever a murder case was studded with fumbling, halting, stupid, uncooperative bungling . . . politeness to people whose place in this situation completely justified vigorous, prompt and efficient police work—the Sheppard case has them all . . .

"I reached the conclusion that an attempt on the part of influential people, public officials and friends was being made to intrude on the free flow of justice . . .

"We just walked in and raised particular hell. The challenge was too great. There was no reason why the case shouldn't be handled like other murder cases."[1]

The trial, which began in mid-October, lasted 47 days and required two million words in 9,534 pages of transcript. It was reminiscent of the celebrated Lindbergh kidnaping trial. Thousands of tourists flocked to the Sheppards' lake-front home. So crowded was the courtroom with press representatives that for a time there was no room for the 66 veniremen.

Approximately three-quarters of the nation's leading newspapers gave the story front-page play. In Los Angeles, for example, 2,500 miles away, the Sheppard case got second or equal billing to the smog controversy, that city's biggest local story in months. Boston dailies were running at least one front-page picture a day, while Chicago papers were using banner headlines and page-one photos even before the trial began. New York's evening papers and tabloids gave the story the full treatment.

Some reporters became personally involved in the trial. The *New York Post* said of the late Dorothy Kilgallen's coverage for its competitor, the *Journal-American:* "Looking at the headlines [on her stories] . . . it became increasingly difficult to tell the reporters from the principals . . . We momentarily expected to hear that she had been chosen to deliver the summation or, at least, to be a surprise witness."[2]

An international touch was provided by Fabian of Scotland Yard (Inspector Robert, retired) who covered the trial for the Scripps-Howard newspapers. In his final report, Fabian confided that he had made up his mind on hearing testimony that lights were on in the Sheppard home about 2:15 a.m., when "things were happening there." The inspector had no difficulty in imagining Dr. Sam "rushing upstairs in a fury and unmercifully attacking his wife."

Finally, after press and prosecution had exhausted the "other woman" angle, the verdict was delivered: guilty of murder in the second degree. Sheppard was sentenced by Common Pleas Judge Edward Blythin to life imprisonment, with parole possible in 10 years. Within the year, Sheppard's father was dead, and both his mother and his father-in-law had committed suicide.

There were many who retained serious reservations about the role of the press in the proceedings. Everett Norlander, then managing editor of the *Chicago Daily News*, considered the Sheppard story grossly overplayed and in large part "disgraceful." He warned that "the press will be answering its critics for years to come on what it has done with this story."

At the end of the trial, the *Toledo Blade* noted that "the press never left any doubt of the verdict it expected, which was not surprising in view of its having plunged so deep into the process of administering justice by its own rules." Later, in a December 22 editorial, the *Blade* declared that "during the long-drawn-out trial the Cleveland papers, and a good many others, treated it like a Roman holiday. With a man's life at stake, they competed with one another in whipping the evidence up into one sensation after another." The Toledo newspaper emphasized that "a fair trial, involving the age-old struggle of the individual against all-powerful government, is the most basic, the most essential of all human rights." For its efforts in this connection the *Blade* received the Ohio Bar Association's first journalism award for outstanding contributions to the administration of justice.

Defense Counsel William J. Corrigan, himself a former newspaperman, sought unsuccessfully a change of venue, and, later, a new trial. "This is a vicious case," he declared. "There are grounds for a new trial because of prejudice against the defendant, judicial error, admission of inadmissible hearsay evidence and Sam's trial by newspapers."[3] He also failed in an attempt to place in evidence copies of Cleveland and out-of-town newspapers in support of his claim that the case was receiving unprecedented and damaging publicity.

Disagreeing with Corrigan's contention that Dr. Sheppard had been indicted and brought to trial because of editorials in the *Cleveland Press*, Chief Assistant Prosecutor John J. Mahon volunteered a comment which seemed to justify publicity if there was enough of it: "As far as articles in the *Press* go, I have seen many articles, such as the space afforded to Sam Sheppard to tell his side of the story. Statements from his lawyers have appeared in the *Press*, setting forth their position. Many articles beneficial to the defense have appeared. We can't control what's published."[4]

Judge Blythin, denying that error was committed by the court in refusing to grant a change of venue, called attention to the universality of the publicity, and the lack of an issue in the case which would tend to build passion or prejudice. He also felt that articles appearing prior to the arrest bore no relationship to the trial itself. Agreeing with Mahon, he pointed out that the defendant, members of his family, and his counsel were fairly prolific in their statements to the newspapers, and Sheppard's "Own Story" had been headlined in unusually bold type on the front page of one Cleveland paper immediately prior to the trial.[5]

On appeal from the Ohio Court of Appeals to the Supreme Court of Ohio[6]—after six previous attempts—Judge James F. Bell substantially affirmed Judge Blythin's view. In spite of the unparalleled public interest in the case and his concurrence with Sheppard and others that the press had enjoyed a kind of "Roman Holiday," Judge Bell ruled that there was no evidence of partiality on the part of the jury. Indeed, "if the jury system is to remain part of our system of jurisprudence," he wrote, "the courts and litigants must have faith in the inherent honesty of our citizens in performing their duty as jurors courageously and without fear or favor."

Of 75 prospective jurors called only 14 were excused because they had formed a firm opinion as to the guilt or innocence of the defendant, Judge Bell pointed out. Moreover, Sheppard exercised only five of his allotted six peremptory challenges to the jurors. Although the evidence was circumstantial, the jury found no reasonable hypothesis of innocence based on the facts.

Sheppard appealed to the United States Supreme Court and was denied *certiorari* (a hearing) on November 13, 1956. In his brief he complained that on the evening before the trial began Radio Station WHK broadcast a debate between Forrest Allen of the Cleveland *Press* and James Collins, city editor of the Cleveland *Plain Dealer*, on the question of which paper deserved more credit for the indictment. Sheppard also complained of a November 22 television interview on the courthouse steps between Inspector Fabian and the judge, the prosecutor and a detective, at a time when the jurors were arriving. Bay Village, the petition stated, was overrun with reporters, photographers and television men. Every move of the Sheppard family and of officers participating in the investigation were covered; interviews with most anyone who would talk about the case were widely disseminated.

"During the days before the trial," Sheppard's petition continued, "the court had erected inside the bar a long table for the use of reporters; one end of that table was within six inches of the last chair in the jury box; a microphone was installed in front of the witness chair connected to three loud speakers in the courtroom . . . Assigned to newspaper, radio and television personnel were all the available rooms on the courthouse floor, including the assignment room, where cases are assigned to other courtrooms for trial. In these rooms the radio and television stations and newspapers had private

telephone lines installed and all other necessary equipment to carry
on their work. Rooms were also assigned to radio commentators on
the third floor of the Courthouse. This is the floor on which the jury
deliberating rooms are located. One such room located next to the
room occupied by the jury that tried this case was used by Radio
Station WSRS, and broadcasting continued from that room throughout the trial, and during the time the jury was in that room during
recess, and during deliberations of the jury.

"Assembled in the hall outside the courtroom were photographers
from the newspapers and television lights were stationed there,
during the entire trial."

No attention was paid by the trial judge to Sheppard's objections
to being photographed, the petition added. A member of the jury
and her family were photographed in their home. The jury as a group
was constantly televised. There was crowding, confusion and a continuing barrage of questions between sessions.

After this hearing was denied, the Sheppard story was kept alive
in the public mind by 30 "confessions," including one in 1957 by a
petty criminal and narcotics addict arrested in Florida. Although
Cleveland authorities discounted his story, Erle Stanley Gardner
and his *Argosy* magazine "Court of Last Resort" entered the case,
gave the Florida drifter a lie detector test, and concluded he was
telling the truth. Gardner asked the Governor of Ohio to allow
Sheppard to be given a similar test but was refused.

Finally when all possible remedies in the state courts had been
exhausted, Sheppard's attorneys were able to bring a *habeas corpus*
proceeding in a federal court, based on the essential argument that
their client's constitutional right to a fair trial had been violated
by a hostile and irresponsible press.

In this petition it was also charged that Judge Blythin had been
prejudiced against Sheppard, and that his refusal to disqualify himself and to order a change of venue in the face of "massive prejudicial publicity" deprived the accused of a fair trial. An affidavit
to the federal court purported to show that Judge Blythin had told
Miss Kilgallen, shortly before the 1954 trial began, that Sam Sheppard "is guilty as hell," though the *Journal-American* reporter herself had previously decided that Sheppard was innocent.

On July 15, 1964, U.S. District Judge Carl Weinman of Dayton
agreed that Sheppard had not been given a fair trial.[7] In a stinging
86-page rebuke to the trial judge and Cleveland newspapers, Judge
Weinman characterized the trial as a "mockery of justice." After
reviewing five volumes of clippings submitted in evidence, the fed-

eral judge contended that inflammatory and prejudicial reporting by all three Cleveland papers—the *Press*, the *Plain Dealer*, and the *News* (since absorbed by the *Press*)—continually implied Sheppard's guilt. One "cheap sob-sister editorial" in the *Press*, he said, "literally screamed" for conviction.

Prejudice may also have been shown, Judge Weinman declared, by the fact that the newspapers kept running pictures of Judge Blythin, who was up for re-election, and gave him pointed advice on how to conduct the trial. In Weinman's opinion, Judge Blythin should have ordered a change of venue; instead he handed over most of the courtroom space to a hostile press. And, contrary to settled law, he allowed Cleveland police to testify that Sheppard had refused to take a lie detector test, then failed to instruct the jury to disregard that testimony.

Judge Blythin, it was pointed out, failed to question the jury regarding a radio broadcast by Bob Considine which compared Sheppard with Alger Hiss. There was also evidence that two jurors had heard a broadcast by Walter Winchell quoting a woman who said she was Sheppard's mistress. Moreover, while the jurors were deliberating, they were allowed to phone their friends.

"If ever there was a trial by newspapers," said Judge Weinman, "this was a perfect example."[8]

A day after the District Court opinion was delivered, Sheppard was released from the Ohio Penitentiary. This time the press rejoiced, for by the end of the week the handsome physician had married Mrs. Ariane Tebbenjohanns, a svelte German divorcee who had corresponded with him while he was in prison. It was a good story, but its mood could not be sustained. Ten months later the 6th U.S. Court of Appeals, over a vigorous dissent, reversed the District Court and ordered Sheppard to resume serving his life sentence. Appellate courts traditionally deal with questions of law, not fact; but in this case the Court of Appeals took issue with the factual content of Judge Weinman's decision and his presumption that the jurors ignored the trial judge's instructions not to read the newspapers.[8a]

Ironically, Sheppard would have been eligible for parole in late 1964. But a parole would leave the guilty verdict unchanged, and Sheppard sought exoneration.

In his second petition to the United States Supreme Court Sheppard reiterated that the press so violated his constitutional right to a fair trial that no impartial jury could have been impaneled to try him. He also claimed that the trial judge failed to protect jurors from outside influences and assigned nearly all the seats in the courtroom to newspaper reporters. On November 15, 1965, the court agreed to review his conviction.

Joined by the Ohio Civil Liberties Union, the American Civil Liberties Union subsequently filed a "friend of the Court" brief urging "the constitutional invalidation of the conviction . . . because the trial court failed to protect the accused from the inherently prejudicial publicity which saturated the community." The brief cited: (1) damaging publicity describing prosecution evidence which varied materially from that introduced by the prosecution at the trial, (2) damaging publicity describing prosecution evidence which would have been inadmissible in court, (3) publicity which made celebrities of the trial jurors, and (4) the accusatory publicity which charged the guilt or attacked the character of the accused. Sheppard's appeal, the brief concluded, gave the Supreme Court an opportunity "to correct at last an egregious denial of criminal due process."

In their arguments before the Supreme Court on February 28, 1966 Sheppard's lawyer, F. Lee Bailey of Boston, and Ohio's Attorney General, William B. Saxbe, differed on the effect of press coverage on the trial, but they agreed that the responsibility for preventing "trial by newspaper" from contaminating juries should be borne by judges, prosecutors and policemen and not by the press. Bailey conceded that a decision in favor of Sheppard would mean that for the first time the Court had struck down a conviction for prejudicial newspaper publicity without proof that any juror had been affected by it. Saxbe countered that to allow Sheppard to attack his conviction with an emotional issue that obscured the overwhelming proof of guilt would be to subvert the jury system.

In its 8-1 decision—Justice Hugo Black dissenting without comment—the Supreme Court agreed substantially with Sheppard's attorney. The trial court erred, said Justice Tom C. Clark in the sole majority opinion, in assuming that it lacked power to control publicity about the trial. Clark censured Judge Blythin for failing to use judicial procedures such as locking up the jury when the publicity got out of hand.

Noting that the Court "has been unwilling to place any direct limitations on the freedom traditionally exercised by the news media," Clark's opinion is nevertheless a detailed indictment of Cleveland journalism, although some of the press practices he deplored—for example, the presentation of Sheppard's statements, identification of veniremen and photography outside the courtroom—are well within accepted professional limits.

Implying bias where bedlam is created by the press, the Court's decision requires judicial control of the news flow on the assumption that editorial judgment is deficient. In consequence it is now incumbent upon the press to reappraise its role in regard to the administration of justice.

While the Sheppard case is a milestone in the search for a higher level of press-bar performance in criminal cases, it is not the first time the Court has addressed itself to the difficult question of how to assure the rights of free press and fair trial.

THE CASE OF "MAD DOG" IRVIN

On April 8, 1955, parolee Leslie Irvin was arrested by Indiana State Police on suspicion of burglary and bad check writing. A few days later the Vanderburgh county prosecutor and Evansville police officials issued press releases stating that "Mad Dog" Irvin had confessed to six murders—including three members of one family—committed between December 1954 and March 1955 in the Evansville area.

A grand jury indictment was returned in the Vanderburgh Circuit Court on April 21. Shortly thereafter, Irvin's court-appointed attorney filed a motion for a change of venue to escape what he called the impassioned atmosphere of Vanderburgh county. The motion was granted, but only to adjoining Gibson county where inflammatory publicity was probably no less intense and extensive. A second change of venue was then sought to a county sufficiently removed from the Evansville locality that a fair trial would be possible; but this was denied because an Indiana statute allows only a single change of venue. Nevertheless, the motion was renewed two additional times on the grounds that it was impossible to find jurors who did not have fixed opinions that Irvin was guilty.

The trial began on November 14. Of 430 prospective jurors examined under *voir dire*,[9] 370 said they believed Irvin guilty. The defendant's attorney exhausted all of his peremptory challenges and when 12 jurors were finally accepted by the court, he unsuccessfully challenged all of them for alleged bias, complaining particularly that four, in their *voir dire* examination, had said they believed Irvin was guilty as charged. Several motions for a continuance were also denied. Irvin was found guilty and sentenced to death.

On January 19, 1956, Irvin's lawyer filed a motion for a new trial, specifying 415 grounds of error which, in his opinion, amounted to a denial of federal constitutional rights. The night before this motion was filed, Irvin escaped from the Gibson county jail; three weeks later he was taken into custody in California and returned to the Indiana State Prison.

In the meantime the trial court had overruled the motion on the grounds that Irvin was an escapee when it was filed and was, in fact, still at large and therefore not within the jurisdiction of the County Circuit Court. Under Indiana law such a motion had to be filed within 30 days of the verdict, and, while he was a fugitive, Irvin's time had run out.

The Indiana Supreme Court affirmed the denial of the motion for a new trial.[10] Irvin then applied to the Federal District Court for a writ of *habeas corpus* under federal law, but that court dismissed his application on the ground that he had not exhausted all remedies available to him in the state courts; and the Court of Appeals affirmed that decision. Both federal courts, in agreement with the Indiana Supreme Court, emphasized that Irvin's motion for a new trial had been properly denied because he was a fugitive at the time it was made,[11] even though the state court had given a good deal of attention to the substance of Irvin's "due process" appeal.

Irvin's appeal on the constitutional question of a denial of due process was then carried to the United States Supreme Court and upheld in a 5-4 decision reversing the Court of Appeals and remanding the case for a decision on its merits. The Supreme Court held that the doctrine of exhaustion of state remedies did not bar resort to federal *habeas corpus* if the petitioner had obtained a decision on his constitutional claims from the highest court of a state, as Irvin had, even though the state court might have based the crux of its decision on other grounds: the fact that the accused was an escapee when his original motion was made.[12] The Court of Appeals reconsidered the case and ruled against Irvin once again. Irvin then brought a second appeal to the United States Supreme Court.

This time in a unanimous decision, the Supreme Court considered Irvin's constitutional claims solely in terms of prejudicial news reporting and concluded that Irvin had not been accorded a fair and impartial trial, that he should have been granted a second change of venue, an Indiana statute notwithstanding, and that, in the circumstances of the case, it was the duty of the United States Court of Appeals to evaluate independently the *voir dire* testimony of the jurors.[13]

It is not required, said Justice Tom C. Clark, speaking for the court, that jurors be totally ignorant of the facts and issues involved, and scarcely any of those best qualified to serve will not have formed some impression or opinion as to the merits of the case. "To hold that the mere existence of any preconceived notions as to the guilt or innocence of an accused, without more," he declared, "is sufficient to rebut the presumption of a prospective juror's impartiality would be to establish an impossible standard. It is sufficient if the juror can lay aside his impression or opinion and render a verdict based on the evidence presented in court."[14]

Every appeal of this kind being of mixed law and fact, the Supreme Court held, would have to be decided on its merits, with the federal judge bearing the responsibility of evaluating independently the *voir dire* testimony of the impaneled jurors and of setting aside findings of impartiality where prejudice is manifest.

And here the community showed a "pattern of deep and bitter prejudice." Curbstone speculation on Irvin's guilt, and on what his punishment should be, dominated press coverage of the case. His past record as a juvenile offender, arsonist, burglar, and army deserter was prominently headlined, and he was described as the remorseless "confessed slayer of six." News stories emphasized the anger of the community by reporting that Irvin's lawyer was subjected to much criticism for being willing to defend him. In a disdainful tone one newspaper editorial rationalized the attorney's participation on the grounds that he would be subject to disbarment if he refused to represent the defendant.

"With such an opinion permeating their minds," Justice Clark concluded, "it would be difficult to say that each could exclude this preconception of guilt from his deliberations. The influence that lurks in an opinion once formed is so persistent that it unconsciously fights detachment from the mental processes of the average man. When one's life is at stake—and accounting for the frailties of human nature —we can only say that in the light of circumstances here the finding of impartiality does not meet constitutional standards . . . With his life at stake, it is not requiring too much that petitioner be tried in an atmosphere undisturbed by so huge a wave of public passion and a jury other than one in which two-thirds of the members admit, before hearing any testimony, to possessing a belief in his guilt."[15]

For the first time, the United States Supreme Court had reversed a state criminal conviction solely on the grounds that prejudicial pre-trial publicity had made a fair trial before an impartial jury impossible. The case was remanded to the District Court and Irvin was retried by the State of Indiana in a less emotional atmosphere.

Irvin was found guilty and sentenced to life imprisonment—a sentence for which he confided to his attorney, he was grateful.

A week earlier, in *Janko* v. *United States*,[16] the Supreme Court, exercising its supervisory power to formulate and apply proper standards of enforcement of the criminal law in the federal courts, reversed a conviction because a single newspaper article in the St. Louis *Post-Dispatch* linked the defendant in an income tax evasion trial to a local "rackets boss" and described him as a "former convict." A defense motion for a mistrial had been denied, but the trial court had repeatedly warned jurors not to read such articles and to disregard anything of this nature that might have come to their attention.

"In the light of the character of the extraneous information contained in the article," said the Court, "we think that, before the jury was finally discharged, the trial court should have assured itself as to whether the jurors had in fact read the article." Instead, when the guilty verdict was returned, the jury was asked a general question —had any juror been influenced by anything that happened outside the courtroom?—a question which begged a negative reply.

Since it was not clear that Janko had been found guilty by a jury "uninfluenced by material plainly prejudicial on its face," the judgment was reversed and the case remanded for a new trial.

Justice Felix Frankfurter, in one of his many emphatic warnings to the press, said in his concurring opinion in the *Irvin* case that *Janko* was reversed because prejudicial publicity had poisoned the outcome—and the Court, he added, was not yet convinced that "the poisoner is constitutionally protected in plying his trade."[17]

PEOPLE V. VAN DUYNE

A Paterson, New Jersey, construction worker, Louis Van Duyne, was arrested in April 1963 on a charge of beating his young wife to death. The story was not an unusual one. After visiting a number of taverns, the 27-year-old husband came to an apartment where his estranged wife was living, chased her out into an alley, and beat her to death. He was tried, convicted and sentenced to life imprisonment.

Van Duyne appealed his conviction partly on the grounds of improper and prejudicial stories having appeared in local newspapers while the jury was being drawn. One such story in the October 7 issue of the *Paterson Evening News* duly noted that "the state is seeking the death sentence for the construction worker accused of brutally beating to death his estranged wife," and added: "Van Duyne was nabbed in a phone booth a short time later. Police quoted him as saying, 'You've got me for murder. I don't desire to tell you anything'." Copies of the paper containing these statements were found in the jurors' assembly room.

The next morning defense counsel brought to the attention of the court the fact that copies of the *Paterson Morning Call* were circulating among the jury panel. Included in the morning story was the following paragraph: "According to police, Van Duyne had been arrested at least 10 times and had once threatened to 'kill a cop.' Authorities reported that after his arrest Van Duyne beat up a man during the summer of 1962 and then threatened Detective William Toomen with a gun." The trial judge ordered the jurors to be locked up "to eliminate any further contact with the press."

The New Jersey Supreme Court[18] could not find in the record sufficient evidence to indicate that newspaper articles had of themselves prevented a fair trial or that they had so infected the minds of some of the jurors as to leave them biased against the defendant. Van Duyne's conviction was affirmed. But the court decided in its November 16, 1964 ruling that it would take no such chances in the future. Included in the decision was an order that police, prosecutors and defense attorneys must not release to the press any information concerning confessions or damaging admissions by a defendant. The court order also prohibited references to an accused's prior criminal record. Theoretically offending officers of the court can be punished under Canons 5 and 20 of the American Bar Association's Code of Judicial Ethics, which generally forbid the leaking of such information; but the Canons have never been enforced even in those states which have adopted them.

In the eyes of the press the New Jersey ruling simply created a news blackout between the arrest and the beginning of the trial. And it is not clear whether the press itself can be punished for digging up its own information, particularly in light of the fact that New Jersey law does not require a reporter to reveal the source of his information.

"The court's intent—to guarantee a fair trial to the defendant and to the state—is admirable but it misses its mark . . .," said the *Bergen Record*. "No one will quarrel with the court's complaint that there have been excesses in crime reporting, that the sensationalist press has played up crime news out of proportion. This new order will not stop that segment of the press from printing rumor. . . . It will instead deny to the legitimate press fulfillment of the responsibility it has to report to the rest of the community all the news factually, completely and quickly. . . . For police and defense lawyers to be encouraged to operate in a vacuum is to encourage still further restrictions of the public's right to know."

The *Trenton Evening Times*, in an editorial, posed these questions:
(1) Will court officers be encouraged by the ruling to conceal facts
which should be made public? (2) Is it the intent of the court that
the public should not be told that a suspect has a long criminal record? (3) Should a defendant, classified as a "public enemy," be
shielded as carefully as another who might be experiencing his first
brush with the law?

In its November 24, 1964 issue, the *Camden Courier-Post* said that
a newspaper reporter will be bound by his conscience to make the
record of a convicted criminal known to his editor. Furthermore, the
public should have information that a habitually vicious criminal,
free on bail pending trial, has a record of assaults upon the innocent.

The court's ruling failed to take account of the earnest efforts of
the news media to strike a just balance between free press and fair
trial, said the *Newark Evening News* in an editorial. "It would be
unfortunate if the court's efforts were used by law enforcement officers to conceal facts of legitimate public concern, something many of
them are only too anxious to do anyway."

Although no meeting of the minds has been reached between press
and bar on this vexing question, the *New York Times* thought the
New Jersey Supreme Court had taken "bold and constructive action
to combat longstanding evil." The *Times* said that the ruling placed
the main burden of responsibility where it properly belongs—on the
officials and members of the bar who disclose pre-trial information.
"Once the police and members of the bar recognize that prejudicial
statements about a defendant are unethical and unprofessional behavior," the *Times* continued, "then sources for this kind of news will
dry up for all of the press, and the problem will largely disappear."

Anthony Lewis, then Supreme Court reporter for the *Times*, thought
the alternative to the Van Duyne decision would be to prevent pre-
trial comment the British way—to punish the press under a contempt
power which was inconsistent with American constitutional norms.
The New Jersey rule, said Lewis, will require a "drastic change in
lawyers' and policemen's ingrained habit of talking with the press."

Jacob Schaad, Jr., a reporter for the *Paterson Evening News*, questioned the effectiveness of the restrictions in terms of reality. "In the
15 years this reporter has covered the courts," he wrote in his weekly
column, "he has learned the greatest method of communication since
Alexander Graham Bell invented the telephone is the courthouse grapevine. It seems that within seconds after a story breaks at the courthouse the boys at Bickford's are talking about it. That's a good three

blocks from the courthouse and even carrier pigeou couldn't do that well."

For Van Duyne's lawyer, Heyman Zimel, the New Jersey Supreme Court ruling had won him a principle but lost him a case. His client remains in prison.[19]

CHAPTER 2

THE OSWALD CASE

"The trouble with crime and punishment as it concerns the press is that it is too interesting and too absorbing and too convincing because it comes out of real life."—Walter Lippmann.

The Sheppard, Irvin and Van Duyne cases serve to bring into sharp focus the 35-year-old confrontation between lawyers and newsmen in their defense of two fundamental rights: the Sixth Amendment's guarantee that in all criminal prosecutions the accused shall enjoy trial by an impartial jury; and the First Amendment's guarantee of free speech and press.

The conflict was intensified by the tragedy of President John F. Kennedy's assassination and the events which followed it. Two weeks after the President's death, the American Civil Liberties Union concluded in a formal statement that had Lee Harvey Oswald lived, he would have been deprived of all opportunity for a fair trial due to the conduct of police and prosecuting officers in Dallas, under pressure from the public and news media.

From the moment of his arrest until his murder two days later, said the ACLU,[1] Oswald was repeatedly tried and convicted in the newspapers, on radio and television by the public statements of Dallas law enforcement officials. As the investigation uncovered one piece of evidence after another, the results were immediately relayed to the public. Oswald's guilt was stated without qualification. The cumulative effect of these public pronouncements was to imprint indelibly on the public mind the conclusion that Oswald was indeed the slayer. Where in Dallas or anywhere else in the country, asked the ACLU, could there be found twelve citizens who had not formed a firm and fixed opinion that he was guilty?

After weighing the right of free press, in terms of the right of the public to be informed, against the right of an accused to a fair trial,

16

the ACLU concluded that the right of fair trial was paramount. The police had erred by capitulating to the glare of publicity and public clamor, and in arranging Oswald's transfer from the city to the county jail to suit the convenience of the news media. The media had erred in not curbing their pressing demands upon the police to publicize the case.

On December 1, 1963, seven Harvard University law professors, in a letter to the *New York Times*, added their criticism of the public spectacle that had been permitted in the Dallas police station, "with its halls and corridors jammed with a noisy, milling throng of reporters and cameramen." A portion of their statement follows:

"Precisely because the President's assassination was the ultimate in defiance of law it called for the ultimate in vindication of law. The law enforcement agencies, in permitting virtually unlimited access to the news media, made this impossible. Not only would it have been virtually impossible to impanel a jury which had not formed its own views on those facts which might come before it, but much of the information released, such as statements by Mrs. Oswald, might have been legally inadmissible at trial.

"It is ironic that the very publicity which had already made it virtually impossible for Oswald to be tried and convicted by a jury meeting constitutional standards of impartiality should, in the end, have made such trial unnecessary.

"We cannot comfort ourselves with the notion that this could happen only in Dallas. It is too frequently a feature of our process of criminal justice that it is regarded as a public carnival. And this reflects our general obsession that everybody has a right immediately to know and see everything, that reporters and TV cameras must be omnipresent, that justice must take a second place behind the public's immediate 'right to be informed' about every detail of a crime. . . .

"As long as we adhere to that notion, and as long as our legislatures and courts are unwilling to protect the processes of justice, we must recognize that the lamentable behavior of the Dallas law enforcement agencies and of the communications media reflect a flaw in ourselves as a society."

In an accompanying editorial the *New York Times* agreed on the ground that televising the trial of Jack Ruby on a charge of murdering Oswald would simply compound the grave errors committed in Dallas. A trial is not meant to provide the public with recreation or the indignities of a national show, said the *Times*, and "when these two duties conflict, we have no hesitation in saying that fair trial should take precedence over publicity." Earlier, the *Times* had expressed its regret in having initially referred to Oswald as the "murderer" without the attendant adjective "alleged."

These views were given greater currency and weight when the Warren Commission reprimanded the Dallas police department for its frantic impromptu press conferences which conveyed misinformation, hearsay evidence, and conjecture to the voracious news media. By divulging specific items of evidence linking Oswald to the killing of the President and Officer Tippit, the prospective jury was given the opportunity of prejudging the very questions that would be raised at the trial.

Some of this evidence would have been inadmissible, said the Warren Report. For example, although Oswald's wife could not have been compelled to testify against him, District Attorney Henry Wade announced before television cameras that Marina Oswald had affirmed her husband's ownership of a rifle like the one found on the sixth floor of the Texas School Book Depository. Moreover, it turned out that Wade was wrong when he said that paraffin tests showed Oswald had fired a gun. The tests merely showed that he had nitrate traces on his hands, which did not necessarily mean that he had fired anything. Police Chief Jesse E. Curry publicized the inadmissible fact that Oswald had refused to take a lie detector test; and on Saturday he reported that "we are sure of our case." Police Captain J. Will Fritz reported that the case against Oswald was "cinched."

Undoubtedly the public was interested in these disclosures, said the Warren Commission Report in understatement. It was proper that the public know which agencies were participating in the investigation and the rate at which their work was progressing. The public was also entitled to know that Oswald had been apprehended and that the state had gathered evidence against him sufficient to support a murder indictment, that he was being held pending action of the grand jury, that the investigation was continuing, and that no additional evidence had been found to indicate that anyone else was involved in either slaying.

But public curiosity, the Report continued, was not to be satisfied at the expense of the accused's right to a trial by an impartial jury. The courtroom, not the newspaper or television screen, is the appropriate forum in our system for the trial of a man accused of a crime.

Conditions at the Dallas police station were likened to Grand Central Station at rush hour and Yankee Stadium during the World Series. In the lobby of the third floor, television cameramen set up two large cameras and floodlights in strategic positions that gave them a sweep of the corridor in either direction. Technicians stretched their television cables into and out of offices, running some of them out the windows of a deputy chief's office and down the side of a building. Men with newsreel cameras, still cameras, and microphones, more mobile than television camermen, moved back and forth seeking information and opportunities for interviews. Newsmen wandered into the offices of other bureaus located on the third floor, sat on desks, and used police telephones; one reporter admitted hiding a telephone behind a desk so that he would have exclusive access to it if something developed.

By the time Chief Curry returned to the building in mid-afternoon from Love Field where he had escorted President Johnson from Parkland Hospital, he found that "there was just pandemonium on the third floor." The news representatives, he testified, "were jammed into the north hall of the third floor, which are the offices of the criminal investigation division. The television trucks, there were several of them around the city hall. I went into my administrative offices, I saw cables coming through the administrative assistant office and through the deputy chief of traffic through his office, and running through the hall they had a live TV set up on the third floor, and it was a bedlam of confusion."

The corridor became so jammed that policemen and newsmen had to push and shove if they wanted to get through, stepping over cables, wires, and tripods. The crowd in the hallway was so dense that District Attorney Wade found it a "strain to get the door open" to get into the homicide office. Police efforts to control the newsmen were unavailing. According to one detective, "they would be asked to stand back and stay back but it wouldn't do much good, and they would push forward and you had to hold them off physically."

On most occasions, Oswald's escort of three to six detectives and policemen had to push their way through the newsmen who sought to surround the suspect. Although the Dallas press normally did not take pictures of a prisoner without first obtaining permission of the police, who generally consulted with the prisoner, this practice was not followed by any of the newsmen with Oswald. Generally when Oswald appeared the newsmen turned their cameras on him, held microphones close to his face, and shouted questions at him.

Oswald's most prolonged exposure occurred at the midnight press conference on Friday night. In response to demands of newsmen, District Attorney Wade, after consulting with Chief Curry and Captain Fritz, had announced shortly before midnight that Oswald would appear at a press conference in the basement assembly room. An estimated 70 to 100 persons, including Jack Ruby, and other unauthorized individuals, crowded into the small downstairs room. No identification was required. The room was so packed that Deputy Chief M. W. Stevenson and Captain Fritz who came down to the basement after the crowd had assembled could not get in and were forced to remain in the doorway.

Chief Curry had instructed reporters that they were not to "ask any questions and try to interview . . . [Oswald] in any way," but when he was brought into the room, "immediately they began to shoot questions at him and shove microphones into his face." It was difficult to hear Oswald's answers above the uproar. Cameramen stood on the tables to take pictures and others pushed forward to get close-ups. The noise and confusion mounted as reporters shouted at each other to get out of the way and cameramen made frantic efforts to get into position for pictures. After Oswald had been in the room only a few minutes, Chief Curry intervened and directed that Oswald be taken back to the jail because, he testified, the newsmen "tried to overrun him."

It is generally agreed that the news media did a remarkably skillful and comprehensive job in providing the American people with almost instant information on the events which were unfolding in Dallas. But their badgering of the police, their aggressiveness in demanding information, and their ignoring of instructions require them to share in the responsibility for the failure in law enforcement which resulted in Oswald's death. The Warren Report concluded: "The promulgation of a code of professional conduct governing representatives of all news media would be welcome evidence that the press had profited by the lesson of Dallas. The burden of insuring that appropriate action is taken to establish ethical standards of conduct for the news media must also be borne, however, by State and local governments, by the bar, and ultimately by the public. The experience in Dallas during November 22-24 is a dramatic affirmation of the need for steps to bring about a proper balance between the right of the public to be kept informed and the right of the individual to a fair and impartial trial."[2]

In immediate response to the Warren Commission's Report, representatives of professional newspaper and broadcasting organizations met in Washington to consider what should be done. One result has been the recommendation by a Joint Media Committee on News Coverage Problems of a voluntary pooling policy for the "orderly, efficient and unobtrusive coverage" of news events such as those that occurred in Dallas, Little Rock, at the University of Mississippi, and during Khrushchev's visit to the United States. In the latter case, it has been estimated that the Columbia Broadcasting System alone used 65 cameras and 375 cameramen and technicians. James Reston of the *New York Times* has expressed the view that there were so many newsmen reporting the Soviet leader's 1959 visit that they changed the course of events. Reporters, rather than playing the role of obscure witnesses of history, became the principal characters in the drama. Newsmen, photographers and their entourages constituted a large proportion of the eager, milling throng which constantly surrounded the Russian visitor. Moscow propagandists were pleased, for who could tell the difference between a working reporter and a Nikita fan.

The widely circulated pooling proposals, recommending numbers and priorities of reporters and photographers for various kinds of events, appear to have the endorsement of the directors of leading professional and news organizations. There have long been standard pooling procedures for coverage of a traveling President, military installations, scientific establishments, and for the coverage of events from parade vehicles or small observation booths. But these are seldom the "problem" situations which arise rarely but spectacularly. The Joint Committee also recommends that authorities in charge of newsworthy events accept a greater degree of responsibility for the formulation of common sense provisions for orderly coverage.

Another response to the Warren Report has been the formulation by the American Bar Association of a three-year, $750,000 study of the responsibility of bar, police and press in assuring a fair trial. And the ABA has joined the American Society of Newspaper Editors, the American Newspaper Publishers Association, broadcasters and press photographers in introspective seminars on the free press-fair trial problem.

The Oswald case may be too monumental and atypical a case to serve as a focal point for a press-bar entente. After a year-long study, the Press-Bar Committee of the American Society of Newspaper Editors concluded in the spring of 1965 that it could not accept the major assertions of the Warren Report concerning press performance. Whatever may be said about the propriety of police and prosecuting officers in Dallas in publicizing facts and falsehoods about the assassination and the suspect, said the editors' Committee, the press performed as reporter, not initiator. To the extent the information purveyed by these officials was accurate, to that extent the press reports were accurate. The press originated no false reports; what rumors there were stemmed logically—not illogically—from information made public by law enforcement officials; they were not originated by the press.

Moreover, the Committee added, Dallas had a policy of cooperation between police and news media; officers were instructed to cooperate with the press. But the upper limits of such assistance had not been set down. Nor were the rights of privacy well defined by custom in the Texas metropolis. If the press does not originate rumors, what would be a responsible policy in disseminating them? Is it not those false and conflicting initial reports which keep conspiracy theories alive?

It was not, of course, mere public curiosity that demanded satisfaction in the Oswald case. The matter was as essential to the citizens of the Republic as any other that can be imagined. Was there time to wait for the winnowing and sifting of fact and error? It is terrifying to contemplate what forms fanatical segments of public opinion might have taken had there been a news blackout, or had only disconnected bits of information been released before the conclusion of Oswald's trial.

Bradley S. Greenberg and Edwin B. Parker, in their collection of essays and research reports on the assassination,[3] find cumulative evidence to support the hypothesis that public fear during the dreadful hours following the President's death was minimized by quick, reassuring information from the mass media. They conclude that "fear and anxiety might have been magnified to the point of hysteria" if news reports following the assassination had not been so reassuring and had not quickly informed people "that the functions of government were being carried out smoothly, that there was no conspiracy, and that there was no further threat."

The political atmosphere of Dallas generated untold erroneous assumptions. But the fact remains that there was no Oswald trial: the role of the police in providing a public setting for his murder before television cameras will be debated for a long time to come.

There have been other important developments in the free press-fair trial debate, though they are less momentous than those tragic events of late November 1963.

CHAPTER 3

THE CAMERA IN THE COURTROOM

"[T]he question on which the Court disagreed is essentially whether the prejudicial potential of televised trials is so uncontrollable and extensive that a violation of due process must follow even when no showing of actual prejudice can be made, and, if so, whether this property of television is so inherent that there is no reason to risk further experimentation."—Dexter Peacock and Don Teague[1]

On September 30, 1937, shortly after the trial of Bruno Hauptmann in the Lindbergh kidnaping case, the American Bar Association adopted Canon 35 of its Judicial Ethics in the following form: "Proceedings in court should be conducted with fitting dignity and decorum. The taking of photographs in the courtroom during sessions of the court or recesses between sessions, and the broadcasting of court proceedings are calculated to detract from the essential dignity of the proceedings, degrade the court and create misconceptions with respect thereto in the mind of the public and should not be permitted."

Canon 35 was amended in 1952 to include television. All states, with the exception of Colorado, Oklahoma and Texas, have adopted Canon 35, or some modifications of it, by statute or by court rules, although court rules do not seem to be binding on state court judges. Rule 53 of the Federal Rules of Criminal Procedure keeps cameras out of federal courtrooms.

Since 1954 numerous bar-media conferences have aired the subject, but the bar has stood fast in its objections to the broadcasting media in the courtroom, compromising only to the extent of deleting from the original statement the provocative phrases "are calculated to" and "degrade the court."

Canon 35 has been reaffirmed in a recent resolution of the Judicial Conference of the United States and in the Supreme Court's decision in the Billie Sol Estes case.

Even the more liberal jurists have rejected the view that the public's right to know entitles the press to broadcast or photograph judicial proceedings. Justice William O. Douglas, for example, has maintained that such coverage imperils fair trial because of the "insidious influences which it puts to work in the administration of justice." The historic concept of a public trial, he says, envisages a small close gathering, not a city-wide, state-wide or nation-wide arena. The television camera would place added tension upon witnesses, and such a strained atmosphere would not be conducive to the quiet search for truth. Unimportant miniscules of the whole would be depicted, says Douglas, and they would be the sensational moments. Judges and lawyers would be tempted to play to the galleries.[2]

In its June 1965 ruling reversing Billie Sol Estes's conviction on a charge of swindling because his trial had been televised, the Supreme Court expressed similar fears.[3] Basing his argument on the premise that fair trial is the most fundamental of all freedoms, Justice Tom C. Clark, in his majority opinion, closed the courtroom doors to television cameras—at least for the immediate future. He was joined by Justices Douglas and Arthur Goldberg.

Prejudice is inherent in a televised trial, said Clark. It could have a prejudicial impact on jurors, witnesses, trial judge, and on the defendant himself. It is not necessary, Clark added, to show precise instances of prejudice caused by television.

Chief Justice Earl Warren, in a vigorous concurring opinion which included seven photographs purporting to show the confusion created by television cameras at the preliminary hearing, concluded that (1) "the telecasting of trials diverts the trial from its proper purpose in that it has an inevitable impact on all the trial participants; (2) it gives the public the wrong impression about the purpose of trials, thereby detracting from the dignity of court proceedings and lessening the reliability of trials; and (3) it singles out certain defendants and subjects them to trials under prejudicial conditions not experienced by others." Moreover, the Chief Justice declared, "To permit this powerful medium to use the trial process itself to influence the opinions of vast numbers of people, before a verdict of guilt or innocence has been rendered, would be entirely foreign to our system of justice."

Justice John Marshall Harlan, voting with the five-man majority, said he would favor future experimentation with the new medium, although he conceded that the "mischievous potentialities" of courtroom television had clearly been at work in the Estes case.

Justices Potter Stewart, Hugo Black, William Brennan and Byron White dissented, partly because they agreed with Harlan that some latitude should be provided for television's future role, and partly because the specific circumstances of the Estes case did not indicate that the defendant had been denied his constitutional rights. Speaking for the minority, Stewart said that "it is important to remember that we move in an area touching the realm of free communication, and for that reason, if for no other, I would be wary of imposing any *per se* rule which, in the light of future technology, might serve to stifle or abridge true First Amendment rights." In effect, Stewart did not wish to escalate the case into constitutional doctrine, for, in his words, "the Constitution does not make us arbiters of the image that a televised state criminal trial projects to the public."

In the judgment of some critics of the Court, including the writer of this book, there was much poppycock in the majority opinions in the Estes case. Television coverage of a trial need not necessarily imply either notoriety or morbid public interest. The public interest may be legitimate. If paid sponsorship is necessary for such coverage, and there is doubt that it is, Justice Clark's notion that this kind of support will have a direct bearing on a juror's vote as to guilt or innocence is idle speculation. And in his commentary on the publicity-mindedness and obsequiousness of the Estes trial judge, Chief Justice Warren impugns that judge's professional competence more than he persuades us of an inherent evil in television coverage or in the scrutiny of a wider public. Certainly the Chief Justice's analogy to a football game with its noisy prognosticators, to the television quiz scandals, to Castro's stadium trials, and to the Soviet Union's trial of Francis Gary Powers does no honor to American journalism; nor is it a credit to the process of judicial reasoning.

Justice Clark's dependence on *Rideau* v. *Louisiana*[4] in his majority opinion seems inappropriate. In that case a 1961 murder suspect was interviewed in jail by a sheriff and their conversation was recorded on sound film. Later that day the filmed interview was broadcast over a Lake Charles, Louisiana, television station and thousands of people in the community heard the suspect confess to murder, bank robbery and kidnaping. Wilbert Rideau was convicted and sentenced to death. Three members of the jury which convicted him admitted, when challenged by his lawyer, that they had tuned in on the interview. A request to have them excused was denied. The conviction was affirmed by the Supreme Court of Louisiana. On appeal to the United States Supreme Court, Rideau's conviction was reversed and Justice Stewart, writing the Court's opinion, said that the televised interview was in fact Rideau's trial: "Any subsequent court proceedings in a community so pervasively exposed to such a spectacle could be but a hollow formality." Rideau was retried, convicted and is now under sentence of death.

The Rideau and Estes cases, in the judgment of Justice Stewart, had nothing in common.

The most surprising characteristic of the majority opinions (especially that of the Chief Justice), is their vague and undefined references to "solemn decorum" and "essential dignity," phrases used at least as frequently as the "public's right to know" to cover up rather well defined vested interests. Weak defenses encourage bold attacks.

Fred Rodell, Yale law professor and long-time student of the Supreme Court, has aptly expressed the alienation he and others feel in regard to judicial preoccupation with ceremonial pretense: "Much of the respect, even awe, in which law and lawyers are generally held by laymen has its source in the aura of solemnity which surrounds the craft from the ponderous language to the musty lawbooks that line lawyers' offices, to, especially, the almost religious ritual of the courtroom itself. The late Judge Jerome Frank used to ridicule this ceremonial solemnity—of architecture, of judges' uniforms, of standardized and stiffly formal court procedure—with a symbolic phrase, 'the cult of the robe.' But he knew that judges and lawyers loved it because it made them and their work, however trivial on occasion, look important and impressive. The idea of opening a courtroom, like a ballpark or convention hall, to television offends much of the profession less because of a fear of unfair trials than because of a fear of detracting from the dignity of the court—and of themselves."[5]

Judge J. Skelly Wright of the United States Court of Appeals for the District of Columbia agrees with Prof. Rodell. Some of our most dignified ceremonies, including church services and presidential inaugurations are televised; Pope Paul didn't find Yankee Stadium inappropriate for a televised mass on his recent visit to New York. "There's nothing solid to this objection," says Judge Wright. "It's all mist." After six days of hearings amid demonstrations, Justice Otto Moore of the Colorado Supreme Court could find no reason to bar modern camera equipment from the courtroom.[6] "That which is carried out with dignity," he concluded, "will not become undignified because more people may be permitted to see and hear."

All objections to the camera in the courtroom may not be invalid. When a University of Illinois teacher of broadcast news dared to ask broadcasters at a May 17, 1964, conference to justify their demands for access to courtrooms, he was greeted with disbelief. Prof. Harry Skornia asked the broadcasters what would seem to be basic questions: How much time would the average newsroom have to spend in covering court trials in full? What is to be done with broadcast executives who equate television news with show business? And how would top management react to testimony in anti-trust suits and litigation involving corporate friends? The Kohler Company hearings in Washington a few years ago, for example, were televised in the morning when management was testifying; yet when labor and Walter Reuther testified in the afternoon, the cameras were strangely absent. The program was sponsored by the National Association of Manufacturers.

Prof. Skornia fears that newsmen would be unable to control what might become courtroom "productions." And big, expensive productions require news, even if it is "made news." (Homer Bigart of the *New York Times*, when covering racial troubles in Little Rock, noted how docile students became a hooting, violent mob when egged on by an irresponsible television crew.)

Not all the broadcasters who attended the aforementioned conference appreciated Skornia's innuendo. One promised never to send his son to the University of Illniois; another shouted from the floor that there was not a broadcast newsroom in Illinois that took orders from its sales department. But such an ideal is seldom realized. A UPI bureau chief reported to the author that during an Illinois primary one station asked that the wire service provide them with a picture and feature story on a candidate because the station had promised such a story in return for the purchase of advertising time. UPI refused.

It is difficult to disapprove some of Prof. Skornia's criteria for live television coverage of trials: qualified court reporters and the exclusion of disc jockeys, salesmen, or TV "personalities"; and a management policy of regularly covering the courts, not just the spectaculars. But his assumption that the training of lawyers necessarily makes them superior to trained newsmen in knowing "truth" when they see it leads him to demand unreasonable conditions. For example, he negates the editing function of news presentation by proposing that the media agree to cover uninterrupted entire trials, even if deadlocked or protracted. He presumes that commercial sponsorship would be distortive, and he is too ready to accept a hair-trigger contempt power to punish newsmen who err. But Prof. Skornia does ask questions that need to be asked.

The most valid objection to the camera in the courtroom is that it has psychological effects on witnesses and jurors that are difficult to measure. Four members of the Estes majority concluded that television causes prejudice although "one cannot put his finger on its

specific mischief." Justice Robert C. Underwood of the Illinois Supreme
Court has pointed out that physical objections to courtroom cameras
no longer concern him. "The factors that give me real concern," he
declared, "are the intangible, psychological factors, and the results
they produce so far as the behavior of individuals is concerned. It
is my frank opinion that the Canon should be redrafted so as to base
it on these psychological factors and not the physical ones."

Judge M. Ray Doubles of the Hustings Court of Richmond, Virginia, also concerned about the psychological effects on witnesses and
jurors, rejects Colorado's policy of leaving the question to the discretion of the trial judge. In a sensational 1956 murder trial, a Colorado
district judge permitted radio stations to make tape recordings and
television reporters to make sound on film movies, despite the specific
request of the accused—the dynamiter of a passenger plane—that
television be excluded.[7] This was followed by the Colorado Supreme
Court's broad evaluation of Canon 35 and its ruling that TV coverage
in the future would be at the discretion of the trial judge. Since the
Estes verdict, the Colorado Supreme Court has prohibited photography
and broadcasting in the courtroom unless the defendant gives his
consent—the stated purpose being to avoid retrials. But this requires
the defendant, says Judge Doubles, to take the affirmative and register
a protest in advance in order to protect himself from such an ordeal.
In his opinion Canon 35 should be redrafted to include a provision
about psychological effects because "The taking of photographs in
the courtroom during session of the court, and knowledge by witnesses
and jurors that the proceedings are being broadcast or televised tends
to prevent the witness from being accurate in his testimony and the
juror from concentrating on his task, and therefore such photographing, broadcasting and telecasting should not be permitted."

In a well-documented volume,[8] the Special Committee on Radio
and Television of The Association of the Bar of the City of New York
speculates on the effect of broadcasting on the administration of
justice. The Committee's concern is largely with pre-trial prejudice
contained in spot news, documentaries, interviews with the accused,
officers of the court, and jurors. An example of the latter problem cited
by the Committee's report deserves consideration.

On February 23, 1961, Melvin Davis Rees, Jr., was convicted by
a federal jury of kidnaping and the murder of two persons. The jury
did not recommend the death penalty. Defense motions for an acquittal
and for a new trial were denied, and the court directed the defendant
to appear for sentencing on March 23. However, on March 22, WBAL-
TV, Baltimore, presented a program in which nine of the 12 jurors

purported to reenact their deliberations. The program had been video-taped on March 12 without the knowledge of counsel or court. For an hour the participants discussed the evidence, the guilt or innocence of the accused, and the advisability of the death penalty.

On the basis of the telecast Rees asked that he be granted a new trial, a mistrial, or that the verdict be set aside. These motions were also denied and Rees was sentenced to life imprisonment. The Chief Judge then appointed two members of the bar of the District Court of Maryland to make a study and report to him on whether the television station had acted in contempt of court. Their report con-cluded that state and case law did not permit a contempt citation, but the court felt nevertheless that the broadcasts had interfered with the orderly processes of justice. "While jurors who sit in criminal cases on petit juries," said the court, "are not bound to secrecy, it is certainly true that the interests of justice are better served if what takes place during the deliberations of the jury are not publicly revealed. For many prospective jurors a new burden will be added to jury service if the discussions which take place in the jury room are to be publicized in this sensational fashion. Moreover, witnesses called on to give disagreeable or embarrassing testimony may be reluctant to do so voluntarily if they know that their testimony and their credibility may subsequently be discussed by the jurors on a television program."[9]

In its 1964 report, the Committee on Civil Rights of the New York County Lawyers Association cataloged its objections to television interference with the rights of the accused.

When a suspect, arrested in connection with a Brooklyn murder, held his head down to conceal his face, a policeman grabbed him by the hair and twisted his head back so that his face could be fully exposed to the cameras.

In another case, Ruben Ortiz and Jesus Negron were arrested on May 30, 1963, in the killing of a police officer on the roof of a Harlem tenement. During an interview with one of the suspects and an arrest-ing officer, telecast on WNBC-TV that evening, these statements were made—

Newsman: "Do you have anything to say, Ortiz?"
Ortiz: "No, sir."
Newsman: "Was it you who pulled the trigger?"
Ortiz: "No, sir."
Newsman: "Who did?"
Patrolman: "One of the perpetrators was hiding behind the door on the roof. The other perpetrator was up on the upper ledge of the roof. As the patrolman

passed the perpetrator behind the door, he had his gun drawn in his hand in which we believed he was looking for one prowler. This perpetrator jumped on top of the patrolman, knocking him to the ground. As the patrolman attempted to rise to the ground, the perpetrator grabbed the patrolman's revolver and shot him in the back three or four times."

Newsman: "Do these men agree as to which one of them did the murder?"
Patrolman: "Yes."
Newsman: "Which one is that?"
Patrolman: "Ruben Ortiz."

An interview with both suspects followed:

Negron: "They got—there's nothing to the charge, you know."
Interviewer: "There's nothing to the charge?"
Negron: "Yeah."
Interviewer: "You didn't do it?"
Negron: "Yeah, there's nothing to the charge."
Interviewer: "What, did your partner do it?"
Negron: "Yeah, yeah, yeah."
Interviewer (to Ortiz): "Did you pull the trigger?"
Ortiz: "No, sir."
Interviewer: "Your partner? Who did?"
Ortiz: "I don't know."

Here a suspect, though denying his guilt, is publicly accused by an accomplice. An arresting officer states as a matter of fact that the same suspect is guilty of the murder, and presents his version of how the crime was committed.

Some New York courts have since banned broadcasting or telecasting anywhere in a courthouse, and the New York City Police Commissioner no longer permits filmed interviews in precinct houses.

The New York County Lawyers Association Committee recommended: (1) Adoption by the Police Commissioner of regulations to discipline any policeman who permits or cooperates in allowing an accused person to be interviewed by reporters in the absence of counsel; (2) Adoption of similar regulations with respect to public statements by police officers referring to admissions by accused persons or facts about a crime obtained in police interviews with the accused; (3) Amendment of the Code of Criminal Procedure to provide that admissions by a defendant could not be used as trial evidence if the police or prosecuting officials had permitted news interviews with the accused while he was not represented by counsel.

Although Judge Joe B. Brown gave in to pressure from the American Bar Association and the Dallas Bar Association opposing television coverage of the Ruby trial, he did permit photographs and interviews in the corridors of the courthouse. At the end of the trial he gave permission for full photographic coverage of the reporting of the verdict, with television controls within his reach. Chief Defense Counsel Melvin Belli's outburst against court and jury after the verdict was read and the undignified stampede of newsmen to provide him with a national forum for his criticism were serious breaches of court rules. Also, the failure of camermen to live up to their promise to use one pooled camera and to shut it off as soon as Judge Brown left the bench provided the bar with the additional argument that TV coverage would make it difficult for the court to control the conduct of attorneys and newsmen. Said the *New York Times* on March 15, 1964: "The case of Jack Ruby was virtually retried on live coast-to-coast television yesterday after the Dallas jury had returned its verdict and the court had been recessed. . . ."

Not all telecasts of judicial proceedings, since the first live coverage of a trial in Oklahoma City in December 1953, have been failures. When KOMU-TV of Columbia, Missouri completed its coverage of a murder trial in which the defendant was acquitted, the defense attorney said to the news director and his cameraman: "I feel your coverage of this trial has been fair and honest. . . . I've had no objections to this coverage, and feel that the public should benefit by such reporting." And Circuit Judge Sam C. Blair was quoted as saying: "Your television coverage should have a salutary effect on the public. . . . Too many, through being uninformed, believe that court procedures are farcical and often feel there are miscarriages of justice. They don't visit the courtroom. If we can bring the court-room to them, they can see how trials are conducted. . . . You KOMU-TV newsmen have done a wonderful job of reporting this trial. Hardly anyone knew you were there. And I hope you'll come back again."[10]

But few experiments with television in the courtroom have been so successful. The grotesque murder of Lee Harvey Oswald before a national television audience hardened the resolve of lawyers and judges to prohibit television coverage of trials and pre-trial proce-dures. And the Estes case suggests that television newsmen may be their own worst enemies. The *New York Times* described TV coverage of Estes' preliminary hearing: "A television motor van, big as an intercontinental bus, was parked outside the courthouse and the second floor courtroom was a forest of equipment. Two television cameras had been set up inside the bar and four marked cameras were aligned just outside the gates. A microphone stuck its 12-inch snout inside the jury box, now occupied by an overflow of reporters from the press table, and three microphones confronted Judge Dunagan on his bench. Cables and wires snaked over the floor."[11]

Where is the compact and non-distractive equipment we have heard so much about? If there are now television cameras measuring 5x4x10 inches and weighing 6½ pounds, as Dr. Frank Stanton of CBS says there are, television newsmen ought to begin using them.

Judges and lawyers for their part, would do well to decide how best to accommodate cameras in the courtrooms of the future. Justice Clark, in his majority opinion in Estes, implies as much: "When the advances in these arts permit reporting by printing press or by television without their present hazards to a fair trial we will have another case." And Justice Harlan in his concurring opinion says that "we should not be deterred from making the constitutional judgment which this case demands by the prospect that the day may come when television will have become so commonplace an affair in the daily life of the average person as to dissipate all reasonable likelihood that its use in courtrooms may disparage the judicial process." In his dissent, Justice Stewart accepts one of the basic arguments of the news media when he says: "The suggestion that there are limits upon the public's right to know what goes on in the courts causes me deep concern. The idea of imposing upon any medium of communications the burden of justifying its presence is contrary to where I had always thought the presumption must lie in the area of First Amendment freedoms."

The Estes decision has given rise to both optimism and pessimism among opponents of Canon 35. Overlooking Justice Harlan's vote for the moment and instead emphasizing what he says in his opinion, Herbert Brucker, distinguished former editor of the *Hartford Courant*, notes that only four of the five justices voting to reverse did so on the proposition that televised trials are constitutionally prohibited. Therefore, a majority of the Court does not accept Canon 35 and the decision is really a victory for its opponents. It is doubtful whether many will read the Estes decision in this way. But Brucker has a point when he says: "What is at issue is whether pictorial and electronic journalism must necessarily, at all times and under all conditions, prevent fair trial. And those who believe that it need not are restive because the prohibitions of news photographers and television is based on subjective antipathy rather than fact."[12]

W. Theodore Pierson, Washington counsel for the Radio-Television News Directors Association is reported to have been "heartened" by the Estes decision because "We did much better than we dared hope."[13]

If the Estes decision is a crack in Canon 35, it is not the first. Canon 28 of the State Bar of Texas states that "The supervision and control of such trial coverage shall be left to the trial judge who has the inherent power to exclude or control coverage in the proper case in the interest of justice." The Canon forbids the use of artificial lighting or the photographing or exposure to radio or television of any witness against his will.

In 1958 the Oklahoma Court of Criminal Appeals, in affirming a lower court conviction, denied that a defendant's rights had been violated by television, and concluded: "We are of the opinion the matter of televising or not televising, photographing or not photographing criminal trials and proceedings . . . is within the sound discretion of the trial judge."[14] Since that case, the Supreme Court of Oklahoma has adopted a rule prohibiting television during actual court proceedings.[15] It is for this reason that Chief Justice Warren observed in a footnote in his concurring opinion in Estes: "Colorado . . . and Texas permit televising of trials in the discretion of the trial judge. The current situation in Oklahoma is unclear."

More pessimistic are those views of the Estes decision as a major setback for opponents of Canon 35. The *New York Times* suggested in an editorial that the decision will probably "block any judicial authorization for televising criminal trials for a long time."[16] *Times* writers Jack Gould and Arthur Krock hold similar views. Gould says the decision will probably keep cameras out of all proceedings "even though the opinion admittedly turned on the 'notorious' nature of the particular trial."[17] Krock believes that although the minority emphasized that courtroom television does not implicitly deny a constitutional right, "the Court as a whole gave the back of its hand to video trial reporting."[18]

Two writers in the *Texas Law Review* have suggested that the nature of television itself will keep it from being served by Justice Harlan's narrow interpretation: "As a practical matter, the opinion of the Court may not be effectively limited by Mr. Justice Harlan's refusal to concur in the holding except insofar as trials of great notoriety are concerned. Only the most notorious trials present sufficient commercial appeal to justify their being televised. Consequently, the only trials that are likely to be televised are those to which Mr. Justice Harlan's reservations would not apply."[19]

The question of notoriety has also puzzled *Editor & Publisher:* "The question immediately arose among lawyers and news media: would the admission of tv cameras to the courtroom raise a routine trial to the status of notoriety?"[20]

The Freedom of Information Committee of Sigma Delta Chi, professional journalistic society, considers the Estes decision "monstrous." While "debate may indeed continue for a long time," said the Com-

mittee's 1965 report, "access to the courts for cameras and microphones may have been snuffed out for an equally long time. The
set-back goes completely back to 1937 when press behavior at the
Lindbergh kidnap trial gave rise to the introduction of Canon 35.
Indeed, that Canon does not carry the weight of law. Last June's
ruling does."

The Estes ruling would seem to have had effects which justify
pessimism. In California, for example, courtroom photographs and
broadcasting have been barred under terms of a rule adopted by the
State Judicial Council. The prohibition includes recesses as well as
formal proceedings. The rationale for this action, in part, is "the fact
that a person being photographed or his voice and speech manner-
isms recorded for broadcast to his friends and neighbors almost invariably has its influence on the behavior of the person. . . . The
hidden camera may be non-distracting as long as pictures are never
shown, but after the secret is out the actors know they are 'on camera'
even though the instrument is concealed." Moreover, intense competition, said the Council, is an influence and the news photographer is
"indefatigable and irrepressible as he attempts to maneuver his
camera and his subject in the effort to obtain a better picture."[21]

Until we have much more evidence than is now available, the court's
arguments for the deleterious effects of television on jurors, witnesses
and defendant may be unanswerable. But these arguments are irrelevant where appellate courts—and the United States Supreme Court
itself—are concerned. Prof. Rodell, Judge Skelly Wright, U. S. District
Judge William Becker, Dean A. K. Pye of Georgetown Law School,
David Berger of the Philadelphia Bar Association, and others see
the day when sound-video tape will supplement the reporter's notes
and provide appellate courts with "living" records of important trials.
Unobtrusive camera equipment will be built into the courtrooms
of tomorrow as it has been built into the deliberative chambers of
the United Nations building. And, in the long run, the camera may
prove to be a more accurate recording instrument than the reporter's
pencil.

Not only will such coverage deter the maladministration of justice,
but it will protect the courts from uninformed attacks, from miscon-
structions and misinterpretations of their work. It may take decades
before suitable trial coverage rules are developed, and the initial
experiments hopefully will be models of excellence—unlike the Ruby
trial or Estes' preliminary hearing. Only then can television's case
be decided on the real issue: is photography and broadcasting inherently harmful to the judicial process so that an impairment of

due process can be assumed without the defendant pointing out specifically how and where prejudice entered the case?

The first comprehensive experiments should be made with the United States Supreme Court itself. Its Monday morning opinions, which fashion national policy, are delivered orally in open court. "It would be a matchless lesson in the meaning of our constitutional rights and principles," says Judge Wright, "for the people of the country to hear the decisions themselves." At present our citizenry is only vaguely aware of these momentous pronouncements and, generally speaking, they are poorly covered by the print media. No reportorial tool is as accurate, as capable of projecting a meaningful and realistic account of an important event, as the television camera. Even the everyday cynic, or the most vociferous critic of the mass media, must accept the proposition that our democracy is predicated on the active participation of the media in the affairs of the land. To reject the press because of its irresponsible elements is no more reasonable than to reject our trial procedure because some lawyers are unethical.

In 1965 the Radio and Television News Directors Association proposed a code of broadcast ethics on legal proceedings intended to encourage broadcast newsmen to conduct themselves with dignity, to keep broadcast equipment as unobtrusive as possible, and to pool coverage where necessary. The underlying purpose of the code is to avoid interference with the right of an individual to a fair trial. In 1959 the National Press Photographers Association adopted Canons of Courtroom Ethics which described in detail cameras and the film and light to be used by still, newsreel and TV photographers. The rules even included restrictions on dress. Were all the canons followed, the courtroom photographer would remain practically anonymous.

Until a successful pattern of coverage filters down from the appellate courts, the Estes decision will effectively protect jurors, witnesses and defendants from the implied bias of the television camera in the trial courts. But the day will come when the blinders will be removed from the lenses of cameras in our courts of law and the people will no longer have to be either a defendant or a fan of "Perry Mason" to understand and appreciate what is going on in the American courtroom. And even in this advanced system, judges will still control the extent to which the camera records, and no witness or defendant will be photographed against his will. There need be no sacrifice of individual rights for a broader participation of the public in governing itself.

CHAPTER 4

SHALL REASON PREVAIL?

"One thing that seems to be lacking in all the talk is appropriate emphasis on one fundamental principle. And it is unfortunate that the more vociferous spokesmen for the press and for the bar seem to have got themselves into the position of adversaries rather than allies in defense of this fundamental principle. The principle to which I refer has found expression in various forms, one of them being that without a free press fair trials would be impossible and without fair trials a free press would be impossible."—Benjamin M. Mc-Kelway, editorial chairman of the *Washington Star*.

Late in December, 1964, the Philadelphia Bar Association drew up a set of guidelines that appeared to be intended to implement the Warren Commission proposals. Although not legally binding, this code would permit only the ranking police officer to make pre-arrest statements, and then only to assist in an investigation. Police and attorneys would be prohibited from releasing any information about prior criminal records, confessions, details of the crime, or admissible evidence. Furthermore, the press was firmly admonished to limit itself in reporting cases that had not yet come to trial.

Although a large turnout of the Philadelphia Bar Association membership adopted the code by a vote of six to one, there was strong dissent in both judicial and press circles. In a television network report,[1] Chief Justice John C. Bell, Jr., of the Pennsylvania Supreme Court expressed astonishment at that part of the code which he thought would encourage crime by removing it from the public spotlight. "The important thing today is to protect the public, not the criminal," said the Chief Justice. "We are in the midst of an appalling crime wave that is sweeping our cities, our state, and our entire country, and instead of considering what they can do to further aid and abet these criminals, they ought to be considering what they can do to aid and protect the law-abiding public."

Chief Justice Bell was supported in these views by Mayor James Tate of Philadelphia, Police Commissioner Howard Leary and District Attorney James C. Crumlish, Jr., who called the guidelines unworkable, emphasizing that "the news media and the district attorney are going to have to use their own judgments in this matter."

A former Pennsylvania Supreme Court Justice and Attorney General, Thomas McBride, felt differently: "I think that most newspaper editors wouldn't know a Constitutional right if they fell over one. . . . If I or any other lawyer or any citizen tampered with a jury in the way that the newspapers do every day in the week in these celebrated cases, he would be thrown in jail summarily, and I have no doubt about that at all, but nothing has been done about the newspapers. They're all afraid of newspapers. That's why you'll find that, in this current controversy, everybody presently in public life is on the side of the newspapers."

The Philadelphia debate continued with newsmen rejecting what they perceived to be a hostile document. The public's right to know is at stake, a city editor contended. William Dickinson, managing editor of the *Philadelphia Bulletin,* pointed out that most pre-trial publicity comes directly from lawyers themselves. "I have," he asserted, "a file in my office of the names of lawyers who have offered to pay our reporters to put in the stories certain information which they thought was favorable to their client or to themselves." A broadcasting executive feared the code would break off vital communication between the accused and the world at large. Moreover, it would undermine our fundamental faith in the jury system by implying that jurors are incapable of making a fair decision when exposed to crime news. Whether we use the information we get or not, said a radio news director, the fact remains that we should be allowed access to this information. Another attempt on the part of the legal profession to gag the press and let the criminal element get away with something, said another news editor.

Members of the bar countered that they had been misunderstood, that they had not meant to gag the press, only to protect the constitutional right to a fair trial. We have our code, you have your code, said a former chancellor of the Bar Association; we are simply suggesting that you comment sparingly on evidence bearing on the guilt of an accused. There are numerous cases, a special assistant attorney general explained, where otherwise valid convictions have been reversed because the jury was impregnated with prejudicial and inadmissible information—such as prior criminal records. The press has no constitutional right to gather news, said Marvin Comisky, Chancellor of the Bar Association. That's a right that the newspapers have created unto themselves. An incontestable point made by the bar is that it has the right to lay down rules of ethics governing its own members.

In Massachusetts a press-bar code, two years in the making, was approved in June, 1963 by the State and Boston Bar Associations, the Massachusetts Newspaper Information Service, and the Massachusetts Broadcasters Association. Although 31 weekly and 26 daily newspapers in the state adopted the code, all Boston dailies, with the exception of the *Christian Science Monitor,* rejected it. Subsequently, lawyers attempted to make the code binding by transposing it into a bill which would make it a crime to publish or broadcast that "any person arrested for having committed a crime has ever confessed to any crime . . . or has ever committed, been suspected of, accused of, arrested for, indicted for, convicted of or acquitted of the commission of any other crime." Justices of the Supreme Judicial Court of Massachusetts in answer to a query from the House of Representatives doubted the constitutionality of the measure, and it failed to get through the legislature. A similarly unilateral effort by lawyers was rejected recently by the Florida legislature.

The best example of a bilateral code is Oregon's "Statement of Principles by the Press and Bar." Although a sensible document providing for a permanent joint committee to hear complaints about violations of the statement, no cases have been brought under it in the three years since it was written. It has no enforcement machinery, and its acceptability to both sides appears to lie in its generality.

Kentucky's Press Association has adopted its own statement of principles on crime and trial news and has invited endorsement by bar associations. Among specific recommendations is one against the use of the term, "confession." "As a general principle," the statement says, "newspapers should follow the policy of stating simply that law enforcement officers have reported that the individual under arrest has made a statement containing damaging admissions." The press statement also recommends that "unless there be clear and overpowering reasons dictated by the public interest, the news media should refrain from publishing prior records of criminal activity." However, the media are urged to seek information for its own guidance and for the subsequent protection of society should there be miscarriages of justice.

"A Guide to News Media and Bar Relations" has been developed in Louisiana to re-emphasize the principle of the presumption of innocence for those accused of wrongdoing. Wyoming has followed suit, and press-bar codes are under consideration in Colorado, Michigan, Virginia, and other states.

As part of its $750,000 project to define uniform standards for the administration of criminal justice, the American Bar Association and the American Law Institute have created a special free press-fair trial advisory committee. Justice Paul C. Reardon of the Supreme Judicial Court of Massachusetts is chairman of the unit. It is working closely with another ABA committee in connection with the revision of the Canons of Judicial Ethics.

A code for judges urging them to prevent lawyers or parties to a case from making statements outside the courtroom is being developed by the National Conference of State Trial Judges. This code is to be distributed to the nation's 3,500 state trial judges with the recommendation that individual states adopt similar codes tailored to local circumstances.

The New York State Bar Association has recommended disbarment and contempt citations for violations of Canon 20 which forbids lawyers to comment on pending proceedings except in extreme cases where circumstances justify a statement to the public based on records and papers on file in the court.

In September 1964, the Association of the Bar of the City of New York set up a special committee to recommend rules for the protection of defendants, with special reference to the impact of radio-television coverage on the administration of justice. The New York County Lawyers Association is also studying the problem.

Ohio lawyers have been warned that they face disciplinary action if they comment to the press in violation of Canon 20. Enforcement of the Canon, the Ohio Bar Association Committee on Legal Ethics and Professional Conduct has declared, "will be vigorous and meaningful whether violation is by prosecution or defense."

In December 1964, Jon O. Newman, United States Attorney for the Connecticut District, issued a memorandum to federal prosecutors prohibiting them from making disclosures to the press involving prospective evidence, statements of witnesses, reports of investigative agencies, and opinions as to the guilt of accused persons. The order did not affect the dissemination of information concerning an arrested person's criminal record, the fact and essential circumstances of the arrest, the name, address and age of adult defendants, the nature of the charge and all events occurring in the judicial process which are matters of public record. "Close questions as to what may appropriately be disclosed are to be resolved against disclosure and in favor of protecting the accused's right to a fair trial," the memorandum added. "To put it simply, if in doubt, keep silent." A few months later, Connecticut State Police Commissioner Leo M. Mulcahy made similar rules applicable to all officers under his charge.

Rules designed to protect the rights of an accused were laid down in 1954 by New York's District Attorney Frank S. Hogan. That such rules do not always withstand public pressures was evidenced in 1964 following the shocking murders of Janice Wylie and Emily Hoffert, daughters of prominent families. Early in the case, police announced that a 19-year-old Negro, George Whitmore, Jr., had confessed to the double slaying, to a third unsolved murder, and to an attempted rape. A mass sigh of relief accompanied headlines such as "Wylie Murder Solved: Drifter Admits Killing 2" which appeared in several New York dailies. Some news stories included Whitmore's detailed "confession" and he was characterized as a "deranged animal," a "horror."

But not all of the pieces seemed to fit. Several newspapers, doubting that the police had in fact found the correct solution to the crime, reversed their field and helped to uncover evidence which nine months later cleared Whitmore of the Wylie-Hoffert murder charge. In the meantime, however, he had been convicted of attempted rape. Suspecting that this trial had not been fair, the prosecution joined with the defense in asking the court to set aside the verdict and order a new trial. Brooklyn Supreme Court Justice David Malbin complied, noting that the jury had been infected with racial prejudice and influenced by Whitmore's previous confession to three murders. "It is inescapable," declared the judge, "that widespread publicity reported by the press, television coverage and radio contributed in no slight degree to the atmosphere of hostility that surrounded Whitmore's trial."[2]

A Rhode Island Superior Court granted a mistrial January 19, 1965 because a defendant's criminal record was published in a local newspaper. In December of 1964 a Nevada Supreme Court Justice advised district attorneys and police to stop giving out information that might prejudice cases. At about the same time a superior court judge in San Bernardino, California granted a mistrial in a murder case on the ground that adverse publicity may have made it impossible to select an impartial jury. And in Pennsylvania a recent state court ruling bans the taking of pictures and the use of recording equipment at hearings before judges, magistrates, aldermen, and justices of the peace.

A 12-man committee under the direction of D. Tennant Bryant, publisher of the *Richmond* (Va.) *Times-Dispatch* and *News Leader*, has been studying the free press-fair trial problem for the American Newspaper Publishers Association. Alfred Friendly, managing editor of the *Washington Post* until recently, has headed a special committee of the American Society of Newspaper Editors dedicated to promoting study and discussion of the issue. Several interim reports have been made.

In March, 1965, an AP Managing Editors Association committee under George Beebe of the *Miami Herald* ventured the following predictions to its membership:

1. It appears that under the First Amendment's guarantee of freedom of the press, codes to regulate the conduct of newsmen are unenforceable. As a practical matter, this is true, too.

2. Pool coverage, while possibly decreasing the flow of information to which the public is entitled, may be necessary in certain situations requiring a minimum number of newsmen.

3. News organizations should consider possible steps they can take themselves to avoid any dangers there may be of news media interference in the administration of justice.

4. Full and frank discussions between news media, the bar, law enforcement agencies and the bench might do much to solve some problems of court and crime news coverage.

5. It may be that problems of this type that arise in a free society can never be solved completely and finally because no one right may override another.

Two months later the Columbia Broadcasting System announced that it had adopted new "standards of self-restraint" in reporting pre-trial and trial information so as to safeguard the rights of both defendant and state to a fair trial. Drafted by Herbert Mitgang, executive editor, and Fred Friendly, former president of CBS News, the guidelines appear to have set a new tone of responsibility for broadcasting in this problematic area. Generally, confessions and prior records would not be discussed until admitted into evidence at the trial, although a news director would be given discretion to disclose the bare fact of a confession if in his judgment it was necessary to do so. The guidelines would not be operative where there were overriding public policy considerations as in the case of a presidential assassination.

To choose a side in the press-bar debate is to invite frustration for there are strong arguments and reasonable men on both sides. A strong bias one way or the other is comforting because it requires a well staged attack on only one battery of contentions. And there is still a propensity for many lawyers to view the problem only in terms of an irresponsible and unredeemable press; and for many newsmen to perceive the problem only in the context of oppressive courts. Editors have no intention of delegating their editorial decisions to judges and lawyers; yet the fact remains that full disclosure does not in every case protect or promote the rights of an accused. Newsmen, on the one hand, would do well to avoid basing their arguments on the premise of an almost perfectly responsible and socially sensitive press. More lawyers must admit that they themselves are the primary source of what may be damaging out-of-court comment.

The press-bar debate has now reached a crescendo and is complicated by lack of unanimity on either side. In 175 years of constitutional government we still have no reliable description of the relationship between publicity and jury verdicts, and no nationally accepted guidelines for the news coverage of criminal trials. The speed and ubiquity of the mass media may serve to exaggerate the seriousness of the conflict—celebrated criminal cases, for example, are blown up out of all proportion. And yet a single case of justice impaired by inflammatory publicity which serves no public purpose may destroy the presumption of innocence, that civilizing legal doctrine which places high value on human life and liberty.

There is, of course, another fundamental right to be considered: freedom of the press and its corollary, the right of the public to be informed. An open society is dependent upon an open communications system. It is essential to the well-being of society that criminal activities be fully reported, that the work of elected and appointed officials be scrutinized, and that the courts of justice function in full view of the public.

President Edward W. Kuhn of the American Bar Association was justified in warning United Press International editors and publishers in an October 6, 1965 address that the Supreme Court will continue to concern itself with criminal appeals based on prejudicial publicity. But he was in error in suggesting that scientific evidence that news coverage does or does not in fact influence jurors is irrelevant. This kind of a foreclosure on the possible results of a systematic analysis of what publicity actually does to influence the outcome of a trial is understandably unacceptable to many newsmen, for it leaves them convicted by hypothesis.

Not only is the American bar advantaged by having the weight of the United States Supreme Court on its side of the debate, but it is also able through its professional organizations to discipline its membership. For journalism, a pluralistic and undisciplined business (as

it should be in an open society), there is no such opportunity. Publishers belong to one organization, editors to another, reporters and
photographers to yet others. In broadcasting, the National Association
of Broadcasters cannot speak for the networks, nor can the networks
speak for local radio and television news directors. American journalism will never subscribe to licensing of newsmen, even if it could
do so under the proscriptions of the First Amendment.

Nor is it fair to assume that newsmen never exercise judgment
or discretion in handling crime news. The sensational cases which
may tempt newsmen to tamper with the rights of an accused are a
miniscule proportion of the criminal cases which come before the
courts.[3] More accurately, it is when the collective judgment of press,
police and prosecutor is inadequate that the specter of justice violated
appears; and it is to a few celebrated cases in this very special catalog
of horrors that we now turn our attention.

Chapter 5

TRIAL BY NEWSPAPER

"Press material prejudicial to the cause of justice is so common that no search is required to find it. The same cannot be said of material which promotes justice."—John Lofton.[1]

In the annals of American crime few cases received wider attention or gave greater impetus to criticism of the press than the famous Lindbergh kidnaping trial. More than 700 newsmen and 130 photographers crowded the tiny town of Flemington, New Jersey, and the mere curious sometimes reached 20,000 in a single day. The small courtroom was converted into a 24-hour news distributing center, and served as a propaganda bureau for both prosecution and defense attorneys.

Newspaper headlines with the impact of "Bruno Guilty But Has Aids, Verdict of Man In Street" titillated readers long before the trial began. During the trial, references to Hauptmann as "a thing lacking human characteristics" or variations thereof were not uncommon. Although New Jersey courts did not appear particularly concerned about possible prejudice, the American Bar Association was. A bar committee report on the trial, written by Oscar Hallam of Minnesota, hardened for a long time legal attitudes toward trial coverage and publicity-seeking lawyers, and proposed firm control from the bench.[2]

Another classic was the trial of Leopold and Loeb in 1924. So clamorous was the press in covering the case that the *Chicago Tribune* threw up its hands in horror and declared: "The dangerous initiative that newspapers have taken in judging and convicting out of court is journalistic lynch law. It is mob murder or mob acquittal in all but the overt act." (But it was a newspaperman who found the clue—a pair of glasses—that broke the case.)

A New York crime commission report in 1927 castigated the Hearst papers for their coverage of the Hall-Mills case; and it was said of the Gray-Snyder trial that crowds jammed the courtroom so thickly that the assistant district attorney had his pockets picked while fighting his way to the courtroom. Billy Sunday, Mary Roberts Rinehart, Dorothy Dix, Aimee Semple McPherson and Will Durant applied their pens and prestige to the latter case for some of the big city dailies. The *New York Journal* polled its readers on the guilt or innocence of the defendant and beat the jury to a verdict by two days.

Attorney Harold Sullivan, who has reviewed a number of noteworthy cases occupying newspaper headlines between 1912 and 1941,[3] tells the story of Molway and Berrett, two innocent men tried for a 1934 murder. The day before the case would have gone to the jury, three others confessed. A *Boston Post* poll of jurors after the trial indicated that all 12 would have voted for a verdict of guilty of murder in the first degree. Once again mistaken identification by eyewitnesses, pressured police officials, and gullible, irresponsible newspapers, says Sullivan, might have succeeded in thwarting justice.

Let us bring the chronicle up to date. On February 7, 1958, delinquency petitions were filed in Chicago against two boys identified as members of a gang who had stripped, beaten and raped an 11-year-old Girl Scout. The two were pointed out by their victim from her hospital bed, and further identified by witnesses as being in a group seen walking down a sidewalk a block from the scene and shortly before the attack occurred.

On the same day, the *Chicago Daily News* published case histories and photographs of the two suspects in an attempt to explain their "vicious behavior." Within a week, however, the two accused juveniles had dropped out of the news because five other boys had been arrested and had admitted the savage attack. "Two other boys mistakenly had been picked up in the case," said the *Daily News* toward the end of a long story reporting this latest development. Such was the exoneration.

Consternation was expressed in some legal circles when, during the 1961 Chicago police scandals, metropolitan dailies informed their readers that two of eight policemen, accused of conspiring with criminals to commit burglary, had made overtures to plead guilty in exchange for light sentences or probation. Defense attorneys, hopeful of a mistrial, were suspected of planting the story. On July 13, the *Chicago Sun-Times,* under the headline "2 Cops On Trial Seek Deal" likened the trial to a poker game—"One of the defense lawyers makes a bet, or an offer. The prosecution raises. It is a game with high stakes." Statements allegedly made to police officials more than a year earlier were liberally recorded prior to being offered in evidence by the prosecution. But the Illinois Supreme Court unanimously affirmed the conviction of five of the policemen who complained that newspaper publicity had denied them a fair trial. A similar petition was recently turned down by the United States Supreme Court. The scandal led to the appointment of a new police superintendent and complete reorganization of the Chicago police force.

At least as agonizing to law enforcement officials was the action of a United States Court of Appeals in 1962 in reversing the conviction for income tax evasion of the notorious Tony Accardo, partly on the grounds of prejudicial trial reporting.[4]

For years Accardo had received wide publicity in the Chicago press as the reputed leader of the syndicate once bossed by Al Capone. He was charged with falsely listing $4,000 in tax deductions for auto expenses as a salesman for a beer company. Selection of his jury began on September 12, 1960. At the end of the first day of *voir dire*, the court ordered the jurors not to read the newspapers or listen to radio or television accounts of the trial. Evening papers reported that Accardo had been arrested 14 times, that he had been found guilty of disorderly conduct, that in 1930 he had been indicted for carrying concealed weapons, and that in 1948 he had been charged with conspiracy to defraud the government as a result of a trip under an assumed name to visit "syndicate hoodlums" at Leavenworth—but "he beat both charges."

Under a September 14 headline—"There's A Capone Echo At Accardo Trial"—a news story related that "in the villain's part this time was Chicago's jet-age Capone—stoney-faced Accardo, the master of muscling legitimate business." On September 27, one Joseph Bronge, Jr., a prosecution witness, testified that Accardo had worked for his father as a beer distributor; he knew Accardo and Accardo had visited his home; his father was now dead, and Accardo was still selling beer. Among headlines in the morning papers were the following: "Murder Victim's Son Takes Stand Against Accardo"; "Gangster Upset By Testimony Of Bronge"; and "Accardo Jury Hears Son Of Gang Victim." News stories told how Bronge's father had appeared before the grand jury which had indicted Accardo, had been indicted himself for perjury, and had been murdered in a West Side beer war soon after. The shooting was blamed on fear by hoodlums that Bronge would tell how he and other beer distributors had been forced to put them on the payroll.

This was too much for the appellate court. In reversing Accardo's conviction, it declared that the trial judge should have, by careful examination of each juror out of the presence of the others, determined the effect of the articles on those who had read them and whether they had discussed them with one another. These admonitions to the jury, said the appellate court, should have been repeated by the trial judge at the close of each day's session.

The newspapers, some of which appeared to know much more about the case than had been made public, would probably have agreed with the dissenting judge who held that, considering the notoriety of Accardo, the trial judge's cautionary instructions to the jury were adequate. Yet the Chicago press could hardly have been satisfied with the outcome of the case. On retrial Accardo was acquitted.

In a celebrated St. Paul, Minnesota, case a prosperous and dapper young lawyer, T. Eugene Thompson, was convicted and sentenced to life imprisonment for hiring a thug to kill his wife. The motive developed at his trial in the fall of 1963 was a $1 million insurance policy on his wife's life and the attractions of a younger woman. Thompson was granted what appeared to some observers to be a futile change of venue from St. Paul to Minneapolis after the Minnesota Supreme Court found prejudice in pre-trial reports of St. Paul newspapers. This was the first change of venue granted by the Minnesota Supreme Court in a criminal case.

Early in the case, the *St. Paul Pioneer Press* quoted police as saying that the mystery was "now completely solved." Coverage of the trial itself was noted for its plethora of wrong predictions of lawyer tactics and its rather feeble attempts to inject color into the proceedings— for example, a posed picture of the "other woman" lying on her bed.

On November 20, 1963, the *Minnesota Daily*, student newspaper of the University of Minnesota, made the following observations on the taste of its professional colleagues:

"It is time to object, newspaper to newspaper, to the coverage of the Thompson trial in the Twin City papers. The St. Paul papers are the worst offenders, but it has gotten so we can't even read a Minneapolis account without throwing the paper down in disgust. . . .

"The last-straw feature was in Sunday's *Tribune*. It was a detailed account of the happy trial attenders who come and make a day of it—something like a carnival. Where there is not news, as over the weekend, the paper makes it. . . ."

The prosecutor, Ramsey County Attorney William Randall, while agreeing that newspapers could generally exercise more discretion, noted that the first break in the case was a press photo of the murder weapon. He welcomed this kind of investigatory assistance as an example of the helpfulness of the press in contributing to the peace and security of the community.

Speaking before a fall 1965 meeting of the Minnesota Civil Liberties Union, Randall declared that a defendant's attorney should have a right to bring questionable police practices to the attention of the public; similarly, the "responsibility on a county attorney is so great that there should be a wide window into his office." Later, in a January 11, 1966 interview with a *Minneapolis Star* reporter, Randall stated that he "used" the press to dispel public apathy toward the case:

"Thompson had a good public image. We had great difficulty in getting his friends and fellow attorneys to discuss his family relationships. . . .

"So, I was to speak at the Rotary Club and I tipped off a reporter to be there, and the newspaper came out with a fine headline—'Randall Raps Public Apathy.' I got the image across—that Thompson was not cooperating with the police, while all along his friends thought he was. It was their pressure on him that brought Thompson to the grand jury for a five-hour conference and also to me for talks."

Randall added that without intensive press coverage Thompson would probably have been able to carry out his plan to resume studies at Northwestern University (Thompson had won a Ford Foundation fellowship) and to win civil suits against seven insurance companies for $1,065,000 in life coverage on his wife. "We prevented a miscarriage of justice," the prosecutor concluded.

Randall clearly believes that rights are best guaranteed when the press has an untrammeled right to print the news. Only a very small amount of criminal news is printed anyway, and for a victimized defendant the law of libel is presumably a substantial remedy.

Is it deep prejudice, or simply gross negligence, that results in a banner headline such as the following which appeared April 6, 1950 in the *Chicago Tribune:* "Iowans Cheer Verdict Freeing Bednasek in Coed Killing?" In the context of the trial of the young University of Iowa student on a charge of murdering his sweetheart, there could hardly be both a "killing" and an acquittal. The headline suggests the Scottish verdict of "not proven." Under similar circumstances, but with a Gallic flair, a French newspaper is said to have concluded its coverage of a sensational trial with the headline: "Monster Assassin Acquitted."

In evaluating the role of the press in the celebrated Caryl Chessman case, Melvin Martin concluded that through ugly headlines and ferocious editorials Chessman had become a symbol of crime itself: "The local community had developed so much hatred and fear of him that it became a considerable political risk to see any merit at all in his defense."[5] When Governor Edmund Brown recommended clemency, according to Martin, "the California press launched an anti-clemency campaign against Chessman, with the *Los Angeles Times* pronouncing editorially that the governor 'have some reservations about turning the creature loose on the community'." The *Los Angeles Herald* ascribed the clemency campaign to "a great wave of blubbering sentimentality," while the *San Francisco Examiner* viewed the movement as the work of pro-Reds and Communists. Other newspapers depicted Chessman as "a madman," "a psychopathic degenerate," and "a depraved fiend." Such fulminations did not end with Chessman's execution.

On July 30, 1959, 15-year-old Peter Manceri was charged with kicking an old man to death in a Brooklyn park. The charge was based on information supplied by a 13-year-old girl friend. The elderly victim had given the police a statement before his death which police had suppressed. Its contents should have cast doubt on the rightness of the arrest. The handling of the story by most New York newspapers reflected a desire for a quick solution, and police were only too happy to oblige. On August 3 the *New York Mirror* reported: "As police reconstructed the story, the boy jumped up and knocked Butler's glasses off. Butler, who had undergone operations for cataracts on both eyes, could hardly see. 'Mind your own business old man!' the boy snarled and started to beat Butler. . . ." The accused was described by an assistant district attorney as "a tough punk . . . sullen . . . defiant," and "one of the most arrogant" he had ever encountered. No attempt was made to find another side to Manceri, to get his own story, or to talk with his parents. The press ignored the fact that his family was being subjected to crank letters and telephone calls.

When the dying man's statement was finally released, it revealed that "two big boys" had attacked him. The charges against Peter Manceri were quietly dropped and he was sent home. One newspaper did not even bother to report this result, although it had covered the story in its every sensational detail up to that point. Were the newspapers less interested in justice than in vengeance in their coverage of the case? The prospective jury foreman said that all the stories he had read prior to the trial "showed that the boy was guilty."

CBS-Television News had serious misgivings about newspaper handling of the case and retold the story in a CBS Reports program, "A Real Case of Murder: The People Versus Peter Manceri," on March 2, 1961.

In the famous Brinks robbery case, the defense vigorously challenged what appeared to it to be a conspiracy between press and prosecutor.

But the First Circuit Court of Appeals[6] denied petitioners' motion for a writ of *habeas corpus* and held that the jurors met the constitutional test of impartiality laid down in the *Irvin* case. Although defense attorneys brought in volumes of newspaper clippings to support their charges of "trial by newspaper," the court said that there were no widespread feelings of rage and revulsion. Sketches of the eight suspects appeared in the newspapers. They were referred to as bandits, and their past criminal records were divulged. The press had taken comfort in J. Edgar Hoover's confident announcement that the Brinks case had been solved and the guilty apprehended. Some of the news stories asserted that the defendants had been involved in earlier murders, but the court found that this was not prejudicial since the "rubbing out of a few small-time hoodlums is not enough to cause any general public clamor for revenge." In distinguishing this case from the *Irvin* case, the court noted that in the latter case 90 per cent of the jurors called had formed an opinion while here only 72 per cent had reached a conclusion—that is 659 out of 1,104 jurors. No wonder that after eight days of examination not a single person had been seated in the juror box.

Chief Judge Peter Woodbury, however, did not seem satisfied with the result for he noted that neither federal nor state courts had any effective means for preventing "trial by newspaper," and he asked that the Supreme Court establish guidelines.

JOHN REXINGER

On July 26, 1957, the following banner line appeared in the *San Francisco Chronicle:* "Sadist Victim: 'This is the Man'—Nurse 'Positive' Ex-Convict is Torture Rapist." The story told of the arrest of young John Rexinger as a suspect in a sex crime in which the assailant had tied up a nurse and her boyfriend at knife point, raped the woman twice, beat her, burned her with a cigarette, pricked her with the knife, and finally cut off her hair with a pair of scissors.

Although Rexinger protested his innocence through long hours of questioning, the *Chronicle* quoted police as saying the suspect had a record of sex crimes, and had served two years in San Quentin on forgery charges. The nurse's escort was less positive than she of the identification, but Rexinger's published photograph bore a remarkable resemblance to a police artist's conception of the victim's description of her attacker. Furthermore, clothes found in Rexinger's apartment were said to match what the nurse remembered her assailant had

been wearing, and a 10-inch knife—not an unusual household utensil
—was cast as the probable assault weapon.

Both the police and the *Chronicle* appeared ready to doubt, at this
point, every statement in the suspect's alibi; and it was suggested that
Rexinger was connected with the attempted shooting of a policeman a
few weeks earlier. Such damaging statements as the following were
contained in stories prominently displayed in successive issues of the
newspaper:

"In an interview with reporters, Rexinger was cautious and at times
testy in his answers yet he appeared to contradict himself at least
once."

"Two tenants living on the same floor as Rexinger characterize him
as insular, suspicious and withdrawn."

"In 1954 he was arrested in Visalia on suspicion of robbery and later
that year he was picked up on forgery charges in Red Bluff. Both
these charges were later dropped. He was sent to San Quentin from
Oakland in 1955 for passing bad checks. Shortly after his release last
January he was arrested on suspicion of rape, but police said the
charge was 'unfounded'."

Such depreciation of a suspect's character hardly anticipates a fair
hearing in court. Rexinger's police record did go back to 1952 and,
among other juvenile difficulties, he had been placed on probation for
statutory rape at 17. But there was another side to Rexinger's makeup.
While in custody it was noted that he was highly intelligent and was
much interested in avant-garde poetry—an inclination which police
were quick to equate with "emotional instability." In fact, the crux of
Rexinger's alibi was that he was in his apartment tape recording
poetic and philosophic vignettes for a University of California ex-
tension course in which he was enrolled at the time he was supposed
to be committing the crime.

He also wrote story plots, and police were certain they had spotted
what they identified as a "Freudian slip" in one of his "stranger"
stories when he said "Abbott" for "Cabot," Cabot being one of his
imaginary characters and Abbott a convicted California sex-slayer of
a year before.

The day after the arrest, the *Chronicle* proclaimed the discovery of a
witness who clearly implicated Rexinger. The story appeared under the
headline: "Gate Park Torture Attack Witness, Cops Dent Alibi of
Suspect."

Although police refused to identify the witness, the newspaper's case
against Rexinger continued to grow. A salesman told police that a few

hours before the crime a man answering the description of the rapist —that is Rexinger—had purchased a car from his lot, and a clerk in a war surplus store identified Rexinger as the man who had bought a pair of manacles.

Held without charge on the technicality of possible parole violation, Rexinger steadfastly maintained his innocence while police "characterized him as a con-wise young man who had been trying to find out from them the exact time of the crime so he could strengthen his alibi." Meanwhile an investigating police officer suggested that the stainless steel knife found in Rexinger's room, and answering the description of the knife used in the assault, was too expensive to have come from the community kitchen in the house where he lived, the inference being that the knife actually belonged to Rexinger and was the one used in the Golden Gate Park attack.

A July 29 headline in the *Chronicle* indicated that investigation of the case was proceeding nicely: "Park Rape—Sadist Suspect Admits Alibi Lie: Cops Crack Alibi of Rape Suspect." Although Rexinger insisted upon a "truth test" either by polygraph, hypnosis or truth serum, he remained in the legally indefensible position of "being unable to clear himself."

It was not until August 1 that the public defender announced that the police had the wrong man. The *Chronicle* so reported on its front page. On the following day the Rexinger story approached its climax. Police assured the district attorney that they were working on new evidence which would leave Rexinger's alibi "pretty well shot," and the newspaper quoted the chief of inspectors as saying, "I am firmly convinced that he (Rexinger) is the man—a brooding, bespectacled express clerk, with a fondness for esoteric poetry, a prison record and three sex crimes on his police record."

But a formal charge was never brought against John Rexinger for on the next day, August 3, the banner headline in the *Chronicle* attested to the newspaper's and the inspector's fallibility: "Sadist Seized . . . Not Rexinger, S. F. Man Admits Assault on Nurse." Melvin N. Bakkerud, an undersized narcotics addict bearing absolutely no resemblance to Rexinger, had confessed the crime and police had found a gold watch, stolen from the nurse's boyfriend, and a "torture kit" in his possession. Perhaps it was a mark of consistency that the *Chronicle* immediately began to "psychoanalyze" Bakkerud, the "Lonely Little Strongman."

But there remained the matter of Rexinger. On August 4 the *Chronicle* reported—as if the thought had never before occurred to it—that the victim's description of the sadist was quite some distance from accuracy. The actual assailant did not have prominent teeth (the *San Francisco News* had billed the attacker as the "Fang Suspect"), he did not wear glasses, as had been reported earlier, and he was a full half foot shorter than the hapless Rexinger. Since the situation now suggested a change in tactics for both police and press, the *Chronicle* manfully reported on August 4: "After yesterday's revelation that a 21-year-old narcotics addict had confessed to the savage crime, police said that they had never considered Rexinger anything more than a suspect."

For Rexinger the damage seemed to have been done. Not only had he made banner news in San Francisco newspapers for 11 straight days, but, in the words of one police officer who had worked on the case, "John Rexinger practically had the pellets dropping"—the reference being to the San Quentin gas chamber. The police helpfully suggested that he leave the city.

There is strong evidence that the *Chronicle* felt either a twinge of conscience or a positive need for self-justification, and on August 7 under the headline, "Rexinger Praises Chronicle," the following story appeared:

"The *Chronicle* was praised by John Rexinger yesterday for its reporting of circumstances which seemed to involve him in the rape to which Melvin Bakkerud finally confessed.

"Rexinger gave Reporter Jack Burby his particular gratitude.

" 'This is to express my thanks to you for being more interested in seeing that justice was done than in selling newspapers,' he wrote to the *Chronicle*.

" 'I would like to thank Jack Burby . . . He worked very hard running down every possible lead I could think of.

" 'The principle of innocence until proven guilty was definitely involved here.

" 'The *Chronicle* defended this principle.' "

Any one of San Francisco's daily newspapers might have been used to tell this lamentable story, for as one observer noted, "News coverage of the case might be compared with the rising strains of a huge orchestra, swelling from crescendo to crescendo."[7]

The *Examiner* "diagnosed" Rexinger as a "schizoid personality with an incipient hysterical psychosis," and at an early stage in the case had used the headline: "Rexinger's Poetic Rambling Indicates He's Sexual Psychopath, Inspector Says." And police were quoted as saying that Rexinger should be in jail for his poems alone. A University of California English instructor thought otherwise, judging Rexinger's literary works as showing "real ability." Overt intellectual interests may be a serious handicap to suspects in police custody. An *Examiner* reporter had further hurt the suspect by evaluating in print evidence he thought he had found against the suspect, flimsy though it was.

The *News* voiced the opinion that the "philosophical discourse (Rexinger's poems and stories) made it clear that he considers himself above the law." More devastating to Rexinger's cause was the alertness of the *News*, and other newspapers, in drawing a parallel between his case and that of Burton Abbott, a convicted slayer. On July 26, the *News* drew attention to the physical resemblance between the two men, printing pictures of both in identical poses. Rexinger's very protestations of innocence became sinisterly Abbott-like.

Rexinger later sued the city of San Francisco for $75,000 for false arrest.

BURTON ABBOTT

In February of the same year, Burton W. Abbott, protesting his innocence to the end, was given two death sentences by a California court for the murder of 14-year-old Stephanie Bryan, daughter of a Berkeley physician. The evidence against the frail, 27-year-old University of California accounting student was purely circumstantial, though unusually persuasive. Stephanie had disappeared on her way home from school. A few months later her body was found in a shallow grave 350 yards from Abbott's summer cabin in the Trinity Mountains.

Police were led to Abbott when his wife reported finding Stephanie's wallet and underclothes partly buried in the Abbott basement. Abbott claimed he had no knowledge of how they had got there, but he was arrested and booked for murder on July 21.

That same day the distraught father of the girl said to the *San Francisco Chronicle*, "He should be removed from society, like cancer, as a safeguard;" and, "Dr. Bryan expressed no doubt that Burton Abbott was the guilty person." On July 22, the *Chronicle*, although admitting that the case was still a puzzle of questions without clear answers, headlined its belief that Abbott's alibi had been "cracked" and quoted police as saying that they were convinced Abbott had killed the girl. Also quoted was a University of California psychiatrist who, after a brief examination of the suspect, concluded that "he is an infantile personality—this sort of act is compatible with his type of personality." Dr. Bryan, the bereaved father, although denying an interest in vengeance, reiterated that "such a man should be removed from the world completely. He is a miserable creature—like cancer that should be cut out and given to a pathologist." They were two important reasons, said the physician, "why such a man should cease to be with us soon:" we should eliminate the chance that he might repeat his crime; and his punishment should be used as a deterrent to anyone else with similar ideas. It is not difficult to appreciate the

father's state of mind, but publication of these highly emotional out-
bursts cannot be condoned.

Through July the newspapers tugged at the string on the circumstantial noose which was tightening around Abbott. The county district attorney was reported to be "satisfied Abbott is the man who
killed her." Bloodstains, though inconclusive, were found on the suspect's clothing. A psychiatrist disclosed that Abbott had checked out
"sex books" at the University library. The district attorney outlined
the case against him, and Stephanie's father presented his own theory
of how the kidnaping was carried out.

It was further suggested in print that Abbott's wife, who had
staunchly defended her husband against the murder charge, had become resigned to his fate; and his brother, in surprise testimony,
called the tubercular Abbott a rugged hiker who had once climbed
a steep canyon—the kind of physical prowess deemed necessary for the
burying of the victim. On July 31 Abbott was indicted.

By mid-August it was clear that both prosecution and defense were
fighting the Abbott case in the press. On August 15, a "Special Report"
took note of the circumstantial nature of the evidence—no motive, no
weapon, no idea as to how and when the crime had been committed,
and no proof of the method of abduction. The next day, the *Chronicle's*
report of the grand jury proceedings was headlined, "Brother Describes
Abbott's Drinking." More than a month later, on September 20, the
Chronicle told Abbott's own story of his ordeal, and chastized the
psychiatrist-witness who, when commenting on the "sex books" Abbott
had taken from the library, speculated: "The details they provide is
such that a guy might smack his lips and say, 'That's for me'." Two
days later, Abbott vainly shouted his plea of innocence in the courtroom.

Less fortunate than Rexinger, Abbott came to trial and after 47
days was found guilty of both first degree murder and kidnaping. He
was sentenced to death and executed.

On January 27, the day after the trial, but before sentence had been
passed, the *Chronicle*, with characteristic lack of subtlety, quoted an
ex-Marine jury foreman as he reflected on what might have been the
temper of the jury in its deliberations:

"Burton W. Abbott was likened yesterday to a mad dog and a rattlesnake by
the foreman of the jury that found him guilty of the kidnap-murder of Stephanie
Bryan . . .

" 'I have no more compunction stepping on him than I would on stepping on
the head of a rattlesnake,' the foreman said in a matter-of-fact voice.

" 'He's just a mad dog that has to be put out of the way.' "

There were some who recoiled at what they considered an example of a vengeful prosecutor using a battery of emotional tricks on an impressionable jury. Of the press coverage, one observer had this to say: "The press covered the trial with a macabre completeness . . . What must be noted . . . is that everyone in the bay area, grade-school children included, had access to the facts of the trial and was ready with an opinion. At trial's end a significant segment of the public was still not completely convinced of the entirely circumstantial case against the student. No murder weapon was found. No proof of motive, opportunity or acquaintanceship between Abbott and the girl was forthcoming."[8]

Whatever the influence of the newspapers and whatever the truth of the case against Abbott, its final solution left no room for correction.

POETRY AND POISON

Decriers of "trial by newspaper" are not particularly concerned with the guilt or innocence of the accused, but rather with what pre-trial publicity might do to an Anglo-American legal precept—the presumption of innocence.

Like John Rexinger, Harlow Fraden had literary interests. On August 19, 1953, 20-year-old Fraden and his school chum, Dennis Wepman, 23, went to the upper-middleclass Bronx apartment of Fraden's parents. They brought with them two bottles of champagne. While Wepman waited in the hall, young Fraden went in, greeted his parents effusively, and proposed a champagne toast to the fact that he had finally gotten a fine new job. Since Harlow, a college chemistry graduate, had been a bit of a wastrel, his parents were overjoyed to drink to this happy turn of events.

By his own admission, Harlow mixed the cocktails in the kitchen, putting deadly potassium cyanide in two of them. When his parents had swallowed the potion and collapsed to the floor, Harlow summoned Wepman from the hall.

"When I entered the apartment," Wepman said in his confession, "I saw Mr. and Mrs. Fraden lying on the floor. Mr. Fraden was still alive. He saw me and said, 'What are you doing here?' He attempted to get up and Harlow, to make certain he was dead, pushed him down and then poured more cyanide down his throat, and also down Mrs. Fraden's throat. To make sure they were dead, we felt their pulses and examined them generally. We were in the apartment about an hour and left." This grim account was carried in the December 18 issue of the *New York Daily News*.

On the day the story broke, New York newspapers presented Fraden's own confession under such blazing headlines as, "Son Confesses Poison Deaths: Pal's Murder Plea Breaks Him," and "Indict Cocktail Murderers: Insanity Plea Son's Best Bet to Beat Chair: Killings Called His Solution to Delusions." Wepman's testimony suggested that the Fradens had been killed for their fortune—Harlow's long-standing hatred of his mother was a secondary motive.

The *Daily News* theorized that Fraden, anticipating his eventual arrest and prosecution, was laying the groundwork for a defense that might show him of unsound mind, while the *World-Telegram & Sun*, in a more clinical exposition, quoted from a psychiatrist's diagnosis: "His insane slaying of his parents . . . far from shocking his own mind appears to be a simple solution of certain imaginary difficulties . . . And after the killing he would emerge without a shudder of regret or a twinge of conscience." Readers were reminded that in 1947, the accused had lighted fires in his parents' apartment and had cut their telephone wires. The fire marshal remembered that he thought the boy peculiar at the time, didn't like him and considered him "a liar and very defiant."

Also detrimental to Harlow's cause—at least in the opinion of the police and press—was his scholarly love of poetry, the *New Oxford Book of English Verse* being his bible—"As Harlow heard himself accused (by Wepman) of pouring additional poison down the throats of his dying parents, he looked up from his poetry and calmly commented, 'He speaks for himself, not for me'."

The two young men were indicted for the double slaying on December 19. Pointing to the large headlines which had accompanied the story for three days, Jerome Spingarn observed that one could not have spent 10 minutes in New York City without being aware of the case, and after three days few hadn't heard the confession, the details of the crime or speculations on its motive. Radio and television, he believed, were equally unqualified in fixing guilt. And he suggested that "such reading before trial and conviction might be a luxury we can ill afford if we are at the same time to maintain our Constitutional guarantee that accused persons are to be presumed innocent until proven guilty and are to be tried before an impartial jury."[9]

THE INNOCENT SADIST

On October 14, 1958, the following headline appeared in the *Chicago Daily News:* "Terrorist Barry Cook Admits Slaying Woman in Park: Saw Victim Sunning Self, Got Urge to Kill—Prisoner." The story underneath began as follows:

"Barry Cook, 24, confessed slayer of Margaret Gallagher, has admitted making more than 200 attacks and attempted assaults on women in this area in the last three years . . ."

On page 5 of the same issue another story headed "Call Killer Most 'Vicious Sadist,' When Cook Had No Other Victim, He Hurt Himself" was followed by a story which stated in part:

"Barry Cook, 24, flabby, pasty-faced admitted slayer of Margaret Gallagher, is described by top detectives as 'the most vicious sadist we have ever encountered.

" 'Since his arrest last February 26 he has twice inflicted wounds on himself, it was learned.

" 'When he had no other victims, he hurt himself.' a detective reported."

Three other Chicago newspapers ran substantially similar headlines on their front pages.

The next day, under the headline, "Barry Cook Confesses: Murder Case Solved At Last," this paragraph appeared in an editorial in the *Daily News:*

"Chicagoans were shocked in 1956 by the daring daylight murder of Miss Gallagher within sight of the Outer Drive. They will be thankful, at least, that *the murderer is in custody and not free to roam the streets* as are others who have committed equally atrocious crimes." (Emphasis added)

Hailing the case as a victory for Chicago police, the *Chicago Tribune* made a similarly positive declaration:

"The police of Chicago can fairly claim to have solved the murder of Miss Margaret Gallagher on the Foster Avenue Beach.

"It remains to be seen if the confession will prove of value in a prosecution of Cook for murder but at least this much has been accomplished: *there is no longer any considerable doubt about who killed Miss Gallagher.* The putative murderer is not at large and as long as he remains behind bars the women of Chicago can feel more secure." (Emphasis added)

Cook had made his confession while serving 14 years in prison on each of seven charges involving robbery and assault on women. The newspapers reported that the admission had come after repeated questioning by the police in the presence of Warden Joseph Ragen. Cook edited the confession but refused to sign it. Within 48 hours Cook was indicted for murder by a grand jury; but repudiating his confession, he entered a plea of not guilty.

On the strength of his unsigned confession, the newspapers continued to pound Cook, some of them going so far as to connect him with other Chicago murders, particularly the heinous killing of 15-year-old Judith Mae Andersen whose dismembered body was found in various parts of the city in 1957. Cook was quoted as saying, "Someday I'll tell you (about Judy) if father lets me."

Miss Gallagher's survivors were quoted as "urging death for Cook," "feeling he was guilty all along," "he should get the electric chair;" and the newspapers gave themselves credit for "solving the terrible crime"—a police detective posing as a narcotics addict had been planted in Cook's cell. On October 16, a *Daily News* story, quoting a police sergeant, was very much to the point:

" 'There's no doubt in my mind at least that Cook killed Judy too,' said Sgt. Charles Fitzgerald.

"Speaking of the Andersen murder, Fitzgerald said, 'The killer slashed it needlessly (the body). It would have made a doctor sick, *but Cook is known to love that kind of gore.'*

"Frank Ferlic, first assistant state's attorney, indicated that the state would ask the electric chair for Cook. 'I'd consider it a helluva lot safer for the public if he got the chair, or went to the penitentiary forever . . . If he is sentenced under the criminal psychopath act, there's too much chance he could get out by behaving himself. And that's the last thing we want for him!' " (Emphasis added)

Just before pre-trial arguments were to begin, the *Chicago Sun-Times* ran a series of articles entitled, "Prelude to a Murder Trial," the avowed purpose of which was to "probe the hidden background of a murder trial and seek thereby to increase its meaning." The following excerpt reflects the tone of the series:

"Barry Z. Cook, whose murder trial begins shortly, entered the basement of a Northwest Side apartment building one afternoon in October 1957.

"He was bent on a sexually motivated attack. The woman he had picked out, by watching the building, was in the basement to do her washing.

"She has recalled that Cook ripped off most of her clothes and struggled with her saying almost nothing as he did so.

"He did not, however, according to the woman, attempt to rape her. In fact, several times when he had forced her to the floor, he sat on her in an apparent show of mastery.

"It was Cook's behavior that afternoon—and his behavior in other attacks on women (which is later admitted)—that caused police to connect him with the slaying of Margaret Gallagher. And it is for killing Miss Gallagher, that Cook is to be tried."

Cook was tried, and in spite of his confession, his criminal record, psychiatric background, and the barrage of press comment on what turned out to be inadmissible evidence, he was acquitted.

Considered in isolation, this tale would seem to give the lie to the power accorded newspapers in influencing jurors. As the *Chicago American* pointed out during the 17-day trial, there was a suggestion of police coercion in getting the confession and in questioning Cook's father. On May 9, the day after the verdict was delivered, the *American* quoted the jury foreman as voting for acquittal because of discrepancies in identification and the patent artificiality of the confession, which was a series of questions and answers rather than an uninterrupted narrative.

DR. BERNARD FINCH

A notorious murder trial was that of Dr. Bernard Finch and his paramour, Carole Tregoff, for the murder of Finch's wife. Both were sentenced to life imprisonment by a Los Angeles county court after a third trial and the most expensive criminal proceeding in California history. Few crimes in recent years have been given as much publicity as this one, but, for the sake of brevity and pertinence, reference will be made only to the *Los Angeles Examiner*.

What actually happened the night of July 18, 1959, when Finch's wife, Barbara, was shot in the back while fleeing across the lawn of her palatial home, is not important to our purposes, nor is it clear. But this is how it looked to the *Examiner*. On July 20 the following banner headline opened the first act of the drama: "Doctor Held in Wife Slaying: Girl Friend Hits Vegas Alibi." In the same issue appeared the "Maid's Story of Terror," in which a frightened Swedish teen-ager was quoted as "begging him (Finch) not to kill me," and as "finding Dr. Finch standing over his wife, holding a gun"—and "those eyes, they were red with anger, I'll never forget it." The youthful maid also quoted Finch as having said to his wife, "Get the keys or I'll kill you, and I mean it." The maid was later to recall that Dr. Finch had "smashed her head against the wall," fired one shot in the garage, and then chased his wife from the place carrying the weapon.

In the following week, Mrs. Finch was quoted as having said, before her death, that if she went through with her divorce plans the doctor would hire someone to kill her. And the *Examiner* added in story and headline that Mrs. Finch, living in mortal terror of her husband, had predicted her own death by Christmas, that Finch's father believed his son "should have been put away," and that Barbara Finch's father, since the crime, hoped his son-in-law would get the gas chamber.

Early in the case, the prosecution was able to announce in large headlines its "Death Plot Theory" which implicated Miss Tregoff and accused Finch of deliberately planning the murder. "Self defense" or "accidental," countered the defense attorney.

At a preliminary hearing in West Covina on July 28, the deputy district attorney linked a do-it-yourself murder kit to Dr. Finch. Before this same prosecutor allowed Miss Tregoff to step down from the witness stand—into the hands of the police—he had wrung admissions from her that she and the doctor had planned to marry, when free to do so, and that they had indulged in intimacies. As far as he was concerned, "It is now evident beyond a reasonable doubt that the two were acting in concert."

Most disturbing, from a defense point of view, was the story and headline which appeared in the *Examiner* on July 30, the last day of the preliminary hearing:

JUDGE BELIEVES DR. FINCH GUILTY
SAYS PAIR LAY IN WAIT FOR VICTIM

"Municipal Judge Albert H. Miller expressed his opinion in a remarkable 28-minute statement as he denied Defense Attorney Ned Nelson's motion for bail.

"The Judge reviewed four days of preliminary hearing testimony in making his ruling.

"At times his summation, in which he said Finch had murder 'in mind' when 'he took after that girl' sounded almost like a prosecutor's final argument to a jury."

In such a way, then, did the *Examiner* help to set the stage for a murder trial which was to span almost a two-year period. Both defendants were convicted.

It would not be difficult to find other qualified accounts for this catalog of horrors. Both press and bar, it would seem, have risked impairing fair trial for full public disclosure in cases where the public interest does not loom large unless that interest is defined in terms of thrill value. It may be argued that the press bears the ultimate responsibility for, as in libel, the crime is in the publication. Certainly it is the press which has borne the brunt of criticism for its traditional handling of crime news.

Harold Sullivan, for example, in his searing polemic, *Trial by Newspaper*,[10] equates the vigor of American journalism with a purely selfish circulation motive, the consequences of which is vicious gossip infringing upon what he calls the sacred right of privacy. Editors and publishers with "Hitler complexes" are primarily responsible for the fact that legal combatants are able to use news and editorial columns as their battleground. Truth and justice are the private preserve of the courts, and those who meddle, beware! The "robber barons" of the "gaudy press", says Sullivan, who ignore this warning will feel the clenched fist of the court's inherent summary contempt power, which will be used so relentlessly that the press "will crawl into court, on all fours, and file affidavits, solemnly averring that it had not the slightest, the remotest intention to interfere with the determination of pending litigation." But what of those cases in which the public interest appears to be very importantly involved?

CHAPTER 6

TRIAL BY OFFICIAL PUBLICITY

"Indeed it is no exaggeration to say that the possibility of controlling communications has now opened up an avenue through which the gap between totalitarian and democratic government can progressively be narrowed, as modern dictators gradually substitute persuasion for coercion, and as democratic leaders acquire the ability to manufacture the consent upon which their authority is supposed to rest."—Francis E. Rourke[1]

President Thomas Jefferson sent a special message to Congress in 1807 in which he announced that Aaron Burr was guilty of high treason. Burr had planned to seize New Orleans, Jefferson said, and then attempt to detach the West from the eastern United States and also conquer Mexico. Burr might have been guilty, John Adams declared, "but if his guilt is as clear as the Noon day Sun, the first Magistrate ought not to have pronounced it so before a Jury had tryed him."[2]

The Presidential practice of stepping into the judicial process and making damaging pre-trial statements persists to the present day.

In March, 1965, President Lyndon Johnson announced to a nationwide television audience the arrest of four men in connection with the murder of Mrs. Viola Liuzzo, Detroit housewife who was shot to death in Alabama while engaging in civil rights activities. Mr. Johnson identified the suspects and reported that they were members of the Ku Klux Klan. "Mrs. Liuzzo went to Alabama to serve the struggles for justice," he said. "She was murdered by enemies of justice who for decades have used the rope and the gun and the tar and the feathers to terrorize their neighbors." Then the President appealed to all members of the organization "to get out of the Ku Klux Klan now and return to a decent society before it is too late."[3]

The *Chicago Tribune* wondered on March 30, 1965, "How can such men expect to receive a just trial when they have been condemned in advance on the highest authority?" And on April 14 the *Los Angeles Times* noted, "Mr. Johnson's comments, addressed to the nation over radio and television, were hardly in keeping with the American legal concept that an individual is innocent until proved guilty." The mother of Collie Leroy Wilkins, one of the suspects, wrote a letter accusing the President of prejudicing her son's trial. "I would like you to explain to me," she said, "why this was done before my son was even interrogated or given any kind of a hearing or trial by jury. I feel like now my son and these other men will not have a fair trial . . . because they were branded guilty before the nation by the President of the United States."[4]

Just three weeks after the President's statement, Attorney General Nicholas deB. Katzenbach, who had stood by Mr. Johnson's side during the television broadcast, released a new set of guidelines to be followed by Justice Department personnel in releasing information to the press in criminal cases.

Most significant in the Katzenbach rules, announced in an address to the American Society of Newspaper Editors, is the door left open for information which, though prejudicial, may include important aspects of the public interest. For example, the circumstances of a person's arrest may involve information vital to the public. An announcement that a man has been arrested on a forged securities charge tells little. But the public interest is served by disclosing as well that millions of dollars in worthless securities were seized at the time of the arrest; that others were sold to unknown victims; and that still others are loose somewhere in the market-place. The public also has a legitimate interest, in Katzenbach's view, in the time and place of arrest, and in facts relating to resistance, pursuit, possession and use of weapons, and the description of items seized at the time of arrest.

(Prior criminal records are problematical.) But Katzenbach notes that "public scrutiny requires information about what kinds of people are becoming involved in the criminal process. Is the problem one of first offenders or repeaters? Does the arrest of a repeated offender result in speedy trial—or is it one continuance after another? Was there undue leniency in prior treatment? Is the arrest a mere harassment of a prior offender? These are social questions which the public has a right, and even a duty, to consider." In any case, convictions are a matter of public record open to any reporter with an interest in checking court files.

The attorney general said his department would not volunteer criminal conviction records, but would respond to a legitimate inquiry having to do with convictions—but not with acquittals—on federal offenses. This rule would not apply to fugitives.

Restricted information would include confessions, or a statement that a confession had been made; opinions of a prosecutor or a law enforcement official about the defendant's character, the nature of the evidence, or comment on credibility of witnesses; and information about investigative procedures such as fingerprint, lie-detector, ballistics or laboratory tests. These restrictions would extend from the time of arrest to the conclusion of the trial. Moreover, the Justice Department would neither encourage nor assist in photographing or televising a defendant, and there would be no distribution of photographs to the news media unless a law enforcement function would be served.

Prohibitions do not include the defendant's name, age, residence, employment and marital status; the substance of the charge against him; and the identity of the investigating agency or the length of the investigation.

The rules have evoked a favorable response from important segments of the press, and other federal agencies appear to be paying some heed. Fred W. Vinson Jr., assistant attorney general in charge of the Justice Department's Criminal Division, told a Senate subcommittee hearing in August, 1965, that the Treasury Department had instructed all its personnel to be guided by the attorney general's policy statement. Treasury bureaus include the Bureau of Narcotics, the Bureau of Customs, the Secret Service, the Alcohol and Tobacco Tax Unit, and the Internal Revenue Service. Vinson said the guidelines also were being followed by the Post Office Department, the Food and Drug Administration, and the Securities and Exchange Commission.[5]

But with pre-trial publicity posing the problem that it does, it is perhaps inevitable that new laws would be proposed to mitigate the free press-fair trial conflict. The most important of these is the contempt bill first introduced by Senator Wayne Morse of Oregon in 1963, amended to provide stiffer penalties and re-introduced in the 1965 session. Senate Bill 290 is stated as follows: "It shall constitute a contempt of court for any employee of the United States, or for any defendant or his attorney or the agent of either, to furnish or make available for publication information not already properly filed with the court which might affect the outcome of any pending criminal litigation, except evidence that has already been admitted at the trial. Such contempt shall be punished by a fine of not more than $1,000."

Unlike some legislative recommendations, this bill does not include newsmen among those liable to contempt citations. It is aimed rather at attorneys—especially United States district attorneys—law enforcement officials and other officers of the court who are in a position to leak information to the press while a case is pending. Newsmen are concerned about the cloak of secrecy such a statute would cast around legal procedures, possibly closing police records to public scrutiny, burying suppressed evidence or testimony which might have public import, and insulating courts and law enforcement agencies from legitimate criticism. And the rights of the defendant himself might very well be jeopardized where a screen of silence could be effectively maintained.

The subcommittees on Constitutional Rights and the Improvement of the Judicial Machinery of the Senate Judiciary Committee recently concluded hearings on the bill. Senator Morse testified that one reason legislation is needed is that the Justice Department guidelines restrict only the prosecution. "For justice to be served, both sides in a criminal case must come before the court and before the jury on an equal footing," he said. "That will not be the case until the same obligations are applied to both sides."[6]

The United States Judicial Conference has recommended similar federal laws to restrict the release of pre-trial information by making it a contempt of court for any federal employee, a defendant or his counsel to collaborate with the press. Individual lawyers and judges also have proposed that legislatures, through narrowly drawn contempt or criminal statutes, condemn specific press practices which appear to create a serious danger of improperly influencing jury decisions. These laws would make editors themselves liable for the reporting of criminal records, confessions, speculations on the guilt or innocence of the accused, and other kinds of information which might be ruled inadmissible by the trial court.

With such a flurry of proposals for legislation to hamstring prosecutors and law enforcement officers on the one hand or the press on the other, the question arises: Wouldn't it be hypocrisy to encourage such legislation while a third party also is involved in providing the public with prejudicial pre-trial information? That third party is the executive and legislative branches of the government, particularly the federal government.

Although Presidents from Jefferson to Johnson have authorized possibly prejudicial pre-trial statements, much of the problem with the executive branch originates, not with the President, but with departments and agencies under his authority. Senator Morse referred, no doubt, to prosecutors but a statement he made while introducing his bill could have broader meaning: "It is hard to understand," said Morse, "how an executive branch of the Government which has been so active in seeking to impose its notions of civil liberties on the various states can refuse to convince by example when it is prepared to coerce by force."[7]

As for the legislative branch, public hearings by committees of both houses of Congress and public statements by Congressmen provide information that frequently comes to public attention later in connection with court cases—information that is not always admissible in court. "If the Government cannot convict a man in court by due process of law," one writer has charged, "it can convict him in the public mind through legislative investigation and then use his testimony as the basis for legal prosecution."[8] Melvin Belli, counsel for Jack Ruby, elaborated on the problem in a colorfully worded letter to the Senate subcommittee holding hearings on the Morse bill:

". . . I think for the Congress to pass S. 290 and at the same time to continue with the well-publicized 'pre-trial statements' of the congressional investigation would be the utmost hypocrisy. . . .

"At the request of the Congress, I brought two colored clients to a congressional hearing several months ago. You were investigating how the hole got in the bottom of the San Francisco National Bank. But my clients were publicly pictured and pummeled by adept and adroit cross-examiners who couldn't have done a better job of character assassination and with more fervor than had they been attorney general of Israel, specially appointed by Ben Gurion to try the memory of Adolf Hitler in special sessions of the supreme court at Tel Aviv beginning at the first blow of the ram's horn on Rosh Hashana.

"This cross-examination was deliberately offered to the press, indeed urged upon the national communication media. Every part of this land saw and heard a cross-examination without rules of evidence, without reply, my clients completely excoriated, and publicly, on Friday. On Monday they were indicted to go before a trial jury for a fair trial."[9]

Ideally federal departments and committees of the Congress are supposed to be discreet in their disclosure of information relating to matters pending in court. But it takes little imagination to conjure up the specter of another Joseph McCarthy emerging from a closed committee room to "summarize" the progress of a Congressional inquisition. The McCarthy scourge illustrates the extent to which the press may become an unwitting accomplice to a legislator purposely using the media to disseminate lies. And some courts have extended the protection of qualified privilege against libel actions to news stories based on these one-sided reports.[10]

The sanction of publicity has been used by Congress with telling effects in other areas of public life as well as in the investigation of subversive activities. The television quiz scandals, organized crime, and union activities are recent examples. Administrative agencies have used publicity as a substitute for litigation, and it has been suggested that the press release is as important a weapon in adversary proceedings before regulatory agencies as the legal brief, and that newspaper publicity will come to occupy more of an attorney's attention than trial strategy.[11]

Libel laws have also been relaxed where executive statements are concerned, whether they are oral or in the form of press releases. One justification is that severe limitations on government publicity, even though designed to protect the reputation of the individual citizen, would seriously jeopardize public debate on matters of pressing public concern. Both secrecy and publicity can obviously be a danger to constitutional rights; and this riddle of democracy is far from being solved. Perhaps the best that can be hoped for is that the courts will continue to demand the highest standards of procedural due process where the privacy of the individual must be disrupted. We know that proof of innocence has a most difficult time catching up with those first dramatic impressions of guilt which can be circulated so widely and rapidly.

Where legislative and executive investigations are involved, a defendant or a witness should be provided with access to defensive publicity.[12] An essential characteristic of an open society is that, on occasion, there be means by which publicity can be organized to rebut a government charge. Publicity, for example, can obviate the danger of secret justice to a defendant; and this is recognized by the fact that almost every step, formal or informal, in a criminal case can be reported with impunity.[13] Although there still is some uncertainty in theory[14] as to where the right of the press to full disclosure ends and individual rights begin, the American press, at least in any comparative sense, is not severely handicapped in covering just about anything that strikes its fancy.

Witnesses and defendants need protection because many of them cannot command the public platform available to a government official. But there seem to be special implications when a principal in a court case is also a Congressman who is able to attract a large audience and try his case out of court. A libel judgment was returned against Representative Adam Clayton Powell of New York after he called a 68-year-old Harlem cleaning woman a "bag woman," or graft collector for police. The courts gave the defendant no opportunity for attacking the verdict so Powell made a speech in the House of Representatives, in which he claimed that his legal difficulties were the result of police corruption.[15]

But our concern here is for the defendant whose right to a fair trial is abridged by pre-trial activities on the part of members of the executive and legislative branches.

For a starting point, we might go back to the night that President Johnson announced the arrest of the four Klansmen in Alabama. The President and the attorney general were not alone before the cameras that night. Standing beside Mr. Johnson was J. Edgar Hoover, director of the Federal Bureau of Investigation. It was Hoover who had announced a year earlier that three men had been arrested in connection with the kidnaping of Frank Sinatra, Jr. According to a witness at the Morse bill hearings, Hoover "made their defense difficult by declaring publicly that each of the three had previous criminal records." Actually, their records contained only arrests, not convictions, and "even that fact would not have been admissible in court if the defendants had elected not to take the stand."[16]

The problem is not limited to the activities of the federal government. For example, two men were arrested in 1957 in Hartford, Conn., after a series of holdups and murders. One of them eventually confessed and implicated the other. (The conviction later was reversed by the United States Supreme Court on the ground that the confession was coerced.)[17] Before the defendants were brought to trial, the acting governor of the state praised the police for bringing "to an end the rash of holdup murders that has plagued Connecticut."[18] At this point, we might echo the question of John Adams and of the mother of the Alabama Klansman: What chance does a man have when he comes to trial if the Chief Executive already has decreed that he is guilty?

The problem of the third party is best illustrated at the federal level, where greater publicity is likely to result. One or more third parties can be seen operating in a number of federal cases—among them, those of Alger Hiss, Bernard Goldfine, Dave Beck, and James Hoffa.

Testimony by Hiss and Whittaker Chambers conflicted when they appeared before the House Committee on Un-American Activities in the summer of 1948. Hiss sued Chambers for libel, and a federal grand jury could see that one of the two should be indicted for perjury. The Justice Department presented its evidence against Hiss to the grand jury and maintained silence in the face of growing public pressure. In fact, one of Hiss' attorneys said at the Morse bill hearings that "I thought in that case the Department's silence was in the best tradition of the law."[19]

It was then that members of HUAC injected themselves into the case. Chambers led committee members to his Maryland farm and disclosed incriminating microfilm hidden in a hollowed-out pumpkin. Over a period of a week, the committee released to the press all but four of about 200 "pumpkin papers."[20] While the disclosures were being made, the grand jury indicted Hiss.

The former State Department official's first trial ended in a hung jury, and prompted a public statement from Richard M. Nixon of California, then a member of the House committee investigating Hiss. Nixon was quoted in the New York papers as saying that the trial judge had been prejudiced against the prosecution. The Congressman made similar statements in a radio interview. Two days after Nixon's first statement, Harold H. Velde of Illinois, another HUAC member, listed six "flagrant examples" of misconduct by the judge. With the newspapers, Congressmen, and even the jurors criticizing the judge, the procedure, and the outcome, the defense asked for a change of venue from New York to Vermont for the second trial. The motion was denied, a new judge presided, and Hiss was convicted on two counts of perjury.[21]

Under these circumstances, it is difficult to disagree with A. J. Liebling's comment that "the great attack on judge and jury that had followed the first trial had obviated any chance of getting a fair jury in New York . . ."[22] And in the midst of the furor was the third party, members of the House Committee on Un-American Activities.

The political power structure changed in the 10 years between the Alger Hiss and Bernard Goldfine cases, but the extralegal public statements by third parties remained depressingly the same.

John Fox, financier who had been publisher of the defunct *Boston Post*, testified before the Legislative Oversight Subcommittee of the House Committee on Interstate and Foreign Commerce that Goldfine had told him of preferred treatment dispensed by Presidential Assistant Sherman Adams in return for gifts from Goldfine. White House Press Secretary James Hagerty told newsmen the next day that Fox's statements were "deliberate and malicious falsehoods."[23]

When Goldfine testified about his various financial dealings, he refused to answer 22 questions on grounds that they were irrelevant to the subcommittee's investigation and that they concerned "matters which are presently in litigation and under judicial consideration."[24] Faced with what was regarded as a lack of cooperation, the subcommittee asked the House to cite Goldfine for contempt of Congress. Speaking for the resolution, Congressman Oren Harris of Arkansas, subcommittee chairman, called the Boston industrialist "an individual who obviously has been getting by with illegal acts in companies where minority stockholders were involved." Not until later did he see fit to add that "no one was on trial."[25] But before the year was out, Goldfine was involved in three separate legal actions besides a contempt indictment by a federal grand jury.

And one can only conjecture on the amount of damaging information that might have found its way into print before Goldfine's trial if his staff had not discovered a conspiracy between the subcommittee's chief investigator and a newspaper columnist. The subcommittee took time out from its investigation to accept the resignation of Baron I. Shacklette after he and Jack Anderson, Drew Pearson's associate, were discovered with a hidden listening device in a hotel room adjoining one occupied by Jack Lotto, Goldfine's press agent.

In the case of Dave Beck, former president of the International Brotherhood of Teamsters, we again find complaints about publicity resulting from Congressional investigations. Beck, in asking the United States Supreme Court for a reversal of a grand larceny conviction, complained that such publicity had made a fair trial impossible.

Beck's petition claimed that early in the investigation the chairman of the Senate's Select Committee on Improper Activities in the Labor or Management Field (the McClellan Committee) announced that the committee had "produced 'rather conclusive' evidence of a tie-up between West Coast Teamsters and underworld bosses to monopolize vice in Portland, Oregon." The announcement also stated that "Teamsters' President David Beck and Brewster (another Teamster leader) will be summoned for questioning on a charge that they schemed to control Oregon's law enforcement machinery from a local level on up to the governor's chair."

On March 22, 1957, newspapers quoted the committee as stating that "$250,000 had been taken from Teamster funds . . . and used for Beck's personal benefit." Four days later Beck appeared before the committee to the accompaniment of such newspaper headlines as: "Beck Takes 5th Amendment, President of Teamsters 'Very Definitely' Thinks Records Might Incriminate Him." The petition also complained that local television cameras had been permitted to cover the hearings. One Seattle station ran an eight-hour live broadcast of the March 27 committee session supplied by its network, and a number of other stations in the Seattle-Tacoma area had picked up excerpts.

On April 12, *U. S. News & World Report* introduced its account of Beck's travails with the caption: "Take a Look Around Seattle These Days, and You Find What a Senate Inquiry Can Do To a Top Labor Leader In His Own Home Town."

Two weeks later, the King County prosecutor announced that a special grand jury would be impaneled in Seattle "to investigate possible misuse of Teamsters Union funds by international president Dave Beck . . ." This was followed by a federal grand jury indictment in Tacoma for income tax evasion. A few days later, Beck was again called to Washington, D. C., to testify before the McClellan committee.

News stories on his second appearance in Washington emphasized that he had taken the Fifth Amendment 60 times during the hearings. On May 20, the day of the convening of the special jury back in Seattle, the chairman of the Senate committee announced that "the committee has not convicted Mr. Beck of any crime, although it is my belief that he has committed many criminal offenses."

The publicity continued after the special grand jury had been convened, said Beck's petition, and during the period in which the prosecutors were gathering evidence by subpoena. On June 11, for example, news stories on the committee hearings described how "Dave Beck, Jr., who even refused to say whether he knew his father, took shelter behind the (Fifth) amendment 130 times, following the example of Beck, Sr., who refused to answer 210 times in three appearances before the committee." The indictment, returned by the state grand jury on July 12, received banner headlines.

In late August, a third grand jury indicted Beck and others on additional income tax evasion counts, and the defendants were again called before the U. S. Senate committee. Further publicity was stimulated when the younger Beck was convicted of larceny charges in late November. The father's conviction in a Seattle courtroom followed on December 14, nine months after his first appearance before the Senate committee. On May 14, 1962, the United States Supreme Court rejected Beck's arguments and affirmed his conviction by the Washington state courts.

Newspaper coverage of the Beck case in Seattle, at least in the early stages, was moderate and subdued; and an unusual reliance was placed on wire copy. The Supreme Court said as much in affirming the conviction: the publicity was neither intensive nor extensive, nor did it deviate from accepted journalistic practice.[26] Observers might conjecture: Did Seattle newspapers fear another libel action by Beck (the *Seattle Times* had felt his sting in 1936); were they protecting him as part of that community's Establishment; or were they genuinely sensitive to his rights as an accused who had not yet been proved guilty? Perhaps the newspapers were doing a better job of insuring a fair trial than was the Senate committee.

The Hiss, Goldfine and Beck cases demonstrate the workings of a third party in dispensing pre-trial information, but any discussion in this area must eventually focus on the problems of James Hoffa, Beck's successor as Teamster president. Unfairness or indiscretion on the part of any branch of government in the realm of individual rights will seriously weaken its case for legislative strictures on news reporting. The three previous cases were concerned mainly with pre-trial publicity fostered by Congressional hearings. But the Justice Department, accused of both indiscretion and unfairness, bears the brunt of the attack in the case of Hoffa, although the charge includes the McClellan committee hearings.

Sidney Zagri, legislative counsel for the Teamsters Union, told members of two subcommittees of the Senate Judiciary Committee that "the impact of the McClellan hearings on millions of TV viewers compromised Mr. Hoffa's position in the minds of the American people, in the minds of prospective or actual members of grand juries or petit juries considering either indictments against Mr. Hoffa or weighing evidence both for and against Mr. Hoffa in current cases." He noted that Hoffa was called as a witness before the committee on 48 separate occasions over a two-year period while indictments were being considered "by 1 or more of 27 grand juries investigating Hoffa during this period."[27]

Hoffa's lawyer, Edward Bennett Williams, also was concerned about the legislature's damage to his client's cause. For four years the McClellan committee held hearings which resulted in 20,000 pages of testimony, filling 59 volumes. "The victims were accused often by rumor and hearsay," said Williams. "If they admitted the accusation, they faced conviction. If they denied it, they faced perjury. And if they stood silent, they faced contempt." Such devices may undermine our traditional legal procedure, Williams believes. If a man cannot be convicted in court by due process of law, he can be convicted in the public mind through legislative investigation and the attendant publicity.[28]

Another writer noted that the McClellan committee conducted itself in the Teamster investigation with more decorum than did the

McCarthy committee and more than is usual for the House Committee on Un-American Activities. "Its purpose, however, like theirs, was not primarily the formulation of legislation, but prosecution by Congress and the newspapers. During the McClellan committee's hearings scores of men were damned publicly without the opportunity to reply, and often through distorted evaluations of the 'evidence'."[29]

Zagri also charged that Senator McClellan, interviewed on a network television program, referred to Hoffa as "a menace to society" and "a threat to our national safety and welfare."[30]

Robert F. Kennedy resigned as counsel for the McClellan committee in order to conduct his brother's campaign for the Presidency. During the televised debates, candidate John F. Kennedy said, "I'm not satisfied when I see men like Jimmy Hoffa in charge of the largest union in the United States still free." He told a reporter that he made the statement "because I think Mr. Hoffa has breached national law, state law." On another occasion during the campaign, the future President remarked: "In my judgment, an effective Attorney General with the present laws we now have on the books can remove Mr. Hoffa from office. And I assure you that both my brother and myself have a very deep conviction on the subject of Mr. Hoffa."[31]

Then at a time when a grand jury had been convened to consider charges against Hoffa, Robert Kennedy appeared on network television and was asked to comment on his brother's campaign statements about the Teamsters' leader. His answer: "I think it is an extremely dangerous situation at the present time; this man who has a background of corruption and dishonesty, has misused hundreds of thousands of dollars of union funds, betrayed the union membership, sold out the membership, put gangsters and racketeers in positions of power, and still heads the Teamsters Union."[32]

Robert Kennedy was named attorney general and the campaign against Hoffa continued. In fact, concern has been expressed about the possibility of a vendetta having been waged against the Teamster's boss by the Justice Department so as to trap him on one charge or another. Four attempts had failed before Hoffa was finally convicted of jury tampering, a charge growing out of a 1962 Nashville trial on conspiracy charges. The merits of the government's case are not our concern. Its tactics are.

Under the headline, "Government's Plan to Oust Hoffa by '64," the *Wall Street Journal* of June 11, 1962, said: "Though their best-laid plans have gone awry in the past, Government investigators are confident they've devised a strategy grand enough in concept to insure the ouster of James R. Hoffa as Teamster president—not this year, but maybe next year, or the year after." A general call to arms indeed.

Hoffa's 1962 Nashville trial led to an interesting sidelight in the running battle. After being cleared of the federal charges which had been brought, Hoffa said that Attorney General Kennedy had tried to tell *Nashville Banner* Publisher James G. Stahlman what the paper "should or should not print" about the trial. Hoffa added that he could provide a transcript of a telephone conversation in which Kennedy had brought pressure to bear on the publisher. How Hoffa got such a transcript was not revealed. But it did exist, and to protect his professional integrity, Stahlman printed it, in full, in the *Banner*.

The conversation between attorney general and publisher came after someone purporting to be a *Banner* reporter called prospective jurors to ask them how they felt about the case which had just begun. Stahlman was so horrified by the prospect of his newspaper being implicated in jury tampering that he offered a $5,000 reward for information leading to the arrest of the imposter. It was at this point that the attorney general stepped in to try to dissuade Stahlman from publishing anything about the incident for fear it would win Hoffa a mistrial. Excerpts from this conversation follow:

Kennedy: ". . . It is the opinion of our lawyers . . . that if a detailed story in connection with this matter were made, it might very well lead to a mistrial in his case. I am sure you are as interested as I am in attempting to bring this trial to a successful conclusion. I can understand your own personal concern as to what has resulted at the trial. I have been subjected to these matters for a period of five years now, and the one thing that Mr. Hoffa is interested in is to obtain a mistrial. . . . If we take any steps now that will lead in that direction, we will play right in his ballpark."

Stahlman: "We are just as anxious to see a successful case against this fellow as you are. We are going to be the last people on the face of the earth to jeopardize that, if it be within our power. . . . A gross injustice has been done to me, my newspaper and my associates on this newspaper, and I feel that it is necessary to put our position in the clear . . ."

Kennedy: "As long as they can get somebody to take public steps, they can get delays, and it doesn't bother them a bit."

Stahlman: "I cannot leave my newspaper in the position of having a false statement made about it or members of its staff."

Kennedy: "These matters require sacrifice by many people."

Stahlman: "General [sic] Kennedy, I have made as many sacrifices for the Department of Justice as any man in middle Tennessee.

I have made many sacrifices for my country and will continue to do so. I am suggesting to you that what has happened has made it necessary for me to defend the reputation of my newspaper, which has existed for 86 years, and I don't intend to have it sacrificed for Jimmy Hoffa, the Federal Government or anybody else."

So the story was printed. And there was no mistrial. Nine weeks later Hoffa was freed when the jury could not agree. We do not know who was villain or hero in the play, but Hoffa had pointed his finger at the attorney general of the United States, whose duty it is to see that justice moves along an unhampered course, for trying to suppress a fact in order to win a conviction.[33]

Other persons have pointed fingers in Robert Kennedy's direction for just the opposite reason—publicizing information that they assume to be prejudicial. In introducing his bill, Senator Morse placed in the record four Department of Justice press releases which he said tended to prejudice Hoffa's case.[34] Three were issued after federal grand jury indictments and presented the government's case; the fourth outlined criminal actions against Hoffa dating back to 1942. A sample paragraph follows:

"Wiretap trials: On May 14, 1957, a Federal grand jury for the Southern District of New York charged James Riddle Hoffa, the late Owen 'Bert' Brennan, and Bernard B. Spindel in a one-count indictment charging them with conspiracy to violate the wiretapping law. The indictment charged that beginning in 1953 the defendants conspired to intercept the telephone conversation of officials and employees of the Teamsters Union at the Teamsters headquarters, Detroit, Mich., who might be called to appear as witnesses before a congressional committee and a Detroit grand jury investigating labor racketeering. The first trial of the indictment resulted in a hung jury, and the jury was dismissed on December 20, 1957. *The newspapers reported that the jurors stood 11 to 1 for a conviction.* Upon retrial the defendants were all acquitted on June 23, 1958." (Emphasis added.)

Williams, Hoffa's lawyer, thought the substance of that charge ironic in light of the fact that at the same time the FBI, a division of the Department of Justice, had announced the existence of 90 of its own wiretaps.

But press releases are not the only kinds of communications in question. Thomas A. Bolan, law partner of Roy M. Cohn, told a Senate subcommittee in March, 1965, that he had been checking on a *Life* article about Cohn published while Cohn was under indictment on 10 counts of perjury and obstruction of justice. During his search of the magazine's files, Bolan found a memorandum dated March 6,

1961, from the Washington bureau chief to an editor in New York. According to the memorandum, the bureau chief had been urged by Kennedy's office to publish an article by Sam Baron, Teamster official who opposed Hoffa. Kennedy "suggested to this man that he make his break via an article in *Life* in the form of a personal exposé of Hoffa," who was under indictment for mail fraud at the time.[35]

Zagri, the Teamsters' legislative counsel, had made the charge earlier in his 1964 presentation to the platform committee of the Republican National Convention. The *Nation* noted Zagri's remarks in its issue of September 7, 1964, and pointed out that the Baron article appeared in *Life* on July 20, 1962, "carefully timed to help establish a climate of opinion highly unfavorable to Hoffa who was scheduled to go on trial in Nashville in the early fall of the same year." The *Nation* also was concerned about two 1964 articles, one in the May 15 issue of *Life* and the other in the May 19 issue of *Look*. Both were sensational revelations by Teamster Edward Partin. These articles, commented the *Nation*, "were clearly instigated by the Department of Justice" as Hoffa was about to go on trial in Chicago. The question at issue, the *Nation* added, "is not whether Hoffa is saint or sinner, a good or an evil influence, guilty or innocent, but rather whether he is entitled to a fair trial."

Zagri referred to the magazine articles again when he testified in August, 1965, before the Senate subcommittees which were conducting hearings on the Morse bill. He noted that the *Look* article was one of three written for that magazine by Clark Mollenhoff, all dealing with Hoffa. "The articles," he asserted, "dealt with matters which could have only been disclosed from confidential information in Government files or in the files of the prosecutor or the grand juries."[36]

Of course, there is another side to the controversy. It would be a mistake to paint Kennedy and the Justice Department completely black and to bedeck Hoffa in the shiniest of armor. Kennedy—by then, the junior Senator from New York—appeared before the same Senate committee that had listened to Bolan's testimony about the *Life* memorandum and denied improper conduct. According to Kennedy, Baron wanted to tell his story to *Life* and he contacted the attorney general, who merely put the Teamster in touch with the magazine. Edward Thompson, the editor to whom the memorandum was sent, called Kennedy's statement "basically correct." And Baron, who was then working in Montreal, confirmed that he suggested the article to Kennedy.[37]

As for the Mollenhoff articles in *Look*, Assistant Attorney General Vinson has denied that the writer obtained information from confidential government files. "Most of the facts reported by Mr. Mollenhoff were available from court files, committee hearings, and other public records to anyone who wished to examine them," Vinson wrote in answer to Zagri's charges. "Any additional facts may well have been obtained by his own investigation as an experienced journalist."

Vinson also commented on the charge of "trial by press release." He stated that three releases mentioned by Zagri and included in the record by Senator Morse were summaries of indictments against Hoffa which had been handed down by grand juries on the dates of the releases. Zagri had said the releases were "slanted from the Government's point of view" but, then, a summary of an indictment, Vinson countered, could do little more than present the government's case. The fourth item was not a general release, but a summary of Hoffa's record "prepared by the Justice Department in response to repeated requests by members of the press for such information from this Department." It was not volunteered, Vinson said, and was sent only to those who made specific inquiries.[38]

In January, 1966, the United States Supreme Court agreed to review Hoffa's 1964 jury-tampering conviction on one question alone: whether evidence obtained from Edward Partin should be suppressed because he was released from jail and planted in the Hoffa organization as a spy for the Justice Department. The court turned down an opportunity to review 20 other questions, including whether Hoffa had been deprived of a fair trial by prejudicial publicity.[39] Therefore, the court is questioning Partin's testimony on the witness stand but apparently not his revelations in *Life* and *Look*.

The paradox for both government and press in pursuing such cases is that overplay leads to charges of irresponsibility and underplay leads to charges of concealment. Certainly the public interest is clear in such matters. The question is: When does news coverage move beyond the bounds of public interest and become an illegal and immoral denial of individual rights? And whose responsibility is paramount, the government source or the news editor who ultimately must decide what shall and what shall not be presented to the public?

The Morse bill means to answer some of these questions. In its framer's own words, its intention is to make meaningful those standards that have been applied by the court in cases where convictions have been reversed "by requiring the defendant to show only that the jury had access to evidence that would have been excluded from the trial because of its prejudicial nature: the burden would then shift to the prosecution to show that it had no adverse effect on the conduct of the trial."

Senator Morse is after prosecutors and their seemingly unbreakable habit of trying cases in the press in defiance of their own code of ethics. He holds no brief for cooperating newsmen, but his bill would not punish them. If the courts will develop no adequate sanction, he feels, the legislature must act. But Morse oversimplifies.

At least these questions remain. How much publicity is actually fomented by prominent defendants such as Hoffa and Beck in the belief that it might help rather than hinder their causes? And does not the defendant have a right to whatever emotional appeal such publicity might have? Furthermore, what of the public interest in cases with wide social ramifications? To what extent should the press perform its traditional watchdog function?

Perhaps the ultimate responsibility lies with the press as a gate-keeper. Allow it full access and let it decide what it will print for both the public and private good. Many critics of the press, however, would say that such a decision cannot be left to the working newsman. They would agree with H. L. Mencken's observation on journalism's pretension to professionalism: "Journalistic codes of ethics are all moonshine. Essentially, they are as absurd as would be codes of street-car conductors, barbers or public jobholders."

But can legislation be the answer? Are any of the three branches of government justified in seeking ways to throttle the press when their own lawyers, committees and departments play such an enthusiastic game of feeding it?

CHAPTER 7

FREE PRESS IN RETROSPECT

"As it is a settled rule in the law of England, that the subject may always address a competent jurisdiction, no legal argument can shake the freedom of the press in my sense of it, if I am supported in my doctrine concerning the great unalienable right of the people, to reform or to change their governments. It is because the liberty of the press resolves itself into this great issue, that it has been in every country the last liberty which subjects have been able to wrest from power. Other liberties are held under governments, but the liberty of opinion keeps governments themselves in due subjection to their duties."—Lord Erskine in defense of Tom Paine.[1]

Freedom of speech and of press, given birth by 18th century liberalism, were grandchildren of the Renaissance, that gradual awakening of human reason and individual conscience. They were perceived as natural rights bestowed by man's Creator, and inviolable against government, a mere artifice constructed by consenting individual wills. But they were rights that literally had to be torn from the grip of authority whatever its form: a Tudor king with his licensing company and secret justice, a repressive and bigotted Parliament, or a Church claiming infallibility. Men died in their behalf, but great protesting testaments against arbitrary power survived.

The radical Levellers, anticipating written constitutions, limited government, and the separation of powers, made as logical an appeal for freedom of the press as can be found. The year was 1649:

"As for any prejudice to Government thereby, if Government be just in its Constitution, and equal in its distributions, it will be good, if not absolutely necessary for them, to hear all voices and judgments, which they can never do, but by giving freedom to the Press, and in case any abuse their authority by scandalous pamphlets, they will never want Advocates to vindicate their innocency. And therefore all things being duly weighed, to refer all Books and Pamphlets to the judgment, discretion, or affections of Licensers, or to put the least restraint upon the Press, seems altogether inconsistent with the good of the Commonwealth, and expressly opposite and dangerous to the liberties of the people, and to be carefully avoided, as any other exorbitancy or prejudice in Government."[2]

The chief instrument for suppressing free speech and press was the law of seditious libel, a broad spectrum of crimes of expression punished by judicial fiat. In 1792 a slight breach in this oppressive jurisdiction was made by the Fox Libel Act which gave to the English jury the right to determine what constituted criminal defamation. Fifty-seven years earlier Andrew Hamilton of Philadelphia had persuaded a colonial jury to perform the same, and what was at that time an illegal, function in acquitting John Peter Zenger who had set type for a criminal libel against the Governor.

Two years after Alexander Hamilton's brilliant defense of a Federalist editor in 1803,[3] the New York legislature enacted a bill allowing the jury to decide the criminality of an alleged libel and permitting truth as a defense when published with good motives and for justifiable ends.

Freedom of speech and press were not spontaneous notions; their definitions gradually emerged from the judicial opinions of Lords Erskine and Camden, from John Locke's "Second Treatise of Civil Government," from clandestine publications of John Trenchard and William Gordon appearing under the pseudonym "Cato," and from the writings of Bentham and Spinoza. In America freedom of speech and press evolved from the libertarian proposals of such men as the Rev. Philip Freneaux, Albert Gallatin, George Hay and Tunis Wortman. The latter's "Treatise Concerning Political Enquiry, and the Liberty of the Press," published in 1800, is considered by one historian to be the pre-eminent American classic on the subject.[4]

All were men of the Enlightenment. They were also men of their time, steeped in a common law which could not condone the idea of willful seditious libel, and bound by the norms of a society which, even with its libertarian spirit, defined freedom of speech and press narrowly. But they would attack speech only when it was brigaded with overt criminal conduct, not the bad tendency of an idea, for they believed strongly in a free marketplace of ideas.

There is evidence that a desire to protect states rights, rather than a highly conceptualized appreciation of free speech and press, provided the basic rationale for the First Amendment. But there is also evidence that James Madison was thinking in near absolutist terms and, in fact, proposed an additional amendment which would have guaranteed freedom of speech and press against state violation. Certainly partisan politics clouded the vision of men then as it does today. Nevertheless, the First Amendment was written in an atmosphere distrustful of the arbitrary powers of government, and, whatever its intention, it gave bold constitutional recognition to the great principle of free expression.

There are some today who read the First Amendment in near absolute terms. Justice Black would place freedom of speech and press wholly "beyond the reach" of Congress and court to prevent restraints in the light of what they think are "more important interests."[5] And he has declared that even libel and slander actions are an unconstitutional abridgement of free speech and press. Alexander Meiklejohn has viewed these freedoms as an absolute right of society to guard its thinking processes, admitting of no exceptions.[6]

Others, notably the late Justice Felix Frankfurter, view freedom of speech and press as one of a number of competing social and individual interests which must be balanced as the particular circumstances require. Anything but an absolute, freedom of expression "is subject to prohibition of those abuses . . . which a civilized society may forbid."[7] Frankfurter rejected the idea that a law which on its face invaded free speech must be presumed unconstitutional.

The trick seems to be to recognize the concurrent individual and social components of these rights. As Roscoe Pound has warned, "When it comes to weighing or valuing claims or demands with respect to other claims or demands, we must be careful to compare them on the same plane. If we put one as an individual interest and the other as a social interest we may decide the question in advance in our way of putting it."[8] Only as a social right can free speech and press stand against a claim of national security. Unfortunately the Court, with Frankfurter's encouragement, has shown regrettable deference to repressive laws in this connection. Similarly, the individual right to a fair trial may be outweighed when balanced against society's need for full disclosure and discussion.

A more general argument for the doctrine of judicial restraint—that is, the non-interference of the Court with legislation—is that the Supreme Court is an undemocratic institution and that the democratic processes of the Congress must not be impaired; power and responsibility shall remain with the people and their representatives. This position is weakened by its dependence upon a 19th century model of representative government which assumes that the "will of the people" is accurately reflected in its Congress. It fails to take into account a decentralized political party system, the existence of well organized and powerful interest groups, a Congress skewed in favor of conservative, and frequently rural, constituencies, and a seniority system which is greatly burdened by one-party states. The will of the people may sometimes be a minority will. A balance of interest test to function safely in an open society must be carefully applied to the facts of a specific case; private and public rights must be considered concomitantly in the light of those facts and weighed against one another in the same scales. There can be no room here for the philosophic preferences of individual members of the Court.

The Supreme Court today is an activist body in that it has assumed for itself a positive governmental role of judicial review. In the first 100 years of its existence it scrutinized social and economic legislation in the name of due process; today its preoccupation is with civil rights and civil liberties. "Those liberties of the individual which history has attested as the indispensable conditions of an open as against a closed society," said Justice Frankfurter in one of his more libertarian moods, "come to this Court with a momentum for respect lacking when appeal is made to liberties which derive merely from shifting economic arrangements."[10] And Justice Brennan has put the matter well in these words:

"The protection given speech and press was fashioned to assure unfettered interchange of ideas for the bringing about of political and social changes desired by the people . . . All ideas having even the slightest redeeming social importance—unorthodox ideas, controversial ideas, even ideas hateful to the prevailing climate of opinion—have the full protection of the guaranties, unless excludable because they encroach upon the limited area of more important interests."[11]

At one time or another all contemporary justices have expressed preference for the freedoms of the mind, though there have sometimes been sharp disagreements as to where they stand in relation to other vital freedoms in specific circumstances. Frankfurter was of the conviction that "no constitutional guarantee enjoys preference"[12] and that "the Constitution does not give us greater veto power when dealing with one phase of 'liberty' than with another."[13]

Neither the common law of England nor the First Amendment settled once and for all the delicate boundaries of free expression. Zealous courts, protecting their dignity and decorum with "immemorial" powers, and frightened legislatures, responding to what John Stuart Mill called "the tyranny of the prevailing opinion and feeling," bear testimony to the fragility of freedom of speech and press.

In an historic case arising under the Espionage and Sedition Acts of 1917 and 1918, Justice Holmes enunciated his famous "clear and present danger" test. The issue was whether the accused, by circulating pamphlets urging people to resist the draft, had violated the Espionage Act. Writing for a unanimous court that said he had, Justice Holmes declared: "The question in every case is whether the words used are used in such circumstances and are of such a nature as to create a clear and present danger that they will bring about the substantive evils that Congress has a right to prevent. It is a question of proximity and degree."[14]

The court's decision in this connection was an attempt to draw that fine line between legitimate expression and expression so brigaded with illegal or anti-social conduct that it must be prevented. A few months later, in a case upholding the conviction of a group of persons who were urging interference with American participation in the Russian revolution, Holmes and Brandeis deserted the majority. In a ringing defense of the widest latitude for free speech and press, Holmes wrote: "It is only the present danger of immediate evil or intent to bring it about that warrants Congress in setting a limit to the expression of opinion *where private rights are not concerned*."[15] (Emphasis added.) The qualification is significant to the free press-fair trial dilemma, and it suggests, of course, that this is no absolutist test, but, as Justice Brandeis was to say later, "a rule of reason" which "can be applied correctly only by the exercise of good judgment."[16]

If "clear and present danger" was ever Supreme Court doctrine, it was only when Justices Black, Douglas, Murphy and Rutledge were together on the bench. Black and Douglas still use the test; and its usefulness is plain where it may discourage premature intervention by the state and provide an opportunity for counter-speech rather than suppression. But its usefulness is not so clear where counter-speech is unavailable or unavailing as in cases of contempt of court (fair trial) or obscenity.[17]

Wallace Mendelson suggests that in 1943 the "clear and present danger" test lost its intrinsic meaning when it was cut loose from its anchor in the distinction between discussion and incitement. It is no longer a guide to decision, he says, but a cloak for "vague but fervent transcendentalism."[18] Moreover, the test has also suffered irreparable damage where it has been replaced by or transformed into a "clear and probable danger" test, or a "bad," "remote" or "reasonable tendency" test. These are retrogressions which hardly express a preference for freedom.

In the Communist conspiracy cases of the 1950s, free speech could not withstand the demands of national security. Bad intent became a crime. Only for Justices Black and Douglas did "clear and present danger" still appear to be applicable. "How it can be said that there is a clear and present danger that this advocacy will succeed is . . . a mystery," said Douglas in the Dennis case. "Seditious conduct can always be punished. But the command of the First Amendment is so clear that we should not allow Congress to call a halt to free speech except in the extreme case of peril from the speech itself. The First Amendment makes confidence in the common sense of our people and in their maturity of judgment the great postulate of our democracy."[19] The Smith Act of 1940, under which the Dennis case indictments were brought, was the first peacetime sedition act since the deplorable Act of 1798.

But fortunately "the clear and present danger" test is not the only means by which the preference for First Amendment freedoms has been sustained. Since the nationalization of fundamental civil liberties —which began in 1925[20] by a process of absorption under the due process clause of the Fourteenth Amendment—no presumption of constitutionality attaches to a statute, state or federal, which on its face appears to severely restrict freedom of expression. Licensing, discriminatory taxation, and other forms of prior restraint are not permitted, and the most strict construction is given to statutes which appear to infringe upon these rights.[21] Higher standards of procedural due process are required where these rights may be jeopardized. Statutes which qualify these freedoms are scrutinized for vagueness.[22] Unlawful intent must be proven, and the burden of proof falls upon the state.[23]

A major difficulty in securing Supreme Court review of constitutional issues has been the requirement that such an issue can be raised only by a person who has standing to sue—that is, by one who has suffered direct and personal injury as a result of allegedly unconstitutional action. In a case involving the NAACP[24] this standing requirement was relaxed. The court allowed the organization, a membership corporation, to assert on behalf of its members the claim that compelled disclosure of the members' names would invade the First Amendment right of free association.

It would be grossly inaccurate to suggest that free speech and press have come down to us in an unbroken line of judgments of ever-increasing certainty. Indeed, judicial doctrines are something less than eternal verities. Although the courts have been responsive to the broad dictates of the First Amendment, the ideal concept of natural rights is no longer "respectable" philosophy. The rise of the urban mass society and the propositions of relativism, irrationalism, existentialism, and behaviorism have tended to shift the locus of free speech and press from the individual to the group—freedom *for* rather than freedom *from*. The individual is seen as the nexus of a complex system of cause-effect relationships emanating from his immediate social environment. The self has meaning only in the collectivity of culture.[25] The problem may no longer be what is permissible speech, but how does one make oneself heard in what is a raucous and largely controlled marketplace of ideas? And how does one enjoy the more passive liberties such as the right of privacy and the right to hear? The mass media are adjuncts of this new social order, and they function in part as agencies of social control disseminating those symbols of conformity which characterize the mass society. For every individual right there are now concomitant social duties, and "the press must know that its faults and errors have ceased to be private vagaries and have become public dangers."[26] Government in the modern society may be the guardian as well as the guillotine of free expression.

Whether we have expanded or shrunk our sphere of essential freedom through this positive re-definition of the concept of freedom of speech and press is a question of great moment. To consider individual rights apart from their social context is to contemplate anarchy; conversely, to permit social rights to subsume those of the individual is to commit oneself to the organic view of society in which the state assumes the rights and the individual merely performs his social duties. Such is the frustration of the modern-day liberal. Platforms in the marketplace are expensive and monopolized, so the cherished freedoms can find expression only through powerful blocs, government, unions, religious and political action groups. The editor himself is part of a social institution which reinforces dominant viewpoints more often than it nutures dissent. The collective will, through the manipulation of electorates and the destruction of a variable public opinion, begins its gradual dissolution of the individual "I" of liberal philosophy. The process may be said to be complete when one asks as did Lenin: "Why should a government which is doing what it believes is right allow itself to be criticized?" And the dominant collective need not be government.

But the transformation is not complete in the democratic societies and individual free speech still has its champions, editors among them. The ideal of free speech and press still grips the imaginations of the citizenry, although the health and vigor of these rights will depend upon their being exercised.

The urgent task for legislator, lawyer and layman seems to be to find that delicate balance between the public and private components of conflicting rights. The fullest development of every human personality is contingent upon the highest degree of individual expression possible in an ordered society—a liberty close to the inner life of man. At the same time, freedom of speech and press as social rights are the keystone of an open society, the freedoms that best guarantee against the destruction of all other rights. This is what the editor has in mind when he sincerely espouses the public's right to know.

Some forms of speech, especially those serving no public function and destructive of other rights, such as the individual's right to a fair trial, will have limits imposed upon them by a court free to make choices between constitutional values in the light of the facts of specific cases. Where the court neglects or postpones its judicial duty, the legislatures may intervene, just as the court has acted where the Congress or the states have been unwilling or unable to protect or promote other constitutional rights. Both are policymaking organs of government.

There is, of course, a middle way out of the free press-free trial maze. It is the way of responsibility and sensitivity, a way which both press and bar must be prepared to take.

CHAPTER 8

FAIR TRIAL IN RETROSPECT

"In all criminal prosecutions the accused shall enjoy the right to a speedy and public trial, by an impartial jury of the State and district wherein the crime shall have been committed, which district shall have been previously ascertained by law, and to be informed of the nature and cause of the accusation against him; to have compulsory process for obtaining witnesses in his favor, and to have the assistance of counsel for his defense."—Amendment VI, Constitution of the United States.

Trial by jury came to America with the colonists. It was affirmed in the Constitution's Fifth and Sixth Amendments. The due process clause of the Fifth Amendment requires that care be taken in all federal courts to preserve the rudiments of fair play in trial procedure, consonant with our common law heritage. The Sixth Amendment guarantees to all persons accused of a crime trial by an impartial jury which, by implication, reaches its verdict solely upon the facts submitted to it by the court, under the court's instructions and guidance. And a defendant is presumed innocent until proven guilty beyond a reasonable doubt.

Although the concept of a fair trial has never been fully defined, it has been suggested that the aim of the Sixth Amendment is "to assure fairness in judicial proceedings through the guarantee of continued availability of certain procedural devices . . . The aim and effect of the amendment . . . is to secure fairness of proceedings, not specific unalterable forms."[1] Perhaps Justice Owen J. Roberts put it more simply when he said that fair trial "is not that a just result shall have been obtained, but that the result, whatever it be, shall be reached in a fair way. Procedural due process has to do with the manner of the trial; dictates that in the conduct of judicial inquiry certain fundamental rules of fairness be observed; forbids the disregard of those rules, and is not satisfied, though the result is just, if the hearing was unfair."[2] Due process may not be as much a technical concept as it is a state of mind.

The first eight amendments originally placed restraints only on the federal government. No application could be made to the states unless the violation involved what Justice Cardozo called "those fundamental principles of liberty and justice which lie at the base of all our civil and political institutions."[3] These principles were not specified.

In the period immediately after the Civil War, the Fourteenth Amendment was adopted in order to protect the civil rights of Negroes against state violations. The states were forbidden to take life, liberty, or property without due process of law, or to deny anyone the equal protection of the laws, and to make laws abridging the privileges and immunities of citizenship. Some of the framers of the Fourteenth had wanted the entire Bill of Rights to apply to the states. In a series of cases brought to the Supreme Court in the next 40 years, this theory was consistently rejected.[4] By distinguishing between state and national citizenship, and by emphasizing that the rights and privileges of federal citizenship do not include the protection of ordinary civil liberties such as freedom of speech and press and fair trial from state power, the court averted, for a time, what was to be a revolution in our constitutional system. That revolution, as has been noted, came in 1925 when the court declared that: "We may and do assume that freedom of speech and press . . . are among the fundamental personal rights and 'liberties' protected by the due process clause of the Fourteenth Amendment from impairment by the states."[5] This construction of the Fourteenth had been foreshadowed in earlier dissents by Justices John Marshall Harlan[6] and Louis Brandeis.[7]

The provisions of the Bill of Rights still impose direct limitations only upon the federal government; it is the Fourteenth Amendment which limits the states. By a gradual process of incorporation, the Supreme Court, in its decisions in specific cases, has lengthened the list of civil liberties which are, again in the words of Justice Cardozo, "the very essence of a scheme of ordered lberty," and therefore must be protected against state power.

But the rate of incorporation has been startling. It now appears that most of the important provisions of the Bill of Rights have come under the shelter of the due process clause, the exceptions being the Fifth Amendment's double jeopardy clause, and the Sixth and Seventh's jury trial guarantees. It is noteworthy that the First Amendment freedoms were the first to be incorporated.

Although the court had said in 1904 that trial by jury is not a "fundamental" right,[8] every state constitution guarantees jury trial, and a state is expected to insure the fair administration of its system. In 1915, for example, the Supreme Court said that a trial dominated by a mob is a departure from due process of law.[9] And in an early Arkansas case, in which five Negro defendants were convicted of murder and sentenced to death, colored witnesses were whipped and tortured and systematically excluded from the jury. Lynchings were averted only by a solemn promise on the part of the court that "the law" would be carried out. Daily newspaper articles helped to inflame the mob. The trial listed 45 minutes and the jury was out for 15. Under such conditions, said the Supreme Court, the convictions are absolutely void.[10] In an important case, *Powell* v. *Alabama*,[11] the court ruled that due process requires state courts to appoint lawyers for poor, ignorant Negro defendants since the right to counsel is of a fundamental character. The Supreme Court has also reversed convictions where the judge appears to have a pecuniary interest in the outcome;[12] where there is racial discrimination in the selection of a jury;[13] and where there is evidence of either psychological or physical coercion of a defendant by police officers.[14] In a Florida case[15] four Negroes made "sunrise confessions" after five days of relentless interrogation; and in a Mississippi case a conviction for murder was based on confessions obtained by brutality and physical torture.[16] Due process was denied in both, said the Supreme Court. Nor can a state knowingly permit a conviction to rest on perjured testimony.[17]

In 1952 a shocked court reversed a California conviction based on evidence obtained from a narcotics suspect by means of a stomach pump.[18] Ten years later, in another California case, the cruel-and-unusual punishment prohibition of the Eighth Amendment was added to the fundamental list and applied to the states.[19] The court in 1956 adopted the rule that all indigent defendants be furnished a transcript of their trial for purposes of appeal.[20]

It is in the last few terms that the Supreme Court has shown a most remarkable preoccupation with questions bearing on the nature of due process, equal protection, and the rights of the accused. Fair trial, of course, is an important element of this concern. In 1963, in the now famous *Gideon* case,[21] a unanimous Court extended the right to be represented by counsel to all felons. Formerly, it had applied only to indigents charged with a capital offense. A year later, in *Escobedo* v. *Illinois*,[22] the court explored the problem of when this right begins, and chose the point at which suspicion begins to focus on a suspect or an accusation is implied. After this point, statements made by a defendant whose lawyer is absent will very likely be inadmissible as evidence at the trial. Similar protections have long been afforded defendants in federal cases through the Federal Rules of Criminal Procedure, which have been affirmed by the Supreme Court[23] and strengthened by the Criminal Justice Act of 1964.

Confessions must be clearly voluntary to be admissible as evidence.[24] Accordingly, evidence seized in violation of the Fourth Amendment's guarantee against unreasonable searches and seizures must be excluded from state court proceedings.[25] Although wiretapping has not been held to constitute a search and seizure violative of the Fourth Amendment, the Supreme Court has forbidden the use of this kind of evidence in federal criminal prosecutions.[26] The states are free to do what they want with it.

In a landmark 1964 case, the Fifth Amendment protection against self-incrimination became part of the Fourteenth.[27] Also incorporated in that term of the court was the Sixth Amendment's right of an accused to be confronted by his accuser[28] The court has also ruled that testimony of a witness promised immunity from prosecution in a state court cannot then be used to prosecute him in a federal court, and vice versa.[29]

In its 1965 decision re *Turner* v. *Louisiana*,[30] the Supreme Court held that a state defendant was denied the right to a fair trial by an impartial jury when the two deputy sheriffs who gave key testimony leading to a conviction had charge of the jury during the three-day trial and had fraternized with the jurors outside the courtroom. Justice Stewart, writing for the majority, reflected the higher standards of procedural due process now demanded by the court when he said: "In the constitutional sense, trial by jury in a criminal case necessarily implies at the very least that the 'evidence developed' against a defendant shall come from the witness stand in a public courtroom where there is full judicial protection of the defendant's right of confrontation, of cross-examination, and of counsel."

"TRIAL BY NEWSPAPER"

Until its 1961 landmark decision in the *Irvin* case, the Supreme Court had not placed pre-trial publicity in the same category with police coercion and mob domination as impairments to fair trial. Generations of press critics had done it for the court. Their charge is basically as follows:

Newspapers have been known to demand the arrest of a suspect while police are still seeking evidence. When a suspect is arrested—and often long before a formal charge is made—eager attorneys and enterprising reporters quote police, prospective witnesses, friends, and next of kin as to the guilt or innocence of the accused. And he is often fitted into patently prejudicial criminal stereotypes. Confessions, whether or not they are later found to have been beaten out of a suspect and are therefore inadmissible as evidence, are treated as conclusive proof of guilt. Potential jurors are offered the recommendations and speculations of amateur detectives and the man in the street. Sometimes newspaper polls attempt to predict possible verdicts or, as in the Jack Ruby case, recommend appropriate punishment. In cases which arouse strong public feelings, the press may become highly partisan, disparaging the merits of one party's case. Reporters may accuse a defendant of jury fixing, a witness of perjury, or a court of bias—before the trial gets underway.

Publication of evidence not produced at the trial, even if of an admissible nature, such as an accused's prior criminal record and other information deliberately kept from the jury by rules of evidence, is subject to the additional objections that it is not given under oath and that there is no opportunity for cross-examination.

The detailed presentation of confessions is especially repugnant to defense attorneys. Edwin Borchard, formerly of the Yale University Law School faculty, cautions that confessions, while they may often be conclusive, need to be scrutinized:

"Persons charged with crime, are not infrequently of defective or inferior intelligence, and even without the use of formal third-degree methods, the influence of a strong mind upon a weaker often produces, by persuasion or suggestion, the desired result . . . Public opinion is often as much to blame as the prosecutor or other circumstances for miscarriages of justice. Criminal trials take place under conditions with respect to which public interest and passions are easily aroused. In . . . cases . . . in which the frightful mistake committed might have been avoidable, public opinion was excited by the crime and moved by revenge to demand its sacrifice, a demand to which prosecutions and juries are not impervious."[31]

This view is echoed by Harold Burtt, a legal psychologist, who suggests that "occasionally persons who are mentally abnormal develop delusions that they have killed someone or committed some crime. Such psychopaths are often subject to suggestion. If one of them is told repeatedly by other people that he has done some particular thing, he is liable to come to believe it."[32]

Speaking to the point with considerably more fervor is Lloyd Paul Stryker, a noted defense lawyer who considers "trial by newspaper" one of the worst evils of our day:

"In trial by newspaper, the defendant has no right to compel the attendance of witnesses or to cross-examine the sources quoted by the newspaper. In trial by newspaper, alleged evidence is presented which has either been directly rejected by a court or which, under no cirsumstances, could be admitted. The statements of alleged witnesses are set forth, but there is, of course, no opportunity to cross-examine them. A trial by newspaper is in every way an ex parte, one-sided affair in which all the safeguards of justice which the courts of the United States and England have worked out through the centuries are ignored. An erroneous conviction can be set aside on appeal if there have been errors by the trial court, but against false or prejudicial evidence introduced by publicity, whether planted by prosecutors or published through the industry of the reporters, the appellate courts can give no redress and, thus, the defendant's right to a fair trial is destroyed. Here is an evil against which no advocate can contend."[33]

Appellate courts, of course, have provided redress to defendants whose fair trial may have been impaired by publicity; and Stryker is perceptive enough to note that all sin is not on the side of the press. Perceptive editors have noted time and again how contesting lawyers, especially prosecutors, skillfully manipulate press publicity to advance their own causes, in direct defiance of their own ethical rules. James A. Wechsler, editor of the *New York Post*, says that the biggest stories in the press coverage of the notorious Minot Jelke trial were those circulated by the prosecution in advance of the court proceedings. "Some of them," he recalls, ". . . were more thrilling as originally whispered to us than they . . . turned out to be in the actual script. It seemed rather astonishing that, after all the advance buildup in which the newspapers received every cooperation from the district attorney's office, the district attorney should ultimately associate himself with Judge Valente's view that this trial was too unpleasant to be exhibited on Broadway."[34] Inevitably, such pre-trial tactics on the part of the prosecutor call for counter measures by the defense counsel, and the ensuing publicity battle pretty well takes the case away from the jury and the rules of evidence.

The fact remains that newspapers themselves have on occasion attempted to bring direct pressure to bear upon jurors. Sixty-five years ago, an Illinois newspaper published the names and addresses of the jurors and suggested that they would now have an opportunity to give the plaintiff "justice."[35] More recently, the press has been accused of exerting the same kind of invidious pressure on a grand jury,[36] and on a sentencing judge.[37]

Few Supreme Court Justices have been more concerned about threats to fair trial than was the late Justice Robert H. Jackson. "The custom of injecting evidence and opinions upon the trial by publicity," he declared in 1950, "proceeds to such a point that verdicts in highly publicized American cases will no more really represent the jurors' dispassionate personal judgment on the legal evidence than do those of the 'People's Courts' we so criticize abroad."

Justice Jackson was particularly sensitive to the impact that a loudly proclaimed and coerced confession might have on the minds of jurors. He also felt that the courts were losing their control of judicial proceedings and that trials were becoming free-for-alls. In his opinion defiant, obstructive lawyers within the courtroom were as much to blame as irresponsible editors outside. In a dissenting opinion in an important contempt case, Jackson viewed the right to a fair and calm trial free from outside pressures and influences no less vital than the right to a free press. "Every other right," he pointed out, "including the right of free press itself, may depend on the ability to get a judicial hearing as dispassionate and impartial as the weaknesses inherent in man will permit."[38]

Since fair trial is another of our cherished rights, we must assume that freedom of the press was never meant to prevent a man on trial for his life from receiving a fair verdict from an impartial jury. The right of the press to publish whatever information comes to its attention does not require that this right be exercised, regardless of the harm done to the individual. A former federal judge suggests that the right to publish inevitably includes the right to refrain from publishing, and he believes that the press cannot disavow its moral responsibility for deciding to publish or not to publish.[39] It is possible to be fully aware of the danger imminent in even the slightest encroachment on the right of free expression without denying the high value that a democratic society places upon human life, as manifested in a system of law which presumes a man innocent until proven guilty, all evidence to the contrary notwithstanding.

CHAPTER 9

BAR-PRESS CONFRONTATION

"There are rights that the accused must have fortified, for after a climate has been created, you could convict St. Peter."—Herbert Bayard Swope, former editor, *New York World*.

"In my opinion, pretrial reporting can and often does serve a useful purpose . . . And a strong and free press . . . is every bit as essential as a sound court system to the preservation of our way of life."—Claude R. Sowle, associate dean, Northwestern University School of Law.

Justice Oliver Wendell Holmes was cautious in urging restrictions on free expression. He drew a line where the private rights of the accused were concerned, and would condone no outside influence "whether of private talk or public print."[1] Justice Stanley F. Reed expressed concern about newspaper stimulation that contributed to "grievous tragedies" in the administration of justice.[2] Justice William O. Douglas, a vigorous champion of First Amendment rights, considers "mass opinion . . . to be a dangerous master of decisions when the stakes are life and death . . . It has no business there. It is anathema to the very conception of fair trial. It applies standards that have no place in determining the awful decision of guilt or innocence. The courtroom at these times is as sacrosanct as the cathedral to be guarded against all raucous, impassioned and foreign influence." Rules of evidence, Justice Douglas has pointed out, are designed to narrow the issues and protect the accused against prejudice. "Judges, not newspaper reporters, fashion and supervise those rules . . . for legal trials are not like elections, to be won through the use of the meeting-hall, the radio and the newspaper."[3]

Justice Hugo Black, a stalwart guardian of the First Amendment, has been highly sensitive to the due process rights of the accused, and would protect from state power all the guarantees of the Sixth Amendment—and in fact all the provisions of the Bill of Rights—

through the due process clause of the Fourteenth Amendment. Although he joined the dissent in the *Billie Sol Estes* case, Justice Black suggested in an earlier case that "our system of law has always endeavored to prevent even the probability of unfairness . . ."[4] More recently, and in another dissent, Justice Black said: "The very purpose of a court system is to adjudicate controversies, both criminal and civil, in the calmness and solemnity of the courtroom according to legal procedures."[5]

In his *tour de force* in the *Estes* case, Chief Justice Earl Warren concludes that the court must take notice of the inherent unfairness of television in the courtroom and rule that its presence is inconsistent with the "fundamental conception" of what a trial should be. It cannot realistically be expected that the court will deviate soon from the deep concern it has expressed during recent terms for procedural due process in criminal trials.

Responsible members of bench and bar are asking essentially for a major cutback on publishable pre-verdict information: statements from defendants, arresting officers, victims, relatives, attorneys and witnesses; references to prior records—usually inadmissible unless the defendant becomes a witness; confessions, and such disclosures as the fact that an accused has either failed to pass or refused to take a lie detector test; and news stories in which the victim is eulogized, or the prime suspect is described by police as moody, defiant, arrogant or unpenitent, or tagged as killer, kidnaper or robber.

By implication at least, the legal profession is encouraging publishers to put sophisticated reporters on court beats, men who will exercise sound judgment and discretion. Some lawyers would favor postponing all reporting until the facts have become part of a court record. Some reject the investigatory role of the press; others take it for granted, assuming that all evidence of criminality will be turned over to a district attorney. Many journalists would agree with these suggestions—at least to the point where the public interest in a case becomes overriding. A good number of lawyers would consider revival of the contempt power or restrictive legislation a last resort, and would favor continuing efforts to work out and adopt voluntary codes of professional conduct.

Except in those Southern courts in which it has been hard to get murder convictions, it is the defense attorney who feels most strongly about the possible influence of press coverage. The public's right to know is a slogan with a hollow ring for lawyers defending unpopular, much publicized, and sometimes penniless clients. Against them stand the powerful, affluent, and fiercely competitive mass media which reward reporters for zeal in collecting facts. For the defense counsel crime news dehumanizes the accused and obliterates reasonable doubt and the presumption of innocence. He knows not what its actual effects might be, but he assumes, with undisguised resentment and helplessness, that it will turn prospective jurors against his client. All too often crime news is information that our evolving judicial system has taken pains to reject: hearsay evidence, testimony which cannot be confronted, damaging past records, and confessions of doubtful validity.

The prosecutor is also an enemy. He passes tips to newsmen with impunity, for his professional codes of ethics are never enforced. Police officers, sheriffs, and court clerks likewise frequently do the same; by the very nature of their vocations, they favor convictions and serve as news sources for the media. The defense attorney dares not communicate with the press for fear that his statements will trigger rebuttals from the prosecution that will imprint guilt more clearly on the public mind. He must admit, of course, that some of his colleagues accept the prosecutor's challenge and vie for press publicity themselves. Melvin Belli, Jack Ruby's chief counsel, instigated a public information campaign that focused on a series of autobiographical articles about his client. While appeals were still pending, Belli wrote a book about the trial. He profited, financially and otherwise, from both the articles and the book. Judge Joe B. Brown was working under contract on a Ruby manuscript while presiding over the case.

The court can use procedural remedies to protect justice, but they are difficult for defense counsel to initiate, and have unattractive side-effects. Moreover, they are expensive. And if a charge does not allow bail or bail cannot be raised, his client must stay in jail as long as the trial is delayed. Counsel has an opportunity to challenge veniremen, but how many prospective jurors will admit prejudice, unless they desire to get out of jury duty?

So the defense counsel stands helpless against the press, the public, and the prosecutor—and sometimes even a legislative committee or a powerful bureaucracy. In such an uneven contest justice is inevitably overrun; only its form remains. Ordeal by publicity has become the great-grandchild of ordeal by fire, water and battle—even if by negligence rather than by design. Harris B. Steinberg, a New York attorney, expresses the frustration of the defense in a plea for deliverance from publicity:

"When you choose to lift that weapon against a man on trial for his life or liberty and you say something which comes to the attention of the jurors, either before or after their selection, but which they are not permitted to hear because of rules of evidence painstakingly developed over the years for the protection of accused persons, you have unwittingly struck a blow not only against that particular man's right to a fair trial, but also against our entire system of constitutional safeguards and controls. It is like bringing down a brick on a Swiss watch."[6]

Not all criticism regarding press interference with fair trial focuses on pre-trial reporting. Inadequate or partial coverage of the trial itself, where one side or the other is featured, where special treatment is given to sensational elements, or where matters stricken from the trial record are emphasized, may also prejudice a cause. Since news reports of the case may differ considerably from the way the case is actually presented to judge and jury, public confidence in the judicial process may be shaken when the verdict is contrary to what the reading, listening or viewing public might reasonably have expected from the news accounts.

Neither bar nor bench appears particularly concerned about establishing that there is a connection between publicity and prejudice. In his majority opinion in *Estes*, Justice Tom Clark fortifies the presumption of prejudice when he says, "The State would dispose of all these observations with the simple statement that they are for psychologists because they are purely hypothetical. But we cannot afford the luxury of saying that, because these factors are difficult of ascertainment in particular cases, they must be ignored." The Supreme Court is seldom confronted with or moved by psychological evidence, and is not very sensitive to it. Bias is implied, and with the major premise secure, the syllogism is completed. There is a certain arrogance here, for the question of influence is neither irrelevant nor unanswerable.

Lawyers are more persuasive when they remind newsmen that their individual rights amount to no more than the rights of all citizens. When these rights are attacked, from whatever direction, vindication, in the final analysis, can be found only in the courtroom. And the justness of the result may often depend on a hopefully representative and open-minded panel of jurors.

Unanimity is as rare among lawyers as it is among newsmen. Claude R. Sowle, associate dean and professor of law at Northwestern University's School of Law, says that his original view that pre-trial publicity is generally harmful to our system of justice has "withered away."[7] Placing his trust in jurors, Sowle believes that a strong and free press is every bit as essential to the preservation of our way of life as a sound court system. In Chicago, for example, there are relatively few cases in which the problem of prejudice might be raised,

and most of the defendants involved probably are beyond the help
of corrective measures. "Men such as Anthony Accardo and Jimmy
Hoffa have been in the headlines for years," Sowle says. "Can anyone seriously contend that a brief, selective, legislatively imposed
pre-trial news blackout in their cases would be meaningful?" Dean
Sowle joins newsmen who insist on proof of harm to defendants.

United States Circuit Judge J. Skelly Wright advocates increased
press coverage of all aspects of criminal justice—from the social causes
of crime to prison rehabilitation, from the policeman on the beat to the
Supreme Court—including television coverage of trials when defendants and judges consent. He would enforce Canon 20, prohibiting
lawyers from releasing prejudicial information to the press; but he
favors the repeal of Canon 35 which prohibits camera coverage of
trials. If, he says, "we live by the First Amendment, we must place
our trust in the maturity of the American people and the responsibility of the mass media."[8]

Judge Wright also finds merit in the newsman's slogan—the people's
right to know—as a reminder that newsmen speak not merely out of
self-interest as representatives of a profit-making industry, but also
out of concern for the legitimate demands of the people that they be
informed. There is strength to the claim that full coverage will sooner
or later expose official corruption, inefficiency, and racial and religious
prejudice on the bench and among law enforcement officials.

Secrecy may menace the rights of an accused more than publicity.
Accused persons have been secretly arrested, maltreated, kept uninformed of their rights, without proper arraignment for long periods
of time and beyond the help of friends, family or counsel.

William Munroe, Washington news director of NBC, illustrates
how publicity can positively aid the cause of justice: A district attorney is known to be fond of charging defendants with misdemeanors
when they should be charged with felonies. He may be lazy, over-
worked, or open to "suggestions." But when a man with a long criminal
record is arrested, and the local media publish that record, the district
attorney is more likely to do his job as it should be done and less
likely to prejudice the state's case. And when a Mississippi sheriff
refuses to permit reporters to see a Negro suspect or refuses to divulge
information concerning the case, who is being protected—the sheriff
or the defendant?

Judge Wright's concern ranges far beyond the limits of the isolated
cause celebre. Crime and trial reporting, in his opinion, should include additional aspects of the criminal process, the cumulative effect
of which will be to increase the public's knowledge of the causes of

crime and society's response to it. His is a call for in-depth reporting of society's contributions to crime: the influence of slums, poverty, illiteracy, unemployment, and mental illness. In its proper context, crime reporting would include penology, parole systems, classification of prisoners, rehabilitation, and efforts to prevent crime as well as to control it.

Here is an invitation to constructive, creative reporting. If there is extensive press coverage of the whole spectrum of crime—antitrust prosecutions, income tax evasions, bribery and official misconduct— the isolated crime of violence will not warrant all the headlines; nor will it suggest that crime is the exclusive propensity of the socially disadvantaged.

Most crime reporting makes the administration of justice appear like a cops-and-robbers game. Society can remain aloof. Prospects of rehabilitation and crime prevention are ignored. Greed or anger are implied to be the only causes of crime. Reality is distorted.

We are also prone to forget, as we glance at blazing headlines, that justice is the goal of our legal system, that the right to a fair trial is basic, and that no civilized person exalts punishment over fairness. To report "Murderer Cheats Gallows," Judge Wright says, is to misunderstand the essential nature of the due process system designed to protect liberties rather than exact revenge.

"Judges must open their minds to the press and together seek more accurate reporting, more experimentation in the scope of what it covers . . . Through cooperation with the press, the untimely publication of inadmissible and prejudicial evidence before and during trials, may be avoided . . . Perhaps the public image of justice is distorted because we have turned our backs to the news media and allowed its writers to draw on their imaginations instead of reality, or on the tiny part instead of the rich whole, in portraying the face of justice."

Word of mouth, in Judge Wright's opinion, is no substitute for informed reportage.

Prof. Louis L. Jaffe notes how intensive news coverage may provide a basis for pressure against law enforcement and court officials who fail to enforce the law; consider the reluctance of Southern authorities to prosecute persons suspected of or held for the murder of civil rights demonstrators. Northern newspapers, and some Southerners, have demanded prosecution.[9]

Some outstanding legal experts would shift the burden of responsibility in the prejudicing of fair trials. Dean Erwin N. Griswold of the Harvard Law School condemns lawyers and police for what he regards as their primary role in disseminating criminal trial information. He would amend Canon 20 to include an *absolute* prohibition against the "release by any lawyer . . . of any material relating to a trial, either before the trial or while the trial is going on. This should specifically preclude appearances of any sort on radio or television relating in any way to the forthcoming trial. It should also specifically forbid the release of any statement to the effect that the defendant has or has not confessed, or that he has or does not have an alibi. It should also specifically preclude the release of evidence that has been offered in court and excluded by the trial judge."[10]

All law enforcement officers should perhaps be controlled by courts through their rule-making and contempt powers. Griswold would adopt England's so-called Judge's Rules: "As soon as a police officer has evidence which could afford reasonable grounds for suspecting a person has committed an offense he shall caution that person or cause him to be cautioned before putting to him any questions, or further questions, relating to that offence"—for example, "You are not obliged to say anything unless you wish to do so but what you say may be put into writing and put in evidence."

It is hypocritical, says Griswold, for lawyers to damn the news media for publishing information which other lawyers give them. In his opinion, it is the duty of the United States Supreme Court to formulate appropriate rules for the federal courts and their employees. Similar rules could be promulgated by the state courts or enacted by the legislatures. Bar associations could give impetus to these proposals. It is up to lawyers to clarify the ground rules.

Milton R. Wessel, a member of the New York bar, agrees that much prejudicial publicity is the product of the statements of official participants in the judicial process—police, prosecutors, defense counsel and judges—whose motives in generating public comment may be political ambition or the craving for a favorable public image. "Their press releases, prepared digests, tips and innumerable other stimulants to publicity," says Wessel, "are approved, or at least condoned, by bench and bar alike on the theory that the information furnished is based on underlying data which is public somewhere, and that the officials have a right not to seem to be hiding behind the shield of confidence."[11]

Wessel believes that without the initial stimulation provided by publicity-minded lawyers few cases would ever become public spectacles because the press would have neither the inclination nor the manpower to keep up with them. But when the lawyers tag a case as sensational, the press will often follow it through.

In one case, a special assistant to the Attorney-General of the United States, assigned to prosecute a case, volunteered information to a local radio station about the defendant's criminal record. Coincidentally, the prosecutor was also counsel for the radio station. The defendant was described as a woman with a long record of arrests on charges of prostitution and illegal liquor sales. The information was broadcast at least three times during the week preceding the trial. The woman was convicted, but because she was unable to show that jurors had been prejudiced by the broadcasts, her conviction was sustained on appeal.[12]

Chief W. H. Parker of the Los Angeles Police Department tells of a case in which the defendant's attorney held press conferences in a rented hotel suite, amply supplied with liquor, so that he could disseminate his client's protestations of innocence.

In *Henslee* v. *United States*,[13] a federal court had this to say about publicity inspired by a U.S. attorney: "The U.S. attorney is the representative not of an ordinary party to a controversy, but of a sovereignty whose obligation to govern impartially is as compelling as its obligation to govern at all; and whose interest, therefore, in a criminal prosecution is not that it shall win a case, but that justice shall be done. As such, he is in a peculiar and very definite sense the servant of the law, the twofold aim of which is that guilt shall not escape or innocence suffer."

THE PRESS DEFENDS ITSELF

The press itself is entitled to a fair trial. Its arguments are strong, its spokesmen lucid. And it can stand on a distinguished record.

An inscription on the facade of the Amarillo (Texas) *Globe-Times and News* declares: "A newspaper may be forgiven for lack of knowledge but never for lack of courage." The *Globe-Times* tested its courage in 1960 when editor Thomas Hazzard Thompson directed a city crime investigation that led to the resignation of a county judge and to his subsequent disbarment, the indictment of several law-enforcement officers, a number of gambling convictions, and the election of a reform slate of local officials. For Thompson and his newspaper, the investigation also led to a 1961 Pulitzer Prize for Distinguished and Meritorious Public Service.

The story began when a daily column by Thompson criticized Judge Roy Joe Stevens for chronic absenteeism, for issuing driver's licenses indiscriminately to any Amarillo youngster who would take the trouble to drive 15 miles to the neighboring community of Canyon, and for keeping a law office on the Potter County side of Amarillo while representing Randall County in which Amarillo is partially located.

What appeared to be a personal feud between editor and judge became a matter of social consequence when a grand jury indicted Stevens and three other men for attempting to bribe a juror. Following a change of venue to Wichita Falls, 230 miles away, Stevens was acquitted. One reason advanced for the acquittal was the belief of the jurors that Stevens was the victim of a political vendetta.

Sensing that law enforcement had broken down in Amarillo, the Texas House of Representatives launched a secret, two-month investigation culminating in three days of public hearings which became the Panhandle's most sensational exposé. The estranged wife of a king-pin Amarillo gambler came out of protective custody to testify that law enforcement and the courts were linked with organized gambling. Also testifying were law officers, gamblers, prostitutes, and a man awaiting trial for murder.

By this time the *Globe-Times* was in something less than a mellow mood. Its March 24, 1960, banner story began: "Randall County Judge Roy Joe Stevens waxed belligerent when he appeared before the House General Investigating Committee here this morning. The Amarillo criminal attorney and county judge hedged, argued and squirmed as the committee tried to fire questions at him in an effort to disclose dereliction of duty in his office."

"Coverage of the hearings," said editor Thompson, "proved to be the biggest test for on-the-spot reporting of a running event in the paper's history. The very nature of a legislative hearing—some call it a wide-open public argument—brought out the best in the entire staff." Two local television stations covered the hearings live and complete, requiring the newspapers to scramble for fast, accurate and detailed reporting—plus interpretation.

During the hearings, many citizens of Amarillo and the surrounding area stayed home to watch or hear the proceedings on TV or radio. Merchants felt that sales were hurt because of the blanket coverage. Other citizens complained that the press, by its sensational coverage gave the city a black eye. But the city's reputation had already suffered. The investigation indicated criminal activity and moral turpitude on the part of the judge, the sheriff's office, and some other local law enforcement officials. Two days after the hearings, Stevens resigned as county judge.

Thompson's argument was that if a city does not clean up its own mess, someone else will do it.

Other American newspapers have shown that they can make a positive contribution to law enforcement and the administration of justice. A Georgia judge was forced to resign after a June 16, 1959, editorial in the *Atlanta Constitution* revealed that he was implicated in the protection of law violators. At the same time, a public prosecutor who was shown to have accumulated $300,000 on an annual salary of $15,000, resigned under pressure.

The *Gary* (Ind.) *Post-Tribune*, after a 10-year battle, was instrumental, a few years ago, in bringing to light a partnership between government and crime in Lake County, Indiana, which was later aired by a United States Senate Subcommittee. One result of the investigation was the resignation of a chief deputy prosecutor.

The *Portland Oregonian* won plaudits in 1957 for its exposure of the attempt of racketeers to dominate city government. The disclosures led to the resignation of a prominent district attorney and a number of police officials. All of the information was published prior to any arrest or trial, as it must be in such cases.

There is nothing new about this responsible watchdog function of the press. In 1934 the *Sacramento* (Calif.) *Bee* sparked an investigation of political machine influence in the appointment of two federal judges in Nevada. A subcommittee of the Senate Judiciary Committee examined the records, denounced the appointees, and the entire Nevada machine was overthrown in the next election. The *Scranton* (Pa.) *Times*, in 1945, brought about the resignation of a federal district judge by disclosing deplorable conditions in his jurisdiction.

In 1949 the *Chicago Daily News* and the *St. Louis Post Dispatch* shared a Pulitzer Prize for uncovering the names of 51 Illinois newspaper editors, publishers, and reporters on the state payroll, most of whom were doing nothing for their pay.

One of the most significant newspaper investigations was that conducted by George Thiem of the *Chicago Daily News* in 1956. In six weeks of arduous digging, he uncovered evidence that showed Illinois State Auditor Orville Hodge had stolen more than $2,000,000 of the taxpayers' money by nepotism, payroll padding, bogus contracts, fraudulent expense accounts, illegal expenditures and phony checks. Thiem won a Pulitzer Prize for his efforts and Illinois adopted broad reforms to discourage such corruption in the future.[14]

Gene Goltz of the *Houston Post* received the 1964 Heywood Broun Memorial Award and a Pulitzer Prize for a series of articles which led to the indictment of the mayor and other municipal officials, and the resignation of the city attorney of Pasadena, Texas, a Houston suburb. The charges were felony theft and conspiracy involving public funds. Goltz pursued his investigation despite physical attacks and repeated threats of violence against him and his wife.

Also in 1964, two reporters and a photographer of the *Philadelphia* (Pa.) *Bulletin* won a Pulitzer Prize for exposing collusion between a numbers racket and police in South Philadelphia. Eighteen dismissals and suspensions from the police department and a renewed city campaign against vice resulted.

A series of investigative articles by Oscar Griffin, Jr., editor of the *Pecos* (Tex.) *Independent* first called attention to the financial dealings of Billie Sol Estes which later proved to constitute a massive fraud against the United States government.

Concerned about increasing restrictive measures against press coverage of criminal proceedings, Alfred Friendly of the *Washington Post* recently introduced a series of case histories in *The Bulletin* of the American Society of Newspaper Editors to show how the press has positively served the cause of justice.

The Robert Snead Williams case is one in point. On a spring day in 1950 two 14-year-old girls reported to a policeman that a man had exposed himself before them near American University in Washington, D.C. Williams was identified by the girls as the offender. The 45-year-old Williams, a father and trustee of All Souls Unitarian Church, was arrested and held incommunicado for four hours. Ten days later he was tried and convicted. Fortunately for Williams the trial judge had not acquiesced to the request of his lawyers that the trial be closed to the public. As it turned out, the embarrassing publicity saved Williams' reputation. A guilt-stricken reader wrote two letters to the prosecutor and subsequently confessed the crime. Williams was granted a new trial and acquitted, grateful for the newspaper publicity which had elicited the confession.[15]

News reporters are not always satisfied with the conclusions reached in routine police reports. Gregory Cruz, a 22-year-old Puerto Rican clerk, was shot three times by a police detective who thought Cruz was a murder suspect. However, Cruz was never charged with murder. Instead he was charged with felonious assault on and resisting a police officer, and with carrying a concealed weapon—a pair of pliers. The detective was suspended for "excessive use of force," while the critically hurt Cruz made a slow recovery, with the charges still pending against him. Skeptical reporters found witnesses who confirmed Cruz's story that he was stopped, searched and beaten by the detective he thought was robbing him. In February 1965, a grand jury, acting on this information, dropped the charges against Cruz.

In the Whitmore case, mentioned earlier, New York reporters found witnesses ready to testify that the accused had been 120 miles away when Janice Wylie and Emily Hoffert were murdered. It appeared that the police—who had written Whitmore's confession for him—held this information also. Considerable editorial pressure was exerted before the district attorney dropped the first-degree murder charges, nine full months after Whitmore's initial arrest.[16] "If this had not been a celebrated case," said an assistant district attorney, "if this case hadn't got tremendous publicity, if this was what we so-called professionals call a run-of-the-mill murder, Whitmore might well have been slipped into the electric chair for something he didn't do." Such an admission, said Robert L. Bartley of the *Christian Science Monitor,* is a strong argument for full disclosure.

Emmett Dedmon of the *Chicago Sun-Times* has recounted that newspaper's major contributions to justice in the past 20 years. Joseph Majczek was convicted of killing a policeman in an attempted holdup of a speakeasy. His scrubwoman mother's faith in his innocence came to the attention of reporter James McGuire, and a year-long investigation by the paper disclosed that the woman who owned the establishment and who had been the chief prosecution witness had falsely identified Majczek under police threats to put her out of business. In 1945 Majczek was granted a full pardon and voted $24,000 by the Illinois legislature for his 13 years of wrongful imprisonment. The story was later the basis of a movie, "Call Northside 777."

When a grand jury failed by one vote in 1951 to indict Michael Moretti, a state's attorney's policeman who had shot and killed two unarmed youths and wounded a third, the *Sun-Times* vigorously demanded that the case be reopened. The newspaper uncovered Moretti's political connections, the false statements he had made when he became a policeman, the protection afforded him by the assistant state's attorney before the grand jury, and the fact that his act had been an unprovoked killing in drunken anger. Subsequently he was indicted for murder and sentenced to life imprisonment.

In 1964 the same newspaper brought to an end an era of immunity for eight B-girl clip joints in a Chicago district dominated by the Cosa Nostra. Evidence gathered in police raids had been consistently quashed in court until the political dynamics of the situation were exposed and the mayor's office and Internal Revenue Service were stimulated to act.[17]

These cases suggest that the American press is more than a mere spectator to the parade of crime and corruption in our contemporary society. And in communities where crimes against Negroes or minority groups are traditionally tolerated, full publication of the facts about the crime and the suspect may protect rather than obstruct justice. The same is true where the malefactor has friends in high places or is closely aligned with the political structure of the community. What can silence accomplish in such circumstances? Whatever guidelines are adopted, what guarantee does the press have that lawyers are playing fair and square, or that they are honestly serving the cause of justice?

A rather unique view of the question is that of Hugh R. Dillon, editor of the Southern Michigan prison inmate newspaper, *The Spectator*. Dillon is a former victim of news coverage who nevertheless fears that official secrecy would open the door to more disastrous abuses. Why don't lawyers spend more time truth-seeking and less time engaging in a battle of wits? Dillon asks. "Too many times men have gone to prison because of clever subterfuges by prosecutors adept at withholding from a jury information that would favor the defense. . . . Also many men have gone to prison because of lack of preparation or initiative on the part of their lawyers." Dillon's conclusion is that if he had to make a choice it might be better to be at the mercy of the news media than subject to the mercy of officials permitted to operate in secrecy.[18]

Gene Blake of the *Los Angeles Times* tells of the official secrecy surrounding the brutal beating of several Mexican-American prisoners in the city's Central Jail. When concerned newsmen finally did get the story, grand jury indictments were returned, several policemen were convicted, and others were disciplined.

It was an alert court reporter for the *Washington Post,* Jack Landau, who first recognized the vast implications of the Bobby Baker case while covering what could have been a run-of-the-mill civil suit. Without subsequent investigative reporting, long before an inquiry by the Senate Rules Committee, it is doubtful that Baker's extraordinary operations would have come to light. And yet it is difficult to imagine a case in which the public could have a greater legitimate interest. Here indeed was an invisible empire built upon the influence and respectability of the highest reaches of government.

The efforts of the fourth estate in connection with exposés of this kind often go unheralded, possibly because the press has never been particularly proficient in telling its own story. A few years ago the *Wall Street Journal* presented a carefully documented account of the outside business interests of a number of federal judges. Two young reporters for the *Louisville Times* and the *Nashville Tennessean* who became observant "prisoners" were able to bring about substantial penal reforms in their respective states. The *Cleveland Plain Dealer* played a major role in the investigation and subsequent conviction of the Cuyahoga County recorder.

On February 19, 1966, a Florida court found Joseph Shea innocent of a murder for which he had served six years in prison. Shea had been sentenced to a life term for the slaying of a 23-year-old airline reservations clerk. Evidence which placed Shea 65 miles from Miami the night the young woman was killed and other evidence which opened the door for a second trial was unearthed by *Miami Herald* reporters.

New York City's newspapers protested vigorously when the son of a Bronx judge who had been involved in the 1963 highway deaths of five persons was freed by three other Bronx judges. Acquitted on misdemeanor charges of drunken and reckless driving, 25-year-old Gareth Martinis was tried again in the summer of 1965 on a charge of vehicular homicide. That trial resulted in a hung jury and Bronx Supreme Court Justice Samuel J. Silverman dismissed the indictment on the grounds that Martinis had been placed in double jeopardy by the second trial. But the New York City bar criticized the Bronx district attorney for presenting what was considered an ill-prepared case in the first trial.

Innumerable stories of the aforementioned type illustrate the commitment of elements of the American press to the protection of the public interest. Those few presented here suggest that, like all other areas of government activity, the administration of justice needs constant scrutiny. And the press itself as a social institution must bear public surveillance, engage in the kind of critical self-examination found in periodicals such as the *Columbia Journalism Review,* the *Nieman Reports* and the *Saturday Review,* and consider the kind of outside criticism now being directed toward it by the American bar.

Many responsible editors are, of course, exploring the difficult free press-fair trial problem with those members of bar and bench who recognize that there is lack of self-restraint on both sides. Most newsmen are as sensitive to the ideals of fair play and justice as lawyers. The crux of the disagreement seems to focus on divergent views of what the public should know about a criminal case and what the influence of such knowledge will be on the outcome of a trial which may follow.

Herbert Brucker, the widely respected former editor of the *Hartford Courant,* raises key questions by reciting the case of a dope pusher who came before the Connecticut Superior Court—for a third time, after two previous convictions for violating the state's narcotic act. After the defendant's second conviction, the state legislature had made a life sentence mandatory for a third narcotics conviction. The new law had been discussed widely. At the beginning of the trial, the judge cautioned newsmen not to publish the fact of a mandatory life sentence for fear the severity of the penalty would sway the jury against a guilty verdict. Aside from the fact that the new law was already a matter of public record, Brucker asks: "Was it not material to the public understanding of the proceedings that the legislature had made a life term mandatory?" Is the judge always right when he asks that some part of the truth be suppressed?[19]

Editors fear that in such cases judges assume responsibility for editorial decisions. But this function editors will not relinquish; being the least naive among us, they know there are cases when "the fix is on" and when neither public nor prosecutor is much interested in impartial justice.

The danger of silence, as it is imposed upon the press in the English system, is illustrated by the Christie case. John Christie was hanged for the murder of six women, a crime to which he confessed. However, another man had been hanged for the killing of two of these women. Might not investigating reporters have prevented this tragic lapse in English justice? Perhaps. But in England an editor can be held in contempt for publishing findings before a trial has concluded.

In an address before the Criminal Law Section of the American Bar Association meeting in London in July 1957, Percy Hoskins of the *London Daily Express* complained of secrecy in the administration of British justice. "We do not wish to see in this country a system of trial by newspaper," he said, "but the present law of contempt is certainly much too rigid. . . . The power of the judges in this respect is still practically arbitrary and unlimited."[20]

Hoskins told the story of Neville Heath, who had killed a woman in the West End of London. The only evidence against him was identification by a taxi driver. Newspapers cooperated with a police appeal not to publish Heath's picture, although pictures of him were available in their morgues because of his air force career and a previous conviction for fraud. The police were afraid that a defense counsel could argue that the taxi driver remembered him only because of newspaper photographs. On the other hand, the public was entitled to know that a sex maniac was on the loose. A few days later, Heath struck again in an even more brutal murder. It is possible, Hoskins argued, that the victim might have lived had she been forewarned by newspaper pictures.

What would have happened in Philadelphia, Mississippi, if there had been no newspapermen prying into the disappearance of the three civil rights workers in the summer of 1964? Would the bodies have been found, and would there have been any indictments for the murders?

Brucker and others, willing to put their faith in the rational fairness of the average juror, conclude that secrecy is simply not worth the serious risks it entails. Better that the clash between bar and press continue.[21]

Some representatives of the press are more choleric and passionate in presenting their points of view. Writing in the January 1964 issue of his "Editor's Notebook," John S. Knight, editor of the *Detroit Free Press*, justifies close coverage of criminal cases as an obstacle to the "criminal scum and crooked officeholders" who would "rob, kill and loot the public treasury," as well as to "shady criminal lawyers, working with sleazy law enforcement officials, who far too often make a mockery of justice."

Alexander F. Jones, late editor of the *Syracuse Times-Herald*, whose newspaper was charged with multiple counts of prejudice in a *Syracuse Law Review* article,[22] was fond of challenging lawyers "to produce one case where newspapers have so hounded any individual or influenced any court or jury that a man was sent to prison in a miscarriage of justice." He was prepared to guarantee that if such a case could be found, he would produce 10 where citizens won freedom from prison through the ceaseless efforts of hardworking newspapermen.

Ralph Sewell, a past president of Sigma Delta Chi, professional journalistic society, objects vigorously to suppression through managed news or codes of journalistic ethics drafted by lawyers and accepted by a supine press. There can be no "truth in news" if reporters are shackled by punitive restrictions and forced to accept a bar association's concept of what should and what should not be printed.

One of the clearest voices in the press-bar debate has been that of Clifton Daniel, managing editor of the *New York Times*.[23] He concedes that the press in its zeal to publish sometimes does violence to the rights of a defendant, even if unintentionally and without malice. Competitive, probing, and working against deadlines, newsmen are frequently bad-mannered; they may distort the news by swarming over an event and making it something it probably would never have been. The press cannot reasonably object to the desire of bar, bench and police to put their own houses in order—provided that the free flow of news to the public is not impaired. But the press will not submit to censorship; it will not give the editor's chair to politically-minded lawyers and judges. "We do not believe," says Daniel, "that a law degree necessarily makes a man more civic-minded than a degree in journalism, or that elevation to the bench is equivalent to canonization."

Journalists ought not surrender their freedom to publish anything that is said or done in public—this side of libel or generally accepted standards of decency and good taste. Policemen and lawyers who make outrageously prejudicial statements should, on occasion, be quoted. "We will not," says Daniel, "yield up the privilege of publishing anything said in open court . . . or surrender the power of the press to expose and criticize the acts of public officials, including prosecutors and judges." The British system is unacceptable to him because it inhibits the traditional investigatory role of the American press. The press, he contends, will not submit to repressive legislation, or accept compulsory codes of conduct which would be unenforceable anyway. But he concedes that the press should continue to participate in discussion, to work on codes of ethics, to react more sensitively to the rights of defendants, and to be responsive to justifiable admonitions and directives from the bench and bar.

Mutual distrust between press and bar has frustrated cooperative efforts to resolve the conflict. Several bar associations have become highly attuned to the desirability of enforcing Canon 20 of the American Bar Association's Code of Judicial Ethics and its equivalent in the various state bar associations. The New York State Bar Association has gone so far as to recommend disbarment proceedings and contempt citations for serious infractions. Edward Bennett Williams, a Washington attorney noted for his courtroom defense of unpopular causes, says of Canon 20: "If lawyers would abide by this rule, most of the difficulty would be overcome. Prosecutors would, of course, have to apply a tight rein on the information which the police give to the press. . . . Defense lawyers would likewise have to refrain from putting out exculpatory material and previews of the defense. Only the courts and appropriate disciplinary committees of the bar can enforce compliance with the rule. But if compliance were rigidly enforced, it would go a long way toward the elimination of 'trial by newspaper'."[24]

However, Canon 20 has been ignored even in those states which have adopted it. Not a single case has been brought against an offending lawyer or judge in the 50 or more years since the Canon was written.

Press criticism of bar attempts to put its own house in order, to determine what its own ethical standards are to be, is sometimes sincere, sometimes sanctimonious. The press tends to defend itself against the charge of prejudice by blaming lawyers for being co-operative, even enthusiastic, sources of crime news; when lawyers exert efforts to proscribe their colleagues, as District Attorney Hogan did in New York in his refusal to release confessions to the news media, the press attack the policy as constituting a press "gag," a news "blackout" or an "iron curtain" of censorship. The press is, of course, genuinely concerned and worried about the drying up of primary news sources.

Two highly developed professional norms appear to be in conflict here. Deeply ingrained in the American bar is the professional norm which is best described as the "will to win—at any cost." Coupled with the political ambition of some prosecuting attorneys, this deep-seated standard of performance has had the effect of sometimes placing questionable tactics above truth, of setting as the objective the winning of the fight rather than the finding of the facts. The late Judge Jerome Frank, a realist in American jurisprudence, said "the 'fight' theory of justice is sort of a legal *laissez-faire*"—a theory which we have come to distrust in the economic field.[25] Recently the American Bar Association and the American Law Institute have taken steps to plug some of the holes in the adversary system.

No less ingrained are the professional norms which at least partly determine the newsman's approach to this subject. News is his paramount value. He defines situations in terms of news values, acts and reacts in terms of them, and is too often more interested in what he considers news than in the unvarnished truth. Unfortunately single-minded emphasis on the dramatic story sometimes blinds journalists to values such as fair play, integrity, and respect for the defenseless individual.

Combine two such professional drives in a criminal case which contains the elements of a *cause celebre* and the need for self-restraint, or self-regulation, becomes apparent.

Perhaps some accommodation between free press and fair trial could be made if slogans, catch-phrases and professional insularity were put aside. The advocates of free press or fair trial make a mistake when they arrogate to either constitutional principle an importance which ignores or unfairly subordinates the other.

Journalists are no more unanimous than lawyers in appraising their proper role in the presentation of crime and court news. The more sophisticated and younger reporters reflect an increasing sensitivity to the grossness of some press practices. Anthony Lewis, a distinguished *New York Times* writer, suggests that although the public interest is often cited by the press, desire to provide titillation and entertainment is usually the real motive for lofty demands to get the facts and admit the cameras.[26] Too often the press forgets that a public trial is not for its benefit but for the benefit of the accused.

In appealing for approval of the Kentucky Press Association's Statement of Principles, adopted in June 1965, Norman Isaacs said that anyone who attempts to claim all virtue is on his side is a fool. "What has grown up in this country of ours," said the executive editor of the Louisville *Courier-Journal* and *Times*, "has been a vast unwitting conspiracy on the part of good men. The policeman wants to do his job well. He wants to be regarded as able and efficient. So does the prosecuting attorney. And the judge. And the newspaper editor. All good men, all wanting to be successful in what they do—and all bound up in a system which does violence to the right of Americans to be considered innocent until proven guilty."

John McMullan, assistant managing editor of the *Miami Herald*, believes that much press criticism could be eliminated if newsmen would simply avoid editorializing in handling crime material. Save compliments for the police and unflattering characterizations of the accused until after conviction, he suggests. Be cautious in using such terms as "murder," "suspect," "solution," and "confession." And don't be a sounding board for either defense attorney or prosecutor.

Dr. Frank Stanton, president of CBS, has said flatly that "such practices as publicizing alleged confessions, declaration of guilt made by police, and attempts to try cases in the press, away from the safeguards of the courtroom, ought to be eliminated in a just society." But he agrees with Judge Wright on the need for more extensive, more immediate, and more compelling reporting of significant proceedings and judgments by the higher courts in which broad public policies are enunciated but neither witnesses nor juries are involved.

In the *National Press Photographer*, an editorial writer presents this reflection on Dallas: "If the news profession itself does not soon suggest precisely how it can inform the public without arousing its resentment, we may go down in history as the generation which refused to obey the imperatives of a new professional self-discipline and mature conduct in the new public arena of news-gathering itself —and consequently exposed the hallowed press freedom to attack and media to arbitrary controls."

Newsman Harry Reasoner put it well in a recent CBS documentary, aptly titled "Fair Press and Fair Trial," when he said: "All sides, it seems to us, are aiming at fair press and fair trial. And the way you get that is by fair play—by self-restraint and good taste. At times, news media overstep the bounds, and so do lawyers, and prosecutors and police. (And he could well have added Congressional committees, executive officials and others who have become past masters of the leak, the well-manipulated news story.) But there is nothing wrong with our press and bar that can be cured by any one party trying to dictate to the other."

It is doubtful whether the organized press will retreat much beyond the non-binding recommendations the Press-Bar Committee of the American Society of Newspaper Editors made to its membership in April 1965 as a "useful and constructive course of action":

1. To rededicate itself to the principle of reporting criminal affairs with restraint, good taste and scrupulous regard for the rights of defendants, including the presumption of innocence, fair treatment and fair trial by unprejudiced jurors;

2. To reaffirm its obligation to provide the public with full, objective, prompt and honest information about criminal affairs, law enforcement and the administration of justice;

3. To reject as impractical and harmful attempts to restrict necessary news coverage by rigid regulations unduly limiting reporting of criminal and legal matters or suppressing information about them;

4. To undertake with open-mindedness and sincerity frequent discussions with the law enforcement agencies, the bar and the bench, at all levels, for the purpose of creating mutual understanding of the problems involved, correcting abuses, resolving complaints and furthering both full news coverage and fair trials.

Those who would restrict the right of the press to investigate, to comment fully, and to criticize the administration of justice in the most vehement terms might read again the words of Chief Justice Hughes in an important 1931 case[27]—words which have startling currency for our own day: "Meanwhile, the administration of government has become more complex, the opportunities for malfeasance and corruption have multiplied, crime has grown to most serious proportions, and the danger of its protection by unfaithful officials and of the impairment of the fundamental security of life and property by criminal alliances and official neglect, emphasizes the primary need of a vigilant and courageous press, especially in great cities."

Fifty years earlier, James Paterson,[28] an Englishman, expressed the same ideal in more flowery terms perhaps, but no less effectively: Freedom of the press is "the freedom with which skillful writers can animadvert on the conduct of all public men and public measures,

acts as a check on every kind of misgovernment, and baffles most of
such attempts sooner or later. It gives dignity and a sense of security
to the whole people when they know that some champion will be
forthcoming or is ever on the alert, able to meet all comers, whenever
an abuse is discovered, a grievance felt, or an evil is to be redressed,
and that there is no machinery by which an interested party can be
sure of enforcing absolute silence."

CHAPTER 10

JUDICIAL REMEDIES

"There is really no conflict between the right of courts to control the publicity of pending causes and real freedom of the press. Control by the courts of such publicity arises necessarily out of their duty to give individual litigants a fair and impartial trial. . . . Any government that fails to accord to its citizens this natural right to justice will forfeit its claim upon their loyalty. In fact failure of the courts to protect litigants in this respect might well result in the destruction of freedom of the press itself."—Justice Harlan in *Patterson* v. *Colorado* (1907).

The Sixth Amendment to the Constitution guarantees trial by an impartial jury in a federal criminal proceeding. State constitutions generally contain similar provisions. In the absence of well defined constitutional or legislative policy, state and federal courts exercise wide discretion in assessing the effects of press comment on their proceedings. Generally, however, they are highly sensitive to outside influences where jury panels are concerned.

In 1950 a white girl in Florida was allegedly raped by three Negroes. Within hours three suspects were in custody. A local newspaper, reporting that they had confessed, helped to transform an already furious public into a mob, which stormed the jail in a lynch attempt, burned the home of one of the accused, and forced another's relatives to flee the community in fear of their lives. The inflammatory newspaper content included a cartoon which appeared while the grand jury was deliberating, picturing three electric chairs and captioned, "No Compromise—Supreme Penalty."

The state militia finally had to be called out to maintain order, and judicial rules had to be strictly enforced to keep weapons out of the courtroom. On trial, the defendants were sentenced to death, although their purported confessions were never offered in evidence by the state. At the same time, the defense offered, and the court rejected as irrelevant, evidence of brutal beatings of the defendants while in custody. On appeal to the United States Supreme Court, the convictions were reversed *per curiam* on the ground that Negroes had been purposefully excluded from the grand jury. Justice Robert H. Jackson, in what is now a frequently cited opinion, emphasized that prejudicial publicity had been a more significant obstruction to justice:

"But prejudicial influences outside the courtroom, becoming all too typical of a highly publicized trial, were brought to bear on this jury with such force that the conclusion is inescapable that these defendants were prejudged as guilty and the trial was but a legal gesture to register a verdict already dictated by the press and the public opinion which it generated . . . Newspapers published as a fact, and attributed the information to the sheriff, that these defendants had confessed. No one, including the sheriff, repudiated the story. Witnesses and persons called as jurors said they had read or heard of this statement. However, no confession was offered at the trial. The only rational explanations for its nonproduction in court are that the story was false or that the confession was obtained under circumstances which made it inadmissible or its use inexpedient."[1]

The Supreme Court underlined the haphazardness of authority for the confession story by citing the editor's own words: "The information is based on articles in the various daily papers and personal conversations I had with people generally. . . . If articles appear in those papers that have stood the test two or three days without denial or corrections, based on my previous experience as an editor, I assume them to be true . . ." Justice Jackson was appalled; he found it "hard to imagine a more prejudicial influence than a press release by the officer of the court charged with defendants' custody stating that they had confessed, and here just such a statement, unsworn to, unseen, uncross-examined, and uncontradicted, was conveyed by the press to the jury." Newspapers, Jackson added, in the enjoyment of their constitutional rights, may not deprive accused persons of their right to a fair trial.

Although a jury untouched by human passions may be an illusory goal, it is not unreasonable to suspect that pre-trial publicity of this sort very likely jeopardizes a fair trial, especially in cases of murder or atrocious sex crimes that create an initial shock in the communities in which they take place. Impairment of a fair trial may also be a danger in cases involving espionage or treason, or other crimes about which there is already an acute sensitivity.[2]

The *Irvin* decision of 1961, as has been noted, was the first time a state criminal conviction was reversed by the Supreme Court solely on the grounds that pre-trial publicity had created "so huge a wave of public passion" that a fair trial for the accused before an impartial jury became impossible. The court took notice of the fact that Irvin's confession was announced, as well as his offer to plead guilty if promised a 99-year sentence. The prosecutor was quoted as being determined to secure the death penalty. One news story dramatically related the vow of a Kentucky sheriff to devote his life to getting Irvin executed for a murder alleged to have been committed in that state. On the second day of the jury selection, the bitter and angry feelings of the community were emphasized in print. Spectators were quoted as saying, "my mind is made up"; "I think he is guilty"; and "he should be hanged." Finally, and with remarkable understatement, a headline reported that "impartial jurors are hard to find." An examination of the 2,783 pages of the jury selection record shows that, 370 of 430 prospective jurors entertained some opinions as to guilt—ranging in intensity from mere suspicion to absolute certainty.

The *Sheppard* and *Irvin* cases are important because they illustrate what has become the chief legal remedy for justice believed to have been contaminated by publicity: *an appeal for reversal of a conviction under the due process clause of the Fourteenth Amendment.* This appeal does not always succeed.

In a California case, an elderly man, Fred Stroble, was convicted of first degree murder for the brutal, ice-pick slaying of a six-year-old girl. The conviction was affirmed by the Supreme Court of California[3] and appealed to the United States Supreme Court[4] partly on the ground that a fair trial had been impossible due to inflammatory newspaper reports inspired by the district attorney. The bases for the complaint, as laid out by Justice Tom Clark in a majority opinion affirming Stroble's conviction, were these: newspaper reports, relying on a confession released by the district attorney on the day of the crime and later accepted as evidence at the preliminary hearing, referred to the accused as a "werewolf," "fiend" and a "sex-mad killer"; at a conference called by the governor and a legislative committee to consider the problem of sex crimes, the district attorney was reported under front page headlines as having said that he did not see why sex offenders "shouldn't be disposed of the same way" as mad dogs.

Although the Court chastised the district attorney, it pointed out that at no time during or before the trial had Stroble or his attorneys requested a change of venue. There was nothing to show, said the Court, that the jurors had read the newspapers, and, in any case, the jurors were carefully examined by the trial court for prejudice. Moreover, the confession was introduced in evidence at the trial anyway. Stroble's mistake seems to have been his failure to make an early showing that newspaper accounts had aroused such prejudice as to prevent a fair trial.

Justice Felix Frankfurter, as was his custom in these cases, registered a strong dissent which focused on the prosecutor's antics: "To have the prosecutor himself feed the press with evidence that no self-restrained press ought to publish in anticipation of a trial is to make the State itself, through the prosecutor who wields the power, a conscious participant in trial by newspaper, instead of by those methods which centuries of experience have shown to be indispensable to the fair administration of justice . . . I cannot agree to uphold a conviction which affirmatively treats newspaper participation instigated by the prosecutor as part of the traditional concept of the 'American way of the conduct of a trial.' Such passion as the newspapers stirred in this case can be explained (apart from mere commercial exploitation of revolting crime) only as want of confidence in the orderly course of justice . . . The moral health of the community is strengthened by according even the most miserable and pathetic criminal those rights which the Constitution has designed for all."

Using the standard it had adopted in the *Irvin* case, that is one of implied bias, the Supreme Court in May, 1962[5] affirmed the conviction for grand larceny of Dave Beck, the former West Coast Teamsters boss. Beck's petition cited the voluminous and adverse publicity in the Seattle media as an invalidation of his conviction under the due process clause of the Fourteenth Amendment.

In approving the trial court's refusal to grant Beck either a change of venue or a continuance, the Supreme Court saw no reason to accept a blanket presumption of prejudice against him. Prospective jurors were examined carefully and out of 52, only eight admitted bias or a preformed opinion as to the defendant's guilt. Six others, who suggested that they might have formed an opinion, were excused. Of those selected for the jury trial, each indicated that he was not biased, that he had formed no opinion as to Beck's guilt which would require evidence to remove, and that he would enter the trial with an open mind disregarding anything that he had read about the case. Justice Frankfurter took no part in the opinion.

There is perhaps the tacit recognition in the Supreme Court's opinion here that publicity and free expression concerning court proceedings of this kind serve the public interest. Moreover, press scrutiny may discourage tendencies toward inefficiency, corruption and the political domination of police and judicial authority. The fair and impartial administration of justice is as much the proper concern of the general public as it is of the prisoner at bar. Press publicity, within proper bounds, may also provide checks and balances against attempts to pervert justice, which are inevitable so long as justice depends upon human beings.

Reference was made earlier to the important case of *Rideau*,[6] another state court conviction reversed by the United States Supreme Court. Here the suspect in a robbery, kidnaping and murder was filmed confessing to a sheriff. The filmed interview was widely broadcast on television the following day. A subsequent request for a change of venue was denied, Rideau was convicted, and the Louisiana Supreme Court affirmed. In reversing, the Supreme Court said: "we do not hesitate to hold, without pausing to examine a particularized transcript of the *voir dire* examination of the members of the jury, that due process of law in this case required a trial before a jury drawn from a community of people who had not seen and heard Rideau's televised 'interview'. 'Due process of law, preserved for all by our Constitution, commands that no such practice as that disclosed by this record shall send any accused to his death'."

Interestingly, Justice Clark, who had written the *Irvin* opinion, dissented in *Rideau* because he could find no "substantial nexus between the televised 'interview' and petitioner's trial, which occurred almost two months later . . . it is an impossible standard to require that tribunal to be a laboratory, completely sterilized and freed from any external factors. The determination of impartiality, in which demeanor plays such an important part, is particularly within the province of the trial judge. And when the jurors testify that they can discount the influence of external factors and meet the standard imposed by the Fourteenth Amendment, that assurance is not lightly to be discarded." The burden of showing prejudice or unfairness must be borne by the accused, Clark added, unless the circumstances are unusually compelling, as in the *Irvin* case. Considering these two cases together, clear guidelines simply do not emerge.

Exercising its supervisory capacity over the lower federal courts, the Supreme Court in 1959 reversed the conviction of Howard R. Marshall[7] who had been found guilty of unlawfully dispensing drugs without a prescription from a licensed physician, in violation of a federal statute. The trial judge had correctly refused to permit the government to introduce evidence that Marshall had previously practised medicine without a license; but some of the jurors read newspaper articles alleging that Marshall had a record of two previous felony convictions and that, while posing as a physician, he had prescribed restricted drugs for Hank Williams, the popular country-style singer, who died shortly thereafter. The judge, on learning that these news stories had reached the jurors, summoned them individually to his chambers and inquired if they had seen the articles. Seven of them admitted they had, but assured the judge that they would not be influenced by them, felt no added prejudice to the defendant, and could decide the case on the evidence presented. The judge delivered cautionary instructions at the close of the trial; a conviction followed; and a subsequent motion for a mistrial was denied.

In an 8-1 decision, the Supreme Court said simply that publicity, so prejudicial that it could not be offered in evidence, was no less prejudicial when it reached jurors through newspaper accounts. And, as a general rule, the court added: "The trial judge has a large discretion in ruling on the issue of prejudice resulting from the reading by jurors of news articles concerning the trial. Generalizations beyond that statement are not profitable, because *each case must turn on its special facts.*" (Emphasis added) A similar result was reached two years later in the *Janko* case, referred to in earlier chapter.

Lower federal courts have faced the same difficult issue, and have had the same problem in deciding whether bias should be actual, or whether an implication of bias is sufficient grounds for a reversal. The trend seems to favor the latter standard.

In *Briggs* v. *United States*,[8] the United States Court of Appeals said that newspaper articles quoting witnesses who were under indictment for perjury were injurious enough to the defendant to necessitate a reversal of his conviction. The court held that: (1) The defendant did not have to question the jurors to see if they had read the papers—and such a course might even have been harmful to the defense; (2) The defendant did not have to prove that the jurors had actually read the newspaper—the appellate court assumed that they had; and (3) Although the defendant had not asked for cautionary instructions, the trial judge should have given them anyway. The question, said the court, is not whether any actual wrong resulted, but whether it created a condition from which prejudice "might arise."

Three defendants in the *Powell* case[9] were charged with conspiracy to violate a federal law prohibiting certain activities affecting the armed forces during wartime. At one point in the trial, on the motion of the defense counsel, the judge excused the jury while objections to evidence submitted by a former American prisoner of war were being considered by the court. The contentious evidence implied treason, a crime with which the defendants had not been charged. The defense subsequently asked for a mistrial when San Francisco newspapers— which had been allowed to remain in the courtroom—published news stories suggesting that the judge had declared the defendants guilty of treason. So flagrant an abuse of the principle of trial by impartial jury was this in the mind of the United States attorney that he said the defense need not press the motion for the Government had no desire to try the defendants in anything but the fairest atmosphere, and there was a strong possibility that this had been destroyed by the newspapers.

The defense motion reminded the newspapers that "the doctrine of freedom of the press is not for the benefit of the press but for the benefit of the people, and newspaper publishers have a high degree of responsibility to preserve that doctrine."

In the *Coppedge* case[10] a defendant was indicted on 16 counts of breaking and entering, and forgery. Newspaper stories disclosed that a witness, who had been observed by jurors refusing to take the stand despite repeated directives from the court, was in mortal terror of the defendant. The news reports also said that Coppedge was currently serving a term in the penitentiary for violent assault upon this witness's brother, that the prosecutor thought the accused a vicious criminal, and that the judge doubted that the witness could be protected from the defendant, either in or out of jail.

A motion for a mistrial was denied in the United States District Court, but this judgment was overruled by the Court of Appeals on the ground that a careful inquiry should have been addressed to the jurors individually as to the possible influence of the articles upon them, for "it is too much to expect of human nature that a juror would volunteer, in open court, before his fellow jurors, that he would be influenced in his verdict by a newspaper story of a trial." It would have been impossible, the court added, to have repaired in the mind of any reasonable juror the damage done to Coppedge's cause by the newspaper articles.

The arrest of Francis Henry Bloeth as a suspect in three murder cases a few years ago in Suffolk County, New York stimulated intense press coverage for three weeks prior to the trial. Bloeth's confession and the results of a psychiatric examination were announced. The prosecutor was quoted as stating: "Bloeth must go to the chair"; and the defense reportedly said: "He is as mad as a hatter." An opinion poll conducted by the defense attorney showed that almost all of 210 persons interviewed in the county knew of the confession and considered Bloeth guilty. A death sentence for first degree murder was affirmed by the state courts. Ruling on a *habeas corpus* petition, the United States Court of Appeals held that the jury was sufficiently biased to deprive Bloeth of due process. All jurors except one had read of the case, although all stated they could set their opinions aside.[11]

The conviction was reversed, ostensibly on grounds of implied bias in both prosecution and defense statements.

Substantially the same conclusion was reached in *United States* v. *Smith*[12] when a federal district court judge in Vermont reversed a state conviction because the jury, despite disavowal of bias, had been selected after exposure to newspaper accounts of the defendant's prior arrests.

State appellate courts also seem to be keenly aware of the publicity problem, and some have appealed for guidance from the United States Supreme Court.

In a prosecution for murder, the Supreme Court of Florida held that a juror should have been dismissed, who when examined on *voir dire* was not sure he could render a verdict without being influenced by what he had read and heard about the case. The juror was also a close friend of the victim's husband. Applying the "fixed" versus "fleeting" opinion criterion, and assuming that any doubt should be resolved in favor of the defendant, the court granted a new trial.

Justice O'Connell, speaking for the Florida court, said that the effect of publicity, either favorable or unfavorable to the accused, is without question one of the most perplexing problems in the administration of justice in both state and federal courts. And, he declared, "we have totally failed to solve it." The Florida jurist considered the English contempt power effective but incompatible with American constitutional traditions. Hinting at the need for statutory direction from the state legislatures, and declaring that the only solution for the present may lie in voluntary restraint on the part of the press and the application of the contempt power to police and prosecutors who feed the media, Justice O'Connell concluded:

"As long as the Constitution of this State guarantees an accused trial by 'an impartial jury' the people of this State through their government in all its branches at all levels and all the institutions fostered or permitted under it are solemnly bound to do that which is necessary to preserve such a trial to every accused, whether he be innocent or guilty. This responsibility can not be escaped nor can failure to furnish such a trial be excused on the ground that under existing conditions publicity, particularly of sensational crimes, is so generally disseminated that it is impossible to empanel a jury of persons who are free from knowledge of the crime and of preconceived opinions of the guilt or innocence of the accused. Rather the answer is to remove the condition which creates the extrajudicial knowledge and preconceived opinions."[13]

But the difficulty experienced by appellate courts in deciding whether or not to reverse faulty convictions is illustrated by a recent case heard in the New York Court of Appeals. The defendant, convicted of managing a professional boxer without a license, appealed when the trial court denied his motion for a mistrial based upon prejudicial newspaper publicity. The judge had questioned the jury and found that those who had read the supposedly damaging articles had done so with varying degrees of intensity. Two jurors were excused and the others declared that they had not been influenced by the press. The Court of Appeals, with one dissent, found that under such circumstances there had been no abuse of discretion, and upheld the conviction—but with this wistful postscript: "Perhaps a day will come when either the Court [Supreme Court of the United States] will find a way to achieve a real balance between 'fair trial' and 'free press,' or newspaper publishers will assume responsibility in the matter and see that their employees refrain from publishing accounts reflecting upon a defendant whose trial is imminent or actually in progress. Until such time, however, we must assess each case on its own facts. The ultimate and vital question for decision is whether jurors were capable of rendering an impartial verdict and of deciding the case solely on the proof received during the trial."[14]

The Supreme Court declared positively in the *Irvin* case that the failure of a state to accord a fair hearing to one accused of a crime violates the due process clause of the Fourteenth Amendment; a trial by jury is not fair unless the jury is impartial; and a jury is not impartial when it is impregnated with prejudice invoked by an unfriendly press.

Lower federal and state courts, in attempting to follow *Irvin*, have proceeded pragmatically, presuming bias on the part of jurors only where publicity has been widespread or particularly vindictive. *Irvin*, of course, has provided defense attorneys with a useful precedent for attack on lower court convictions of their clients; and it is now commonplace for defense counsel to appear in court with scrapbooks containing, for example, newspaper clippings, and circulation, readership and population statistics. Billie Sol Estes' attorneys presented 11 volumes of pretrial press clippings. This tactic may prove increasingly embarrassing to newspapers held responsible for the upsetting of otherwise valid convictions.

But the relationship between publicity and jury verdicts is still fuzzy, and it is impossible to specify what factual showing a defendant must make in order to prove that a fair trial was denied. Although the due process appeal will continue as the primary argument for reversals of convictions, there are other procedural remedies, the importance of which are suggested in Justice William O. Douglas' proposition that "our remedy for excessive comment by the press is not the punishment of editors, but the granting of new trials, changes in venue, or continuances to parties who are prejudiced."[15]

CHANGE OF VENUE

Although a defendant may seek a change of venue (transfer of the trial to another jurisdiction) by claiming prejudice in the community, courts have generally been hesitant to grant the motion; and press publicity alone is usually insufficient grounds unless it has so aroused public hostility toward the accused that a fair trial appears to be impossible. This requirement was met in a federal prosecution in New York City.[16] The New York Crime Commission, investigating waterfront conditions, had uncovered rather startling information which it aired in the press several days prior to the trial of the defendant, reaching its most intense level on the morning when the jury was impaneled. Newspapers referred to the accused as a "mobster," a "gang leader" and a "dock racketeer," and made repeated insinuations regarding his past and to events unassociated with the crime charged in the indictment. The court considered the publicity "intense, critically timed, and indubitably prejudicial," creating a climate so hostile that the defendant could not be accorded a fair and impartial trial. Invoking Rule 21(a) of the Federal Rules of Criminal Procedure,[17] the motion for a change of venue was granted.

Similarly, in a Maryland case,[18] a denial of a motion for a change of venue was reversed by a higher court where a newspaper printed an alleged confession in a murder case, the defendants' homes were broken into, and police had to be called to restrain a dangerous mob.

But derogatory publicity alone does not warrant a change of venue, even though false and reflecting upon the accused himself, or expressing the belief that he is guilty.[19] In *State* v. *Taborsky*,[20] a highly publicized case, the motion was denied. Admitting that the case had attracted unusual publicity, the court nevertheless ruled that there was no evidence before it indicating prejudicial results from news reports.

Beginning on February 25, 1957, the *Hartford Times* reported Taborsky's past criminal record, which included a murder conviction, and reminded its readers that the accused's release from prison four years earlier did not mean that he had been exonerated. A police officer was quoted as saying that Taborsky's story didn't hold water. On February 28, a headline conveyed the damaging accusation of an alleged accomplice, one Culombe: "Culombe In Eight Confessions

Says Taborsky Was 'Mad Killer' In State's Crime Wave." Pictures and news stories described both suspects as "killers." On the following day, the *Times* reported that Taborsky had planned to "shoot his way out of court." An accompanying editorial commended the police for bringing the crime wave to an end.

The court appreciated the impact of such publicity but doubted that there were many people in the county who would be unwilling to give the defendants a fair trial. The judge refused to apply the standard of *Shepherd* v. *Florida* since he did not believe that "southern prejudice" could exist in Hartford County, Connecticut. "So strongly is the American system of justice embedded in the minds of our citizens," said the judge, "that outraged feelings usually give way to a desire for orderly procedure."

Four years later, the Supreme Court of the United States reversed Culombe's conviction on the ground that his confession had been coerced,[21] and was therefore inadmissible as evidence. But it was much too late to reconsider his partner Taborsky's original motion for a change of venue.

The chief difficulty with this remedy is that there is frequently no place for a defendant to go, considering the ubiquity of the mass media. Broadcasting and telecasting do not respect state or county lines. In addition, it may pose a financial hardship for a defendant and his counsel to go to trial in another county; and there is no assurance that the new environment will be any more hospitable. Moreover, the defendant is giving up his constitutional right to a speedy public trial by an impartial jury of the county or district in which the offense is alleged to have been committed, a guarantee provided in federal and most state constitutions.

Change of venue motions generally impose upon the defendant the added burden of showing, to the reasonable satisfaction of the court, that a fair and impartial trial would be impossible in the original community; and even in jurisdictions where the change of venue is liberally granted, appellate courts hesitate to reverse a trial court's decision on this question.[22]

It has been suggested that existing legislation should be broadened to give the courts greater discretion in granting changes of venue on the ground of prejudicial publicity. The trial court should also be permitted to choose the county or district for a re-hearing, preferably one where emotional fervor is at a minimum.[23]

Another suggestion for a solution to the problem is the locking up or sequestering of a jury during the course of the trial. The difficulty here is knowing in advance when prejudicial material will appear in the press, and where a newspaper carrying such material might un-expectedly turn up. There is also the possibility that jurors will feel resentment against the defendant who requests that they be locked up, for such an order is obviously a serious inconvenience to them. For this reason and because of the added expense to the state, this remedy is seldom used.

In addition to the change of venue, some states use what is called a change of venire. Here the place of the trial remains the same, but a panel of jurors is drawn from a different county and imported to the scene of trial.

MISTRIAL OR NEW TRIAL

A mistrial, usually sought during a trial, may be declared by a court of original jurisdiction. At the conclusion of a trial, a new trial may be ordered either by a court of original jurisdiction or by an appellate court reversing a lower court's determination. Appellate courts reverse to correct the mistakes of a lower court, mistakes which could include the denying of a change of venue, a mistrial, the granting of a new trial; failure to excuse jurors who have been challenged for cause; failure to grant a continuance; or the improper instructing of a jury by a judge.

Since more than one of these motions can be made simultaneously, they are sometimes difficult to distinguish in specific cases. And in the use of all of these, the only guidelines emerging from myriad court opinions are that (1) much reliance is placed on the discretion of the trial judge, which means that "tainted" convictions may be allowed to stand,[24] and (2) the burden of showing prejudice is on the defendant, a burden of extraordinary difficulty when, as in some cases, jurors are prohibited from testifying that the publicity did prejudice their conclusions.[25] The courts have also recognized that the press has a constitutional right to publish news and fair comment,[26] and "antiseptic" trials are therefore not to be expected.

In an 1879 case, the United States Supreme Court recognized the fact that intelligent jurors were likely to have opinions on matters of public interest, and laid down the flexible rule that when the issue of partiality was raised it would have to be tried, "as far as the facts are concerned, like any other issue of that character, upon the evi-dence."[27] It added that the finding of the trial court upon the issue ought not to be set aside by a reviewing court unless the error is manifest.

An early Illinois statute provided that "a juror shall not be dis-qualified because he has formed an opinion based upon rumor, or upon newspaper statements about the truth of which he has expressed no opinion, if upon oath he states that he believes he can fairly and impartially render a verdict in accordance with the law and the evidence."[28] Its constitutionality was affirmed by both the Supreme Court of Illinois and the United States Supreme Court. The former case, appealed from the Criminal Court of Cook County, grew out of Chicago's Haymarket Riot for which eight defendants stood trial. The State Supreme Court noted that the jurors had been carefully examined. Then, relying on an earlier case,[29] it made that difficult distinction between opinions of a "light and transient character" and those of "strong and deep impression."[30] The United States Supreme Court held that, as interpreted by the state court, the statute did not deprive the defendants of the right to a trial by an impartial jury— that is, due process of law.[31]

In a later case, Justice Oliver Wendell Holmes, speaking for the court, upheld a lower court's denial of a motion for a new trial in a capital case made on the grounds that the jury was allowed to separate during the trial, and that during the separation they saw newspaper headlines bearing on the case. "If the mere opportunity for prejudice or corruption is to raise a presumption that they exist," said Justice Holmes, "it will be hard to maintain jury trial under the conditions of the present day."[32] However, in a 1963 case,[33] the Massachusetts Supreme Court presumed prejudice because the jury was allowed to separate, and, since the trial court had denied the defendant's motion to poll the jury after damaging articles had been published, it was impossible to rebut the presumption of prejudice.

The general rule that has evolved in the federal courts—and that the states have followed—is that even a preconceived opinion as to the guilt or innocence of a defendant being tried on a criminal charge, based upon newspaper reports and which would require some evidence to remove, is insufficient to disqualify a juror or result in a mistrial or reversal, if that person satisfies the judge that he will fairly decide the case on the evidence and the legal principles laid down by the court.[34]

Questions as to whether news accounts are actually prejudicial, whether they are read by the jurors, and whether they are influential in the light of the judge's instructions, are questions to be decided by both federal and state trial judges in the exercise of their sound discretion. And the burden is on the complaining party to show abuse of discretion on the part of the trial court.[35]

Where a misleading article appeared in a local newspaper after the trial had begun, and was read by some of the jurors, a federal court held in *United States* v. *Pisano*[36] that the purity of the trial had not been affected where the trial judge had advised the jurors to ignore the article. In a Louisiana case[37] it was held that the reading of prejudicial stories did not constitute a ground for reversal where the trial court pointed out factual errors in the articles and specifically asked that they be disregarded.

A new trial was also denied in *United States* v. *Wolf*[38] where jurors testified that they remembered little of what the offending articles had contained, and that they would not have been influenced in any case.

It has also been held that if it does not appear the jurors have read the newspaper, a verdict will not be set aside simply because the stories were published before the trial.[39] And where the evidence of guilt is overwhelming, a reversal may not be warranted. In a Pennsylvania case,[40] the court said that proof of the defendant's guilt was so overwhelming that even a preconceived opinion reached by reading newspaper accounts of the trial, whether favorable to the accused or not, would have failed to sway a juror.

Courts have also denied relief where the defendant appeared to be at least partly responsible for some of the objectionable material reaching the jury.[41] If the reading of news accounts by a jury during the trial is known to a defendant and he makes no objection at the time, he may waive his right to a new trial or mistrial.[42] In a 1930 Kentucky case, a United States District Court said that even if articles have been prejudicial, the defendant's failure, upon learning that the jury had read them, to move for a new trial or to request an instruction from the judge, was fatal to his belated motion. It would be unjust, said the court, to allow a defendant to sit idly by in anticipation of a favorable verdict and withhold his objections to the proceedings until the verdict turned out to be unfavorable.[43]

Affidavits by a jury stating that newspaper stories will not prejudice their thinking can make it difficult for a mistrial or new trial motion to succeed, although there is some question as to when such affidavits should be presented.[44] Admonition of a jury by a judge[45] and the retraction of an offensive article by the newspaper also make it less likely that such motions will succeed.[46] A fair and accurate account of a trial cannot be used as grounds for a new trial motion.[47]

After their arrests on spy charges, Julius and Ethel Rosenberg faced an understandably hostile press. On July 18, 1950, the *New York Mirror* quoted J. Edgar Hoover as saying that the defendant is "another important link in the Soviet espionage apparatus." On August 12, an assistant U.S. attorney who was prosecuting the case, was reported in the *Daily News* as blaming the Korean War on the Rosen-bergs. In *United States* v. *Rosenberg*[48] a federal court severely repri-manded the prosecutor for a press release he had given to the *New York Times*. But since the defendants had made no motion for a mis-trial, the court assumed that the prosecutor's statement to the press had not, in the opinion of the Rosenberg defense, prejudiced the jury. And the defense, after an adverse judgment, cannot then ask the court to adopt a contrary assumption.

In a 1953 Maryland case,[49] the free press-fair trial issue was sharply focused, as was the reluctance of some courts to grant motions for a new trial. George Edward Grammer had been found guilty of the murder of his wife and sentenced to be hanged. His motion for a new trial was denied by the Supreme Bench of Baltimore City, and so he appealed to the Maryland Court of Appeals. Grammer pointed to the extensive television, radio and newspaper coverage of the crime, before and after indictment, which, he said, was fostered by prosecution and police. The Baltimore state's attorney and two Baltimore County as-sistant state's attorneys had appeared on a television news program, and an announcer, although indicating his unwillingness to prejudice the case, had read the charge against Grammer. Also, a Dr. Fisher appeared on a University of Maryland TV show entitled "Death and the Law," with the prior approval of the state's attorney, and described his job as a medical examiner, using the Grammer case as an example. Dr. Fisher used a news photograph of the death car with a stone lodged under the accelerator to describe his theory of how the crime had been committed. He did not tell his audience that the picture had been staged while the car was impounded on the police lot.

Grammer complained that the state had denied him a presumption of innocence and had convicted him of premeditated murder before he entered the courtroom. It had also deprived him of his free election of a jury trial and his opportunity of a fair hearing before a judge.

The Court of Appeals took the extraordinarily unsympathetic view that the nature and facts of the crime made publicity inevitable—citizens were intrigued by the near perfection of the crime and the "other-woman" motive. The facts themselves had been the inspiration for most of the publicity, said the court, and Grammer and his family had contributed much of it. Citing the famous *Baltimore Radio* case,[50] the court said that a charge by the state's attorney, or an indictment by the grand jury, clearly and obviously implies that the police believe the accused to be guilty, and the public would naturally gain the same impression. There was no showing that the defendant could not have obtained a fair and impartial jury, the court added, since newspaper accounts gave no hint of anger, hatred or intense resentment in the community. Moreover, Grammer did not make use of any of the procedural remedies open to him when prejudice appeared to be interfering with the fair administration of justice during the course of the trial. And besides, the publicity in the *Stroble* case and the *Baltimore Radio* case had been much more damaging and inflammatory than in this case. The judgment of the lower court was affirmed.

But motions for a new trial or mistrial do not always fail. In a case in which Treasury agents inspired newspaper comment to the effect that a plaintiff's tax refund claim was an "attempt to loot the Treasury," a new trial was granted. The court assumed that such news reports were "well calculated to prejudice" the jury, and had been read by them.[51]

In *United States* v. *Ogden*,[52] the defendant was charged with the illegal sale of oleomargarine, and the Pure Butter Protective Association had hired a Philadelphia newspaper to look into the matter. The newspaper concluded that Ogden had been selling oleo "by the ton." An appeals court decided that the butter forger deserved a new trial because he had been tried in the columns of the newspaper and declared guilty and denounced as a criminal before there had been an impartial trial in a proper tribunal.

A new trial was also granted in *Griffin et al.* v. *United States*,[53] where in a prosecution for conspiracy to defraud the federal government, a lower court was said to have erred in not withdrawing a juror and granting a new trial after a prejudicial newspaper article had circulated among the jury. The news account quoted the prosecuting attorney as saying that five of the defendants had offered to admit their parts in the conspiracy and turn state's evidence, that three of them had already signed written confessions, and that two had pleaded guilty.

A guilty verdict was reversed by the United States Supreme Court[54] when the *Wichita Daily Eagle*, in a murder trial, reported that the defendant had once before been tried for his life and that he had given up all hope of winning the present case. The jury read the story while they were deliberating.

While an accused was on trial for rape, articles appeared in two local newspapers stating that the defendant had (1) confessed to two murders for which he would be tried later, (2) had boasted of attacks on more than 50 women, (3) had been described by police as a vicious degenerate, and (4) had been arrested while attempting to attack another woman. The court found that at least one of the offending reports had been read by all the jurors. On the assurance of the jurors that they had not been influenced, the trial continued, over the defendant's objections, and he was convicted. An Illinois appeals court held that the news stories were so prejudicial as to require a new trial.[55]

While a jury was trying to decide between the death penalty and life imprisonment for a defendant, one of the jurors prevailed upon the foreman to read a newspaper story aloud decribing how the defendant, a convicted murderer, had celebrated the end of his parole by killing another man. The jury, which up to that time had been divided, voted for the death penalty. The Texas Court of Appeals said the accused was entitled to a new trial.[56]

Mistrials have also been declared where a newspaper reported the defendant was guilty of another felony;[57] where an article predicted that the testimony of the accused's own children would send him to the chair unless refuted;[58] where it was reported that attempts to bribe the jury on behalf of the defendant had taken place;[59] where a newspaper story suggested that the defendant had planned a jailbreak if found guilty;[60] where an article included a purported dying declaration prejudicial to the accused and inadmissible as evidence;[61] where it was stated that a defendant had several times before been convicted of abortion;[62] and where the defendant, a public official, was reported to have been involved in many shady deals and that several mass meetings had been held to remove him from office.[63] And where a newspaper presented its own interpretation of the evidence in a manner hostile to the defendant and instructed the jury on what weight to accord it, the court said there were grounds for a new trial.[64] In a state which does not permit comment on the evidence by the trial judge, an article purporting to convey the opinion of the judge as to the facts of the case warranted a new trial.[65] A mistrial was also declared where a newspaper ran a photograph showing the grave of a murder victim with the caption, "Say Widow Planned Burial Prior to Burgess Slaying." The woman had been charged as a conspirator and accessory in the murder of her husband.[66]

The problem of overcoming the prejudicial effects of publicity after a case has been given to the jury is complicated by the fact that jury deliberations are secret. An accused usually has no way of ascertaining whether a jury has actually seen the possibly prejudicial news articles. Inducing a juror to impeach his own verdict and admit that he disregarded the court's admonition is a formidable obstacle for a defendant to overcome. And in moving for a new trial, it is well settled that the testimony of jurors will not be received by the court either to support or to impeach their verdicts.[67] The reasons for this rule are (1) there would be no end to litigation if verdicts could be set aside because jurors did not understand the law or could not accurately weigh the evidence, and (2) a contrary view would encourage tampering with the jury after the verdict.[68]

In ruling on a motion for a new trial or mistrial, the court need only consider whether the nature of the news report was such that the jury could not avoid having been influenced by it in reaching their verdict. Juror affidavits are useful only in bringing to the attention of the court contact with publicity, not in showing its influence upon the verdict. The decision whether or not to grant the motion is entirely up to the court. Therefore, the defendant bears the heavy burden of convincing the trial judge that the publicity must have influenced the jurors and their verdict.

For the past 25 years at least, it has been a rule in federal courts that in criminal cases where jurors are permitted to separate, the court must admonish them not to communicate with anyone on any subject connected with the trial, and not to read published accounts of the trial.[69] Where this rule is broken, federal courts will often reverse convictions.

Since the granting of a new trial may be unfair to the party who wins at the first trial, courts are properly reluctant to grant such a motion unless there is evidence that at least some of the jurors have read the offending articles.[70] Affidavits testifying to such extraneous influences or other instances of misconduct on the part of jurors will be accepted by the court. If the offending articles are strong enough, the court will imply bias. Such a presumption of prejudice is especially strong where a defense attorney learns that the jury has read these kinds of news stories during the trial and the trial judge refuses or neglects to interrogate the jurors as to their influence. The presumption is also strong where the defense attorney does not find out that the jury has read prejudicial news reports until after a guilty verdict has been brought down. Where prejudicial articles are read prior to the trial and the defense has an opportunity to question the veniremen on *voir dire*, the presumption of prejudice is generally overcome by the juror's assertion that he can act impartially on the evidence.[71]

The major disadvantage of mistrial or new trial motions is the tremendous financial and psychological cost it imposes upon the defendant when he must stand trial for a second time. This is especially true in cases that have whetted the public's curiosity.

After veniremen are sworn, a defendant is allowed an unlimited number of challenges for cause during the *voir dire* (literally "to speak the truth") examination when prospective jurors are questioned to ascertain whether they are incompetent to serve by reason of having an interest in the cause or of having a prejudice which might affect their impartiality with respect to a defendant. When a jury has been sworn, the defendant still has a stipulated number of peremptory challenges—usually from 15 to 20 in a criminal case.

In the federal system, the general rule in the absence of statutory direction, has been that an unqualified, fixed or decided opinion that might interfere with the exercise of a fair and impartial judgment, disqualifies a juror for cause.[72]

In an 1850 case, *Commonwealth* v. *Webster*,[73] Mr. Justice Shaw said for the court: "The opinion or judgment must be something more than a vague impression, formed from casual observation with others, or from reading imperfect, abbreviated newspaper reports. It must be such an opinion upon the merits of the question as would likely to bias or pervert a candid judgment upon a full hearing of the evidence. If one has formed what in some sense may be called an opinion, but which yet fell short of exciting any bias or prejudice, he might conscientiously discharge his duty as a juror." The same conclusion was reached in *Coughlin* v. *People*[74] where the Illinois Supreme Court reversed a lower court and sustained challenges to two jurors:

". . . The holding of this and other courts is substantially uniform that, where it is once shown that there exists in the mind of the juror . . . a fixed and positive opinion . . . as to the guilt or innocence of the defendant he is called to try, his statement that notwithstanding such opinion, he can render a fair and impartial verdict, according to the law and the evidence, has little, if any, tendency to establish his impartiality . . . It is difficult to see how, after a juror has avowed a fixed and settled opinion as to the prisoner's guilt, a court can be legally satisfied of the truth of his answer that he can render a fair and impartial verdict, or find therefrom that he has the qualification of impartiality, as required by the Constitution."

The fact that a prospective juror has heard and talked about a case, or has read about it in a newspaper, will not disqualify him if he declares that in spite of any opinion he may have reached he can still give both parties a fair and impartial hearing.

Some courts have ruled that opinion formed solely from a casual reading of newspaper reports lacks the fixed quality needed for disqualification.[75] The source of information is immaterial, except for its importance in determining its fixed or transitory nature. Generally the trial court's discretion, even in borderline cases, will not be challenged by an appellate court. The rule seems to be that newspaper reports are ordinarily too unreliable to influence a fair-minded man when he is called upon to pass upon the merits of a case—unless upon *voir dire* examination he appears to have a fixed opinion.

This is how a defendant's attorney might handle a *voir dire* examination:

Q. "Mr. Wilson, have you read anything about this case in the newspapers?"

A. "Yes, when it happened there was a lot about it in the papers, and naturally I read something about it."

Q. "Do you remember specifically anything you read?"

A. "Not specifically; it's quite some time ago."

Q. "Did you read any of the newspaper accounts of the proceedings on the former trial of the case?"

A. "Yes."

Q. "Did you discuss the newspaper reports of the case with anyone?"

A. "Well I probably did; a lot of people were talking about it."

Q. "Based upon what you read and the conversations you had with people, did you form any opinion in the case one way or the other?"

A. "Well, at the time I did."

Q. "Was that an opinion as to the guilt or innocence of the defendant?"

A. "Yes."

Q. "And was that what you talked about?"

A. "Naturally."

Q. "Mr. Wilson what was the opinion which you say you formed and expressed?"

A. "Based upon what I read I said I thought he was guilty."

Q. "Is that your opinion still, Mr. Wilson?"

A. "I guess it is; I have heard nothing to change it."

Q. "Is it a fixed opinion?"

A. "Well, yes, until I hear something which makes me change my mind."

Q. "In other words, it would require evidence to remove the opinion?"

A. "Yes sir."

Q. "Do you think that opinion is so fixed that it would prevent you from rendering an impartial verdict?"

A. "Well, I believe I could decide the case on the evidence all right."

Q. "Have you any doubt about it?"

A. "Well, at the end of the last trial I had my mind made up, and that might stick in my craw in this case; I don't know."

Defendant's attorney: "Challenge for cause, your Honor. The juror says he has a fixed opinion, that it would take evidence to remove it; that it might affect his verdict."

The court: "He doesn't say he has a fixed opinion which would bias his verdict. That's the language of the statute. However, in view of his other answers, I think I will sustain the challenge."

Comment: "The *voir dire,* as a whole, indicates that Mr. Wilson would not make a fair and impartial juror. He declares to having a fixed opinion based in part upon newspaper accounts of testimony given on a former trial (a source more highly regarded than newspaper comment)."[76]

Challenge of a juror is rare in England. English law does permit a question to be put to a juror to show that he is incompetent, but the question must be based on specific evidence. Neither prosecution nor defense is permitted to go on a fishing expedition in the hope of discovering unexpected evidence of bias.[77]

A few courts, contrary to the preponderance of legal authority, adopt the premise that it is not always possible for an individual to prevent his predispositions from determining his conclusions. Unconscious presumptions derived from news reports may be as damaging as conscious ones, and declarations of impartiality are not enough to vitiate the possibility of prejudice.[78]

In *State* v. *Caine,*[79] a new trial was ordered on the ground that jurors had read newspaper accounts and comment; and their affidavits attesting to their impartiality were insufficient to overcome the probable influence of the reports. The unconscious influence of such accounts, said the court, would be far more likely to affect the result than an influence which was conscious and therefore resistable.

This principle was followed to some degree in a 1954 federal case.[80] A defendant named Juelich was convicted of the murder of a deputy United States marshal. The district court denied a motion for a change of venue, and the defendant appealed, largely on the basis of public prejudice resulting from newspaper and radio publicity. In rather lurid banner headlines, newspapers had referred to Juelich as a murderer with a long record who had confessed his crime to the F.B.I. Each of the 12 original jurors testified on *voir dire* examination that from the publicity he had formed an opinion that the accused was guilty, and it would take some evidence to change it. The United States Court of Appeals said that forcing a defendant to trial before a jury, every member of which had entered the jury box with the opinion that the defendant was guilty, was reversible error, and that a motion for a change of venue or a continuance should have been granted.

In the use of this remedy, the courts are in a quandary. They have developed no method of measuring the actual influence of press publicity on a juror, and they have balked at the testimony of expert witnesses, for example the testimony of a psychologist at the Rosenberg treason trial. The crucial question is left to the juror himself, and few jurors will impugn their own capacity for detachment and objectivity. The alternative is to depend upon the intuitive power of lawyers; but who can look into the mind of a juror and identify bias with any sense of confidence? We take the juror at his word, unless, as in the *Irvin* case, the evidence is overwhelming. One critic of this procedural device wonders "how a juror who is of the opinion that the defendant is guilty and who admits that it will take 'some evidence' to change his mind can be a competent juror when the state has the burden of proof and the defense is under no obligation to offer any evidence."[81]

Edward J. Ennis, general counsel of the American Civil Liberties Union, recommended in his testimony before the Senate Subcommittee hearings on the Morse Bill that a "challenge for cause" be instituted by statute or by Amendment of the Federal Rules of Criminal Procedure. This provision based on a prospective juror's knowledge of facts about a case received from the press would eliminate the juror and thus eliminate the speculation on whether he could be a fair juror despite this knowledge. Such a challenge for cause, in Ennis' opinion, would act as a strong deterrent upon government attorneys, investigators and other personnel connected with the trial of criminal cases, who would hesitate to release facts to the press if the consequence might be a substantial delay in the trial. Many experienced judges and lawyers are not satisfied that a juror can in his deliberations completely separate what he learned in court from what he has learned out of court.

CONTINUANCE

Motion for a continuance is designed to postpone a trial until prejudice has died down. Among the disadvantages to the defendant of a continuance are that it interferes with the right to a speedy trial, it allows time for witnesses to disappear and for their memories to dim, and, if the defendant is not able to make bond or the offense is not a bailable one, it requires him to remain in jail pending trial. In the *Brinks* robbery case,[82] for example, the defense sought to exploit the constitutional conflict between fair trial and speedy trial: prejudice would outlast any period during which a trial, properly called speedy, might be had. Therefore the defendants could never be constitutionally tried at all. The Supreme Judicial Court of Massachusetts held that the publicity, though instigated by law enforcement officials and improper, did not entitle the defendants to release on the theory that they could never be constitutionally tried. This was no setting for apathy, said the court, and the newspaper coverage undoubtedly extensive was commensurate with a crime of colossal proportions.

The question remains as to how to know when the effects of prejudicial publicity have worn off—a point upon which defense attorney and court may strongly disagree. There is also the possibility that the lengthened span of litigation might provide an opportunity for even wider circulation of publicity, and past publicity can always be revived.

A motion for a continuance rests on the same grounds as a motion for a change of venue, with wide discretion given the trial court. The general rule is that the defendant must take the initiative in moving for a continuance, or he loses the right.[83]

An important federal case[84] illustrates the use of this procedural remedy. Denis W. Delaney, an official of the Internal Revenue Service, had been indicted on charges of bribery in an income tax case. Immediately prior to the trial, a congressional committee investigating the case had issued a great deal of unfavorable publicity. The defendant was given an initial six-week continuance, but when he asked for more time he was turned down. He was later convicted, but the conviction was reversed by the Court of Appeals on the ground that a longer delay should have been granted.

The court drew attention to the flamboyant front page headlines and colorful feature stories which emphasized the more dramatic aspects of the testimony before the committee. These were supplemented by radio and television "exploitation" of Delaney's difficult situation. National attention was focused on the case by a *Life* magazine article entitled, "The Hands in the Taxpayer's Pockets: The Truman Administration's Worst Scandal is in the Making as Corruption is Found Throughout Internal Revenue Bureau."[85] A photo of Delaney was included.

Concerned with the fact that the committee hearing had afforded a public preview of the prosecution's case, the Court of Appeals said in part: "It is fair to say that, so far as the modern mass media of communication could accomplish it, the character of Delaney was pretty thoroughly blackened and discredited as the day approached for his judicial trial on narrowly specified charges. . . . The present case presents an unusual situation not covered by any precedent in the Supreme Court. . . . This is not a case of pre-trial publicity, of damaging material, tending to indicate the guilt of a defendant, dug up by the initiative and private enterprise of newspapers. Here the United States, through its legislative department, by means of an open committee hearing held shortly before the trial of a pending indictment, caused and stimulated the massive pre-trial publicity, on a nationwide scale."

The court here was unwilling to assume that the average juror is so endowed with a sense of detachment, so clear in his perception of his own mental processes that he can confidently exclude even the unconscious influence of his preconceptions. And the court viewed with displeasure the "fatalistic acceptance" given trial by newspaper, which required the use of ineffective procedural devices in an attempt to insulate jurors from publicity. Delaney was given a new trial.

The dilemma was illustrated by the late Judge Learned Hand in the 1950 trial of Dennis and other leaders of the Communist Party. When it was urged that it would be impossible to get an impartial jury because of the heated public feelings against Communists, Judge Hand disagreed. To wait for public feeling to subside, he said, would be to put off the trial indefinitely. The choice was between using the best means available to secure an impartial jury and letting the prosecution lapse.[86]

INSTRUCTIONS TO THE JURY

By means of cautionary instructions, a judge, in effect, tells jurors they must decide a case purely on the law and evidence and not on extraneous news reports. Adequate instructions by a judge may defeat motions for a mistrial or new trial.

In the 1951 *Leviton* case,[87] the Court of Appeals sustained the conviction of defendants charged with exporting food products to Italy in violation of a Presidential proclamation. A copy of the *New York Times*, containing an inaccurate report that a customs bureau clerk had been offered a bribe by the defendants to suppress evidence and that the defendants were part of a larger ring, had found its way into the jury room. The court reasoned that where the judge had given explicit instructions that the contents of the article were to be disregarded and went on to point out how the offenses set forth in the indictment differed from those described in the article, there was no error in having allowed the trial to proceed.

"Trial by newspaper," said Judge Clark for the court, "may be unfortunate, but it is not new and, unless the court accepts the standard judicial hypothesis that cautioning instructions are effective, criminal trials in the metropolitan centers may well prove impossible." This was by no means a new idea in judicial circles, but it did point up the basically psychological nature of the issue. The late Judge Jerome Frank was incensed by the majority opinion, and in a frequently quoted dissent said:

"My colleagues admit that 'trial by newspaper' is unfortunate. But they dismiss it as an unavoidable curse of metropolitan living (like, I suppose, crowded subways). They rely on the old 'ritualistic admonition' to purge the record. The futility of that sort of exorcism is notorious. As I have elsewhere observed, it is like the Mark Twain story of the little boy who was told to stand in a corner and not to think of a white elephant. . . I think the technique (judge instructions to the jury) particularly objectionable and ineffective here for two reasons. (1) The story was a direct result of confidential disclosures by a government office, of not-in-the-record matters and was not merely the accidental garbling of a confused reporter. (2) The article was no statement of opinion or editorial, but a professed account of court-room evidence calculated to confuse and mislead juror-readers. In such cases, courts recognize that, for all practical purposes, defendants are deprived of their constitutional rights to confront witnesses, cross-examine and contradict them, and object to evidence as irrelevant or incompetent—in short all the elements of a fair trial."

Justice Robert H. Jackson, in an earlier Supreme Court case, reached the same conclusion when he said, "The naive assumption that prejudicial effects can be overcome by instructions to the jury, all practicing lawyers know to be unmitigated fiction."[88]

There is some evidence that strong prohibiting instructions by the judge may boomerang and serve primarily to remind the jury of something it would not otherwise have thought of doing,[89] much in the fashion of a parent's instructions to his children, and often with the same harvest of confusion and disobedience.

More distressing is the fact that some courts have denied motions for mistrial because a defendant either failed to request judicial instructions to the jury or did not demonstrate an abuse of discretion or prejudice on the part of the judge;[90] other courts have held that failure of the judge himself to so charge the jury was, in part, grounds for reversal;[91] and still others have ruled that any kind of charge to the jury is inadequate where articles have been flagrantly prejudicial. The latter proposition supports the notion of implied bias or presumed partiality of jurors where publicity has been widespread as being a sufficient cause for mistrial or new trial. Certainly this has been the rationale of majority opinions in *Irvin, Rideau, Sheppard, Janko,* and *Estes,* Supreme Court decisions which suggest that less confidence is being placed in the efficacy of cautionary instructions to combat prejudicial publicity occurring before or during a trial.

WAIVER OF THE RIGHT TO TRIAL BY JURY

In waiving the right to a jury trial, a defendant gives up a constitutional right and loses whatever emotional appeal his cause might have. Moreover, the state then has only a judge to convince, and in some circumstances this may be simpler than leading a jury of 12 persons to a desired conclusion.

The 1930 Supreme Court decision in *Patton* v. *United States*,[92] requiring both the court and the government to consent to any waiver of a jury trial by a defendant in a federal case, was incorporated into the Federal Rules of Criminal Procedure. It has since been recommended that the Supreme Court consider easing the difficulty of invoking this procedural remedy in light of the fact that the federal courts have allowed waivers of other important rights such as the right to counsel, speedy trial and a public trial.[93] Ronald Goldfarb has recently suggested that three-judge courts be permitted, through constitutional amendment and legislation, to take sensational criminal cases away from the jury. Judges, he believes, because their decisions are subject to appellate review, want to decide cases correctly; and, of course, they are much less subject to extraneous influences.[94] The problem is that judges are much more prone to convict than juries.[95]

THE DUE PROCESS APPEAL

Considering the recent preoccupation of the United States Supreme Court with questions of due process and its decisions in such cases as *Irvin, Janko, Rideau, Estes,* and *Sheppard,* it appears that an "implied bias" assumption will support future appeals under the due process clause of the Fourteenth Amendment. In the important 1961 *Irvin* ruling the Court stated simply that failure of a state to accord a fair hearing to one accused of a crime violates due process; a trial by jury is not fair unless the jury is impartial; and a jury is not impartial when it is impregnated with prejudice catalyzed by a hostile press. The lower federal court rulings in such cases as *Florio, Briggs, Powell, Coppedge, Delaney* and *Bloeth* indicate that the same "implied bias" assumption is being used there. And state courts often take their cues from the federal system.

The courts are to be commended for the pragmatic use they make of these procedural remedies, in lieu of subjecting judge and jury to deep therapy in order to determine the real effects of possibly prejudicial publicity. But substantial problems remain unsolved. Court rulings are confusingly inconsistent. Some imply that a juror's unconscious preconceptions will influence his determinations; others that a mere declaration of impartiality will overcome prejudice. In exercising his discretion, the judge must play a hunch, guessing as to whether opinions are "fixed" or "fleeting," and whether or not particular jurors will follow his instructions. Moreover, any strict insistence on impartiality would paralyze criminal procedure. New trials tend to crowd already seriously overcrowded dockets. Changes of venue seldom neutralize the effects of the ubiquitous modern mass media. Continuance gambles on fading memories and cold evidence. Lawyers may use *voir dire* challenges to indoctrinate as well as to excuse for prejudice.

Reversal of conviction upon a successful due process appeal may inflict a hardship upon the state, but it does reinforce the doctrine of the presumption of innocence, a first principle of Anglo-American law. It also serves notice on the press that it may be responsible for the overturning of otherwise valid convictions.

Lawyers frequently assert that the procedural remedies are not only impractical but fail to punish editors directly and therefore do nothing positive to thwart the adverse effects of prejudicial publicity. Newsmen find unacceptable the presumption of a direct cause-effect relationship between news reports and jury verdicts, and they don't quite trust the lawyers' motives in continuing to pursue the phantom of an unbiased jury.

The impatience of the bar is best reflected in its frequent recommendation that the contempt power of the courts be taken down from the shelf, dusted off, and used with force against out-of-court publications which have a tendency to subvert the orderly course of justice.

Chapter 11

CONTEMPT AND THE CONSTITUTION

"We are a garrulous and querulous people. It would be better if we talked and complained less. But it would not be well if we mended our manners out of fear of fine and imprisonment and not out of a growth in the amenities of civilized living."—Max Radin.[1]

Contempt of court, said Sir John Fox, an English legal historian, has been a recognized phrase in English law from the Twelfth Century to the present.[2] In 1742, Lord Hardwicke identified three kinds of contempt: (1) scandalizing the court itself, (2) abuse of parties who are concerned in causes before the bench, and (3) prejudicing mankind against a person before the cause is heard.[3]

Today, press comment on pending trials is a common form of criminal contempt. It can be punished by fine or imprisonment or both and by the summary, or on the spot, process of attachment (direct committal to prison), with or without examination of the accused and without benefit of jury.

Justification for the summary punishment of constructive or out-of-court contempt is credited to the great English jurist, Blackstone, who depended for his opinion upon the authority of Justice Wilmot's undelivered opinion in *R. v. Almon,*[4] a case having to do with a libel by a bookseller upon the Chief Justice, Lord Mansfield. Wilmot believed the procedure to stand upon immemorial usage, to be coeval with the common law, and to be absolutely necessary to the authority of the courts. A clerical error in drawing up an attachment against Almon led to the abandonment of the case, and the 1765 judgment was never delivered. But it was published posthumously in 1802. Although not mentioned in the reports of the period, the case became a widely cited authority for the summary power to punish constructive contempts of court.

Fox doubted the "immemorial" basis of Wilmot's rule and, in an authoritative treatise, attempted to prove that in early times criminal contempt committed by a stranger out of court was proceeded against like any other trespass in the common law courts, with the assistance of a jury.

The punishment of libels on the court by attachment, said Fox, were arbitrary and oppressive Star Chamber processes, which clashed with the whole system of English law. But Wilmot's undelivered opinion has become legal doctrine. As recently as 1964 the immemorial power was affirmed in a Supreme Court ruling that Governor Ross Barnett of Mississippi was not entitled to trial by jury in a criminal contempt proceeding.[5]

The Wilmot doctrine was incorporated into the law of the colonies, and even in the period immediately after the Revolution, the courts made no effort to reshape the English law of contempt.[6] During the formative period of American law, between 1800 and the Civil War, the legislatures rather than the courts attempted to alter the law of contempt by restricting the summary contempt power to a limited number of misbehaviors committed within the immediate environs of the court. In some statutes, publications were expressly excluded from the list of misbehaviors.

The first such bill was passed in Pennsylvania in 1809 after a bitter court case[7] had drawn attention to the issues. Summary punishment for publication was expressly forbidden, and redress by regular indictment or libel action was substituted. Under the strong influence of Edward Livingston's theory—in his "System of Penal Law Prepared for the State of Louisiana"—that the summary power should be confined to what is said or done directly in the presence of the court, the provisions of the 1829 Revised Statutes of Livingston's native state of New York limited the scope of the summary power. Criminal punishment was forbidden, even after trial by jury, for publications not classifiable as false or grossly inaccurate reports of proceedings.[8]

This reaction against the English common law method of dealing with constructive contempt reached its zenith in the impeachment trial of Judge Peck before the United States Senate in 1831. Peck, a federal judge, had used the contempt power to suspend from practice for 18 months a lawyer who had criticized him. The impeachment failed by a one-vote margin, but within nine days Congress had passed the Federal Contempt Act of March 2, 1831, limiting punishable contempt to disobedience to any judicial process or decree and to misbehavior in the presence of the court, *"or so near thereto as to obstruct the administration of justice."*[9]

Vivid memories of the noxious Alien and Sedition Laws of 1798

—bulwarked as they were by the wide power given the federal courts
in the Judiciary Act of 1789—motivated legislators to deny any
ill-defined concentration of power to the judges. The English common
law power of contempt, being inapplicable to American conditions,
was to have no status in American jurisdictions. By 1860, 23 of the
33 states had enacted similar limitations on the summary power to
punish for contempt.

From the Civil War to World War I, both state and federal courts
gradually circumvented or abrogated these limitary contempt statutes
and reintroduced the English common law rules.

For example, in *State* v. *Morrill*,[10] Arkansas courts invoked the
separation of powers doctrine to get around the Arkansas statute.
Patterson v. *Colorado*,[11] decided in 1907 by the United States Supreme
Court, gave further support to the common law rule that truth is no
defense in a constructive contempt proceeding and provided a rationale for state prosecutions.

The *Toledo Newspaper Company* case[12] finally ratified the causal
construction of the Act of 1831, which had gradually come to prevail
in the lower federal courts. On appeal, the Supreme Court upheld
the conviction of the *Toledo News-Bee* for attributing bias to a judge
in a squabble between the city and a transit company. The majority
opinion misconstrued the 1831 statute as declaratory of the assumed
immemorial scope of inherent power at common law and saw in this
newspaper's misbehavior a "reasonable tendency" to obstruct justice.

In a powerful dissent—which was to be recalled in later cases—
Mr. Justice Holmes renewed the geographical dictates of the "so near
thereto" clause, sought to discredit the summary power (the same
person to be accuser and sole judge), and saw nothing in this particular publication to prevent the judge from doing his sworn duty.

By interpreting the federal statute in terms of reasonable tendency
rather than proximity, this decision nullified the intent of the 1831
Congress to make the crime of contempt specific. The essence of
Holmes' dissent is found in the following sentence: "I would go as
far as any man in favor of the sharpest and most summary enforcement of order in Court and obedience to decrees, but when there is
no need for immediate action, contempts are like any other breach
of law and should be dealt with as the law deals with other illegal
acts."[13]

By bringing a contempt proceeding, the court destroys the defenses
of truth and fair comment and criticism available in libel actions.

In *Craig* v. *Hecht*,[14] Chief Justice William H. Taft recommended trial by jury and judgment by someone other than the aggrieved judge in all cases of constructive contempt. More recently Justice Hugo Black made the same argument, dissenting in *Green* v. *United States*.[15] But the spectre of Wilmot remains, for, in the *Green* case, Justice Felix Frankfurter said that though the historical assumptions regarding the procedure for punishment of contempt of court are ill formed, a century and a half of the legislative and judicial history of federal law based on such assumptions cannot be ignored.

By the mid-1920s only four states—New York, Pennsylvania, Kentucky and South Carolina—still possessed statutes which had withstood judicial efforts to narrow the meaning of legislative restrictions on the contempt power. With the federal courts leading the way, 43 judicial systems had firmly rejected efforts to control the contempt power by legislation. For 20 years after the *Toledo* case, the Act of 1831 posed no obstacle to the summary punishment of contempt by publication in the federal courts.

State courts had likewise cast off their inhibitions, and when an influential minister impugned the motives of a Superior Court judge in a series of radio talks, the Supreme Court of California held him in contempt, notwithstanding a state statute limiting the contempt power to acts committed in the presence of the court.[16]

The main difficulty with such a doctrine was that, in a period when American judges were more and more being called upon to evaluate social and economic laws involving both the public welfare and private rights, their judgments were not open to critical examination. Thus the right to subject the judiciary to the free play of public opinion was curtailed precisely in the country where it was most urgent that it be given the greatest scope.

Possibly under the onus of Franklin D. Roosevelt's court-packing threats in the years immediately preceding World War II, the Supreme Court made a right about face and, in *Nye* v. *United States*,[17] largely restored the discredited interpretation of the "so near thereto" clause and greatly limited the power of federal judges to punish out-of-court contempts. To this day the proper interpretation of this clause is a matter of scholarly debate. But in the *Nye* case, the Court decided that "so near thereto" means physical proximity and should be applied as a geographical rather than as a causative directive. The Court also declared that if the reasonable tendency rule used in *Toledo*—and earlier cases decided under the federal statute—was to be given causal meaning, it would undermine the purposes of the Act of 1831.

BRIDGES: THE COURT TURNS A CORNER

Also during 1941, in what is perhaps the single most important case in the whole field of contempt, the Supreme Court in *Bridges* v. *California*[18] abandoned the "reasonable tendency" rule in favor of the "clear and present danger" test, first enunciated by Justice Oliver Wendell Holmes in the *Schenck* case. We will recall that for Holmes the question was to be whether the words used actually create a clear and present danger that will bring about the substantive evil that Congress has a right to prevent. And it would also be a question of proximity and degree. Words were not to be punished simply because they have a remote tendency to bring about bad acts. More important, for the first time, out-of-court publications relating to judicial proceedings came under the Constitutional protection of the First Amendment rights of free speech and press and would be further protected against state laws by application of the due process clause of the Fourteenth Amendment.

Union leader Harry Bridges, the Times-Mirror Company, and the managing editor of the *Los Angeles Times* were found guilty and fined for contempt by the Superior Court of Los Angeles. The case against the newspaper resulted from several critical editorials written while a trial court was considering appropriate sentences for two men found guilty of intimidating members of a labor union. Bridges was cited because of a telegram he had sent to the Secretary of Labor —and which was published in the newspaper—criticizing a court decision against the CIO, of which he was a leader. In the telegram, Bridges threatened to strike the Pacific Coast with his ILWU longshoremen if the decision was enforced. On appeal to the Supreme Court of California, the decision of the Superior Court was affirmed.

The cases were then appealed to the Supreme Court of the United States on the constitutional question, and that court handed down one decision for the two cases. By a 5-4 majority the California courts were reversed.

The court cast aside technicalities in order to decide what was to be the relationship between contempt and the Bill of Rights. "The question," said the court, "is whether freedom of the courts from duress is so vastly, so immeasurably, more important than liberty of speech that even the possibility of duress excludes the latter liberty."[19]

Lawyers and judges are by no means unanimous in their interpretation of the clear and present danger test, or in its application. But in *Bridges*, and subsequent cases, the Supreme Court construed it to be synonymous with threats to justice which are imminent, immediate, impending, urgent, or, at least, not remote. Fear of future evil was not enough, within the meaning of the test. As distinguished from the reasonable or bad tendency test, the clear and present danger doctrine clearly implies a more libertarian social and political philosophy, for it insists upon a stronger, more positive justification for curtailment of free speech and press.

The state court had punished the *Times-Mirror*,[20] said its attorneys, for publishing views related to a pending cause in violation of state statutes designed to protect fair trial. These statutes depended for their enforcement on the common law procedure of punishing interferences and obstructions of this kind by summary contempt proceedings. The resulting restrictions subordinated liberty of expression to the public interest in judicial impartiality. The Supreme Court agreed.

Justice Black, in his majority opinion for the court, noted that in the absence of a more specific California contempt statute, the state court's decision was "based on a common law concept of the most general and undefined nature . . . and to assume that English common law became ours is to deny the generally accepted historical belief that 'one of the objects of the Revolution was to get rid of the English common law on liberty of speech and of the press.' "[21] He added: "What finally emerges from the 'clear and present danger' cases is a working principle that the substantive evil must be extremely serious and the degree of imminence extremely high before utterances can be punished. Those cases do not purport to mark the furthermost constitutional boundaries of protected expression, nor do we here. They do no more than recognize a minimum compulsion of the Bill of Rights. For the First Amendment does not speak equivocally. It prohibits any law 'abridging the freedom of speech or of the press.' It must be taken as a command of the broadest scope that explicit language, read in the context of a liberty-loving society, will allow."[22]

In *Bridges*, the Supreme Court also considered the question of pendency, and the majority felt that judgments against publications made during the pendency of a case "produce their restrictive results at the precise time when public interest in the matter discussed would naturally be at its height. . . . It is therefore the controversies that command most interest that decisions below would remove from the arena of public discussion."[23]

With regard to Bridges himself, the court noted that he was a prominent labor leader speaking at a time when public interest in the particular labor controversy was considerable. And the majority of the court could see in Bridges' published telegram to the Secretary of Labor no evidence of intimidation of the court or of interference with the course of justice. No longer was pendency to be a mere technical matter; the clear and present danger test would be applied to that question also.

Mr. Justice Frankfurter's dissent was concurred in by Chief Justice Harlan F. Stone and Justices Owen J. Roberts and James F. Byrnes. In *Bridges,* Frankfurter saw claims on behalf of liberties no less precious than freedom of speech and press. His argument emphasized the rights of the states to decide by law what protection should be afforded their judiciary. The divergence of his views from those of the majority is indicated by this fragment of his opinion: "But that the conventional power to punish for contempt is not a censorship in advance but a punishment for past conduct and, as such, like prosecution for a criminal libel, is not offensive either to the First or to the Fourteenth Amendments, has never been doubted throughout this Court's history. . . . The power should be invoked only where the adjudicatory process may be hampered or hindered in its calm, detached, and fearless discharge of its duty on the basis of what has been submitted in Court."[24]

In summary, the majority in the *Bridges* case seemed firmly committed to the proposition that the First Amendment liberties have a preferred place in our hierarchy of constitutional values. The majority held also that the normal presumption in favor of the constitutionality of legislation did not exist for laws which on their face invade one of these freedoms, and the clear and present danger standard for testing the validity of limitations on these freedoms was underscored.

The minority opinion held that the actual likelihood of intimidation is irrelevant and that any language by which anyone attempts to influence the actions of a judge, or language which has a *tendency* to influence him, is a danger to impartial and dispassionate deliberation on his part and is not to be protected by the right of free speech guaranteed by the First and Fourteenth Amendments.

Pennekamp v. *Florida*[25] and *Craig* v. *Harney*[26] gave the Supreme Court an opportunity to carry the argument farther and to restate the freedom-versus-justice issues of the *Bridges* decision with a liberality shocking to some legal observers.

In *Craig,* Justice William O. Douglas said that the "law of contempt is not made for the protection of judges who may be sensitive to the winds of opinion" for "judges are supposed to be men of fortitude, able to thrive in a hardy climate." This seemed to close the door to the summary contempt procedure for the scandalizing of a touchy judge. But it did little to cope with the problem of "trial by newspaper," where a jury might be involved. Nor do the latter two decisions add any precision to the still disputatious meaning of the clear and present danger test.

"To deny that bludgeoning or poisonous comment has power to influence, or at least to disturb, the task of judging is to play make-believe and to assume that men in gowns are angels," said Justice Frankfurter in rebuttal.

But these two cases did resolve for the time being the question of whether a state through the enactment of laws could vest its courts with power to punish publications for contempt and so escape federal dictum. The Supreme Court said it could not.

Zechariah Chafee, Jr., the late authority on freedom of speech and press in America, was particularly critical of the majority opinion in *Pennekamp*. He would not have excused the gross inaccuracy of the offending editorial, which criticized the court for needless delay in returning indictments to a grand jury for correction. At the least, said Chafee, the newspaper should have been required to print a retraction correcting its initial blunder. Chafee would make Frankfurter's concurring opinion in the case—because of its incisive discussion of what should be the relationship between the press and the courts—required reading in every school of journalism, newspaper office and broadcasting station.[27]

It is suggested that the *Craig* case differed from the *Bridges* case in one important particular. In the *Bridges* case there was no prior compulsion to decide the issue one way or another. In *Craig*, whatever compulsion there was to grant a motion for a new trial was given impetus by newspaper publicity (the Corpus Christi *Caller-Times* had joined in a community-wide campaign to secure a new trial in a forcible-detainer case for a soldier serving overseas). The Texas Court of Criminal Appeals made the distinction by suggesting that in *Bridges* the newspaper kindled a fire already burning, while in *Craig* the newspaper ignited the fire.[28]

The Supreme Court disagreed, blaming the layman judge's decision in this nonjury case for the public outcry. But this somewhat absolutist approach to the application of the clear and present danger test has led some lawyers to the frightening conclusion that anything short of actually threatening the court to arrive at a particular decision is permissible comment. In choosing between free press and fair trial, perhaps the majority opinion in the *Craig* case says as much: "But it is hard to see . . . how [the editorial] could obstruct the course of justice in the case before the court. The only *demand* was for a hearing. There was no *demand* that the judge reverse his position—or else." (Emphasis added.)[29]

"No modern Justice questions the primacy of free speech as an element in the political process," Wallace Mendelson has pointed out. "But what is food for politics may be poison for a court and jury. Must words calculated to frustrate the judicial process have the same high respect as words offered for grist in the political mill?"[30]

That Holmes may have subscribed to the same idea is given credence by a sentence from his dissent in the *Abrams* case: "It is only the present danger of immediate evil or an intent to bring it about that warrants Congress in setting a limit to the expression of opinion *where private rights are not concerned.*" (Emphasis added.)[31]

Justice Douglas has made the same point, at least by implication: "*Where public matters are involved,* the doubts should be resolved in favor of freedom of expression rather than against it. Otherwise criminal libel will tend to cast the same shadow over discussion of public affairs as seditious libel once did." (Emphasis added.)[32]

It might appear that the landmark cases discussed above have had the composite effect of abolishing the power of state courts to reach publications that appeared to interfere with the administration of justice. However, the Supreme Court has not yet defined the permissible scope of the contempt power, for *Nye, Bridges, Pennekamp* and *Craig,* and subsequent cases, deal only with criticism directed at a judge and do *not* consider pressures brought to bear on jury deliberations. The distinction is crucial. Is what we expect a judge to bear with professional fortitude disastrous to a jury? The Supreme Court made the distinction in both *Pennekamp* and *Craig.* Justice Douglas says in *Craig,* for example, that none of the landmark cases raises questions concerning the "full reach of the power of the state to protect the administration of justice by its courts." There is a firm suggestion in these cases that the decisions might have followed a different path had juries rather than judges been involved.

THE BALTIMORE RADIO CASE

The United States Supreme Court had an opportunity in the *Baltimore Radio* case[33] to face squarely the issue of "trial by newspaper," to clarify the judge-jury distinction, and to set guidelines for lower courts in their application of the clear and present danger test to prejudicial pre-trial comment in jury cases. By denying *certiorari,* the court elected, unfortunately, to hold in abeyance its judgment on these crucial matters—for what reasons we can only guess. Justice Frankfurter was greatly disturbed by this decision and, in a personal memorandum, took pains to point out that the denial of *certiorari* did not necessarily imply approval or disapproval of the lower court decision. The depth of his concern is suggested in an appendix to the memorandum in which he presents the leading English cases on constructive contempt in order to recommend what American courts *ought* to do to solve this problem.[34]

In 1939, Baltimore newspapers published, under screaming headlines, news stories announcing that Aurelio Marco Tarquinio had confessed in the sensational "Torso Murder Case." There was evidence that the source of most of the information had been the police department. Thereafter, the Supreme Bench of Baltimore City adopted its Tarquinio Rules (usually referred to as Rule 904), which outlined in assiduous detail restrictions on pre-trial comment. There were to be no photographs of an accused without his consent, no issuance by anyone in an official capacity of statements relative to admissions made by the defendant, no forecasting of the future course of action in a case, and no publication of "any matter which may prevent a fair trial, improperly influence court or jury, or tend in any manner to interfere with the administration of justice." Newspapers and some lawyers immediately protested that such sweeping restrictions on news reporting revived the "inherent power" theory of contempt. The Rule stood until 1950.

It was under these conditions that the *Baltimore Radio* case arose. In 1948 Baltimore radio stations carried a series of newscasts on a murder case of wide public interest: An 11-year-old girl had been stabbed to death, and her assailant was the object of an intensive police search. "Stand by for a sensation," promised a radio station announcer when Eugene H. James, a Negro, was arrested on suspicion of the crime. The news broadcasts went on to relate that James had confessed, had a long criminal record, had re-enacted the crime, and had found the hidden murder weapon for police.

Four radio stations were cited for contempt by the Baltimore City Criminal Court for what was, in its opinion, a clear and present danger to the fair administration of justice. The defendant, claiming the broadcasts made it impossible to find impartial jurors, elected to waive his right to a jury trial—a right which is constitutionally guaranteed in Maryland. A change of venue was not suggested because of the blanket coverage of the broadcasts, and defense counsel felt that *voir dire* examination of all prospective jurors would simply compound the injury to James. As is usually the case, the Baltimore court was presented with no affirmative showing that the broadcasts had actually made an impartial jury trial impossible; it accepted speculation on this point by the defendant's counsel as conclusive. The four radio stations were assessed nominal fines, and they separately appealed.

The Court of Appeals of Maryland, in a 5-1 decision, somewhat self-consciously reversed the lower court, holding that its decision and the *rules* under which the decision was made were invalid restraints on the freedoms of speech and press. "It is now perfectly clear," said the Maryland court, "that whatever the law of the state, embodied in its constitution, statutes or judicial decisions, the provisions of the Federal Constitution are supreme."[35] In addition, the court declined to accept the argument that jurors require more protection from potentially prejudicial comment than judges. The prosecution would have brought the confession and prior criminal record before the court and jury in any event. And the rule of exclusion of evidence of prior conviction of unrelated crimes remains a rule of evidence and not a constitutional right. Moreover, a widely recognized exception to the rule is where such evidence may have logical relevance in establishing a behavior pattern as in cases involving sex crimes or abnormalities.

There is a certain air of resignation, however, in the court's contention that the mere fact of arrest, or indictment, implies that the police believe the accused to be guilty, or that the grand jury has found a *prima facie* case. The presumption of innocence totters on such a premise. More agreeable is the suggestion that knowledge that public authorities are active may have a tendency to allay public excitement and fears, so often magnified by word of mouth.

James was subsequently sentenced to death and, on appeal, the same court affirmed the judgment. "We would have difficulty," said the court, "in holding that the same statements that would not be so prejudicial as to require the reversal of a death sentence, could still be so prejudicial as to support conviction for contempt."[36]

Judge Markell, in a dissent which was later to be approved by Justice Frankfurter, thought "trial by newspaper" had been substituted for trial by jury in the case. Two conflicting propositions—neither of which he was willing to accept—represented much of the argumentation on this issue, in his opinion: (a) Prejudice in a jury can always be prevented. So why worry? (b) Prejudice in a jury can never be prevented. So why try? The observation that the two trials (the one in court and the other in the press) reached the same conclusion anyway was, he said "a time-honored apology for lynch law."[37]

Castigating the inflammatory nature of the broadcasts, Judge Markell said that it was unnecessary to make a distinction between intent and effect—the administration of justice would suffer in any event. He suggested that the Maryland court, purporting to follow the Supreme Court decisions—which negate the contempt power—adopted the minority view as to the relation of judges to publications and then departed from that court's decisions, and from the reasoning of all the justices, by applying the disputed doctrine regarding judges, to jurors, to whom none of the justices have applied it. "Unless the Supreme Court says so," he added, "I cannot believe that the broad fundamental right to a fair trial can lawfully be defeated by a blast from the radio."[38]

The failure of the United States Supreme Court to grant *certiorari* has had the consequence of withholding from state courts a clear idea of what are to be their limits in using the contempt power to punish prejudicial pre-trial publications that have their primary effect on jurors rather than on judges. The very fact that the question of applying the clear-and-present-danger test to jury trials arose in the *Baltimore Radio* case gives it a permanent place in constitutional law. That a judicial answer was not forthcoming can only be regretted. The controversial nature of the point at issue is indicated by the fact that the American Civil Liberties Union appeared as *amicus curiae* supporting a free and unfettered press, while the Maryland Civil Liberties Committee stood for the right to a fair trial.

In the present state of the law, it would appear that the press, without fear of contempt of court, may freely comment upon pending jury trials—unless the object of its out-of-court activities is intimidation or violence. Moreover, offenders are not to be punished summarily, but only after indictment and trial by jury. To protect his right to a fair and impartial jury trial, the accused must depend on the procedural remedies discussed in the previous chapter. These devices have consequently gained considerable importance in the American judicial system, and until the Supreme Court deigns to say whether the clear and present danger rule is applicable to pending jury trials, and until it suggests what it takes to constitute a clear and present danger, they will continue to be important.

Justice Frankfurter hinted—upon what authority we do not know—that the court was now ready to arrest, if not actually reverse, the previous trend toward newspaper immunity in judge as well as jury cases, and he seemed to be encouraging state courts to revive summary punishment for press comments, even though they create only a possibility of obstructing justice.

In 1957 the Supreme Court of Illinois,[39] at least spiritually, upheld the contempt conviction of a television announcer who had been sentenced to ten days in jail and fined $100 for commenting prejudicially on a divorce action then being tried in the Superior Court. The essence of his crime was his questioning of the veracity and credibility of witnesses in the pending child-custody proceeding. He had also said over the air that he would do everything in his power to prevent the "legal kidnaping" of the child.

This attempt to influence the outcome of the case, regardless of the announcer's real intent, was said by the court to constitute a clear and present danger to the administration of justice. The prejudicial comments, the court added, were not directed at the trial judge but to the parties and witnesses "to whom there is no reason to attribute a special degree of fortitude."[40]

Doubting that the Supreme Court intended to require proof of an actual interference with the judicial process, the Illinois court relied on *Craig* to support its conclusion that where comment is systematically designed to serve the contrary aim of thwarting the judicial process, it is not constitutionally protected—as in this case where the defendant publicly announced his intention of influencing the outcome. Justice Frankfurter's dissent in *Craig* was cited freely and with approval.

But the lower court decision had to be reversed nevertheless (after much discussion of what seemed to be the main issue), because the trial judge was bound by a state law to grant a change of venue when requested, and he had failed to do so.

In late 1965 the New Mexico Supreme Court unanimously reversed the contempt conviction of Will Harrison, a syndicated political columnist. Harrison had criticized the leniency shown an assistant district attorney charged with manslaughter in contrast with the prison sentence imposed upon a similarly culpable Mexican-American laborer.

C. N. Morris, assistant district attorney at Carlsbad, New Mexico, was involved in a traffic accident on June 22, 1963, in which five members of a Mexican farm worker's family were killed. Morris subsequently pleaded guilty to a charge of involuntary manslaughter while driving while intoxicated. District Judge Paul Tackett put Morris on probation for 12 months and fined him $500, suspending the fine upon his good behavior and the payment of court costs. In a similar case, Elerio Trujillo, involved in an accident in which three persons were killed, was sentenced to a prison term of from one to five years.

Judge Tackett sentenced Harrison to 10 days in jail and assessed him $250 in court costs. Aided by the New Mexico Press Association and the American Society of Newspaper Editors, Harrison appealed. The New Mexico Supreme Court could see no "clear and present danger" to the administration of justice in the newsman's comments.

The 1965 New Mexico Legislature, by unanimous vote, passed a law providing for a jury trial in indirect criminal contempt proceedings, and amended the law relating to the disqualification of judges to extend the provisions for disqualification to constructive contempt proceedings. The Bar Association and the State Supreme Court later revoked Morris' license to practice law.

When Harold James Meriwether, one of Georgia's 10 most-wanted criminals, was put on trial for an armed robbery in which a bystander was critically wounded, the *Atlanta Journal and Constitution* covered the story in the same manner as would have most American newspapers. It reported the fact that Meriwether was under other indictments besides the one for which he was being tried, that he was an escapee from a Georgia prison, and that he was on the "most wanted" list. In its June 3, 1959, issue, the *Constitution* recounted the robbery story, part of which said:

"Other witnesses to the holdup said Meriwether shot Meyers in the back as he tried to get up off the floor after he had been ordered to lie down.

"When Meyers reached for a telephone, Mitchell testified, Meriwether ran into the room shouting, 'I see you, you ———. I ought to kill you now . . . I ought to kill you anyway.'

"Then he fired, the bullet striking Meyers in the back near the spine, passing through his lungs and chest."

Charging that the published material was "calculated to prevent the defendant from obtaining a fair trial and due process of law," Judge Durwood T. Pye cited the Atlanta newspapers for contempt and fined them $20,000.

After a poll of the jury indicated that some of the jurors had read the offending articles, a mistrial was declared. The newspapers argued that Meriwether's past was a matter of official record, and his behavior and trial a matter of public interest that they had a right to publish.

The judge retorted that it was unlawful to circulate "material about the case on trial which is calculated to come to the attention of jurors, selected or prospective . . . whether or not it actually comes to the attention of jurors, and whether or not it related to admissible or inadmissible matter."[41]

The contempt conviction was reversed by the Court of Appeals of Georgia,[42] but only because "courts must follow the law." The appellate judge feared a Supreme Court reversal. Speaking for the court, Judge Nichols rejected the preferred freedoms doctrine and declared that the Supreme Court's interpretation of the clear and present danger test served to sanction "trial by newspaper" at the expense of trial by jury. He hoped that the Georgia Legislature, at its earliest opportunity, would correct a situation that allowed newspapers to intimidate judges, witnesses and parties to an action.

It is noteworthy that the judge depended heavily for his arguments on the minority opinions of Frankfurter in *Bridges, Pennekamp* and *Craig.* The case was later appealed to the Georgia Supreme Court and there affirmed.

In 1952 an irate Georgia judge sentenced two newspaper editors to jail for refusing to print material furnished by him and designed to answer published attacks against proceedings in his court. In the same year, a trial judge in Virginia tried to punish a clergyman for public criticism of him. In both cases, the state supreme courts reversed the convictions.[43]

In *Brumfield* v. *State*[44] the conviction of a news photographer was upheld by the Florida Supreme Court. The judge, attempting to protect a defendant in a rape trial from a hostile community, issued an order prohibiting any photographing of the accused while he was in jail preceding his arraignment. The photographer snapped a picture in the courtroom corridors and, even though the film was not used, he was held in contempt and convicted. The Florida Supreme Court said that the restraining order prohibiting pictures was a valid exercise of the judge's power to control activities in and around the courtroom.

In a 1962 Georgia case, a judge had instructed a grand jury to investigate Negro block voting and to determine if there might be truth to rumors and accusations that such voting was being stimulated by unlawful payments to Negro groups and their leaders by political candidates. The judge's instructions came in the midst of a political campaign, and in order to publicize the investigation, the judge asked all local newsmen to be present in the courtroom when his charge to the grand jury was delivered.

On the next day, with the grand jury still in session, the Sheriff of

Bibb County, himself a candidate, issued a news release criticizing the judge's action. Then he delivered to the bailiff of the court an open letter to the grand jury implying that the court's charge was based on falsehood, that the Bibb County Democratic Executive Committee was responsible for corruption in purchasing votes, and that the grand jury would do well to investigate.

A month later, the sheriff was cited for contempt on the ground that his language ridiculed the investigation, imputed lack of judicial integrity to the court, and presented a clear and present danger to the investigation and to the proper administration of justice in the Bibb County Superior Court.

A day later the sheriff struck again. This time he restated his original charges and said that his defense against the contempt citation would be truth. The court again cited him for contempt on the ground that the second statement presented a clear and present danger to the handling of the first contempt citation.

After a hearing, the trial court held the sheriff in contempt on several counts. The State Court of Appeals upheld the lower court ruling. The Georgia Supreme Court refused to review the case. The United States Supreme Court reversed.[45] In his opinion for the court, Chief Justice Earl Warren distinguished this case from one in which an individual is being investigated before either a grand or petit jury. Here no judicial proceeding was involved, nor was there any showing of a clear and present danger to the work of the grand jury. Instead, the sheriff was a contributor to a stream of public discussion at a time when public interest in the issue was at its height.

But at the same time there is the implication in the words of the Chief Justice that the clear and present danger test may be inappropriate in a case involving trial by jury, and that a showing of prejudice might be unnecessary in such a case if there were statements made which could prejudice the rights of an accused to a fair trial. In other words, bias is implied.

Further guidance from the Supreme Court is needed, for there seems to be a serious contradiction in the court voting to reverse criminal convictions influenced by inflammatory news stories and at the same time voting to reverse contempt citations against newspapers that print such material.

Chapter 12

THE ENGLISH REMEDY

"It appears to us desirable, in considering whether such an act is contempt, to balance, on the one hand, the effect it might have on the litigation and, on the other, the interest of the nation in free discussion."—*Justice*.[1]

In 1957 a pudgy and inscrutable English physician—Dr .John Bodkin Adams—was accused of the murder of a wealthy 82-year-old widow. At the preliminary hearing, it was suggested by the Crown prosecutor that Dr. Adams had accomplished the deed by administering overdoses of sleeping pills. And it was further intimated that other elderly and trusting patients might have suffered the same fate.

These allegations were widely reported in the British press before the middle-aged doctor came to trial, to the consternation of some British jurists. But pre-trial accounts in *Newsweek* magazine, well circulated in Britain, seemed to the Attorney-General to go far beyond the bounds of propriety and proper English practice.

Two fairly long paragraphs in the magazine—innocuous by American standards—hinted at a relationship between legacies left the doctor by other elderly and grateful patients and their subsequent demises. No charge of multiple murder, however, appeared in the indictment. Most irritating to the court was *Newsweek's* observation that "since major criminal trials can make or break the reputation of a British barrister or detective, the ambitions of more than one man were being whetted on the fate of one plump doctor."[2]

Possibly because no one in England could be held directly responsible for the publication, the Attorney-General moved for writs of attachment against London-based Eldon Wylie Griffiths, chief European correspondent for *Newsweek*. The Attorney-General also cited the circulation director of a firm that imports the news magazine and distributes it to the trade, and a firm of news agents and bookstall proprietors who supply the magazine to wholesale houses. The result was a panic among distributors faced with the prospect of having to read every issue of every foreign paper coming into the country. Both companies attempted to retrieve the offending copies and to stop the sale of next week's issue for fear it should contain further dangerous references to Dr. Adams. And they offered hasty and profuse apologies.

Griffiths also hastened to explain that he had had nothing to do with the preparation of the magazine, and that indeed he had not written the offending paragraphs or supplied the material upon which they were based. Lord Chief Justice Goddard's retort was that he should have been better qualified to offer guidance to his American editors on matters relating to Great Britain; and the jurist added that "While this jurisdiction to punish for improper comment on pending proceedings is absolutely necessary for the proper and impartial administration of justice, it is one which must be used with caution, and ought not to be vicariously extended because the real offenders are outside the jurisdiction."[3] No punishment was subsequently imposed upon Griffiths, although the English court seemed sorely tempted. The distributors were found guilty of contempt and paid nominal fines.

After the longest murder trial ever held at Old Bailey, Dr. Adams, thanks to the brilliance of his defense attorney, Geoffrey Lawrence, was acquitted by the jury after only 45 minutes of deliberation.

In his charge to the jury, Lord Justice Devlin indicated his preference for closed preliminary hearings, since they are often quite different from the trial itself. As a postscript to this sensational case, he offered the following significant thoughts to the jury:

"But having said that, members of the jury, I venture to wonder whether, after three weeks of sitting in this court, there is anything left of it that really affects your mind. If you have not learned within those weeks to distinguish between what is solid fact, sifted, gone over again and again, and what is gossip and rumour, then, members of the jury, you will not be the sort of jury that I believe you are and that ordinarily serves in these courts. If you have not learned to distinguish as easily as one can distinguish, if one is an expert, between different textures of stuff—good quality, on the one hand, and shoddy, on the other—between what is evidence and really proves something, and what is mere suspicion, gossip, and of no value whatsoever, then, as I say, you would have learned nothing. But I am completely confident that you have, and I entertain no doubt at all that anything that may conceivably have been in your minds at the beginning has sunk to the bottom, as it were, as the dregs which will trouble you not at all in arriving at your verdict."[4]

In England there is no open warfare between free press and fair trial. Parliament and the courts have clearly given priority to fair trial, and, through the vigorous use of the contempt power, have greatly restricted pre-trial press comment on judicial proceedings. Contempt is a broad and somewhat arbitrary jurisdiction which can be invoked whenever there is a "reasonable tendency" of impairing the administration of justice.

Contempt by publication is a criminal offense at common law, punishable by summary procedure—that is, without benefit of an indictment or a jury trial. The aggrieved party to a civil or criminal suit who thinks his right to a fair trial has been imperiled by the press makes an affidavit setting out the circumstances and through his counsel applies to the court for a ruling. If the court agrees, it orders the committal to prison of the publisher, editor, reporter or printer, unless he comes before the court on a certain day and "shows cause" why the ruling should not be made final. On the appointed day, the hapless editor, having sworn affidavits explaining, excusing or justifying the publication in question, appears in court and through his counsel offers the most abject apologies or attempts to show by argument that no contempt has, in fact, been committed. If the court disagrees, the editor goes to jail and remains there until he can convince the court that he has learned his lesson. Or the court can impose a fine; or both a fine and imprisonment. If the court is convinced that no contempt has been committed, the editor is discharged.

Before 1960 there was no right of appeal from a conviction for criminal contempt, except on the acquiescence of the Attorney-General or the Director of Public Prosecutions, or in cases originating in the dominions or colonies. A group of English lawyers, believing that a contempt charge should be weighed against other matters of public concern such as the right of free speech, initiated appropriate legislation which now allows appeals in all cases of criminal contempt.

English lawyers do not hold press conferences or issue publicity releases. Once a person is arrested, newspapers, on pain of a contempt citation, carefully refrain from publishing pre-trial comment about his confession or his criminal record. English judges apply a "reasonable tendency" test in evaluating the effects of offensive publication; some degree of bad intent must be involved; and there must be evidence of substantial prejudice to the complaining party.

The most serious cases of contempt are those committed during the pendency of a criminal trial. When is a case pending? A leading case is *R. v. Davies, Ex parte Delbert Evans*.[5] A medical practitioner was convicted in the Central Criminal Court on charges of procuring abortions and was sentenced to five years in prison. Before an appeal was heard—although it was not clear to the court whether a notice of appeal had been formally filed or not—*News of the World* published an article relating how the police had been investigating the doctor's case for 20 years, and that the suspect had made and concealed a fortune in ill-gotten gains. Although the court decided that the article in question did not tend to interfere with the administration of justice, and was therefore not a contempt of court, it laid down the rule that after a man has been convicted of a criminal offense, and before his appeal has been heard or the time for appeal has expired, the publication of comments on the case may constitute a contempt of court.

English editors must strive to distinguish between news reporting and commentary. All preliminary and interlocutory proceedings, if open to the public, can be fully reported, but comment must be postponed until after the trial has taken place and a final judgment delivered. An inaccurate or misleading account of a trial is not always a contempt, especially if the error is unintended.

In a 1960 opinion, the Chief Justice of England, Lord Parker, said that although a case is pending until all possibilities of appeal have been exhausted, the significant consideration was "whether the article when published . . . was in all the circumstances calculated really to interfere with the hearing of an appeal, should one be brought."[6] The case at hand, said the Justice, rested more on its particular facts than on any binding legal rule; and here the trial had concluded and an appeal had been lodged when there appeared a rather vitriolic article asserting the guilt of the accused and condemning him as a man of violence. The article was ineffectual, said the Lord Chief Justice, and, "Even if a judge who eventually sat on the appeal had seen the article in question and had remembered its contents, it is inconceivable that he would be influenced consciously or unconsciously by it. A judge is in a very different position to a juryman. Though in no sense superhuman, he has by his training no difficulty in putting out of his mind matters which are not evidence in the case . . ."[7] Nevertheless, Lord Parker concluded, newspapers continue to publish such articles at their peril.

It would seem wise for British editors to reserve comment on a trial until after the issue has been dealt with by the appellate court, especially in light of the fact that an appeal may result in an order for a new trial before a jury. Although English courts have not spoken clearly on the matter, an appeal is generally not pending until a formal written notice of appeal has been served. In a 1921 case, a reporter wrote about a sentence before that sentence had been confirmed, and his editor was fined for contempt.[8]

Where the issue has been settled beyond the possibility of an appeal, judicial proceedings are over and a contempt citation is no longer possible.

THE COSTLY METAPHOR

The severity of the English law of contempt is dramatized by the sensational case of John George Haigh, alias the Vampire. Haigh was accused of the acid bath murders of wealthy women acquaintances whose dismembered bodies were found hidden in his apartment—a veritable house of horrors.

The offending news stories included front page references in the *London Daily Mirror* to a "Vampire" and its characteristic of drinking pulsing blood from live victims. On an inside page was a picture of the 39-year-old Haigh, who had been specifically charged the day before with the murder of an elderly woman. A day later the *Mirror* headlined a page one story: "The Vampire Man Held," and on page two there appeared a feature story with a sketch of a vampire bat. No direct reference was made to the accused, but a dapper man was described as the killer, and the description could appear to fit Haigh— quite enough evidence under English law.

Haigh's arrest had been preceded by a wave of sensational stories in even the more conservative British papers, most of which had described how such a monster might prey on wealthy people and then chemically destroy their bodies. The courts were poised to strike, and they did. Sylvester Bolam, who had been editor of the *Mirror* less than a month, was convicted of contempt and sentenced to Brixton Prison for three months; his publishers were fined 10,000 pounds.[9]

The conduct of the *Mirror*, said the court, was a disgrace to English journalism and violated every principle of justice and fair play which it had been the pride of that country to extend to the worst of criminals. It appeared, moreover, that the newspaper had ignored a warning from the Commissioner of Police not to embark upon a recounting of the grim details of the case. Speaking for the court, Lord Chief Justice Goddard declared: "In the long history of the present class of cases there had never, in the opinion of the Court, been one of such a scandalous and wicked character. It was of the utmost importance that the Court should vindicate the common principles of justice and, in the public interest, see that condign punishment was meted out to persons guilty of such conduct. In the opinion of the Court what had been done was not the result of an error of judgment but was done as a matter of policy in pandering to sensationalism for the purpose of increasing the circulation of the newspaper."

As a further ominous warning, the Lord Chief Justice added, "If for the purpose of increasing the circulation of their paper they should again venture to publish such matter as this, the directors themselves might find that the arm of that Court was long enough to reach them and deal with them individually. The Court had taken the view that there must be severe punishment."

In a 1956 case, crime reporters for *The People* gathered damaging information on one Micallef who was allegedly engaged in the business of purveying vice and managing prostitutes. The headline over an article in the widely circulated daily exclaimed: "Arrest This Beast."

What those responsible for the headline did not know was that the man whom they had so diligently investigated had been arrested three weeks earlier and had already been committed for trial. On motions for actions against the proprietors of the newspaper, its editor, and the reporter responsible for the story, the Attorney-General accepted the plea that none of the respondents knew that criminal proceedings against Micallef were underway.

No matter, said Lord Chief Justice Goddard. Whether or not those responsible knew of the arrest was immaterial to the question whether a contempt had been committed, since the plea of *mens rea*—a guilty mind—was not a necessary element of contempt. The test of guilt, said Lord Goddard, was whether the matter complained of was calculated to interfere with the course of justice, not whether the result was intended. The truth or the falsity of the report was not at issue. The Court also noted that the offending article gave in a sensational manner details of the accused's relationships with persons of bad character and previous convictions, the number of which were exaggerated tenfold. Publishers, editor and reporter were assessed heavy fines.[10]

The decision did not sit well with English journalists nor with some segments of the legal profession. Brian Inglis, writing in *The Spectator* noted that defense attorneys had cited 1889 and 1906 precedents in which the judge had decided that guilty knowledge *is* an essential element of contempt. But, said Inglis, in its opinion the High Court had dismissed these, basing its decision instead on 1806 and 1742 cases in which the judges had decided that knowledge was *not* an essential ingredient of contempt. Inglis strongly recommended that precedents before the 1820s, at the earliest, be handled gingerly, since the press was not then in any sense a fourth estate, and judges largely took their orders from the Government.[11]

The British Section of the International Commission of Jurists took a similar view, stating: "We consider that in general it should be a defense to any charge of contempt in relation to matter alleged to prejudice any judicial proceeding that the alleged contemner neither knew nor had any reason to know or suspect that such proceeding had begun."[12] Recent legislation has incorporated this recommendation; it has also incorporated the rule that a distributor—as in the Dr. Adams case—be allowed to prove that "he had not examined the contents of" any publication distributed by him "and had no reasonable cause to suspect that" it contained matter in contempt of court.[13]

Where a newspaper published an alleged confession while the suspect was in custody under a warrant but had not been brought before a magistrate, the court levied a heavy fine. "Even if a confession had really been made," said Mr. Justice Darling ,"it might still have been contempt to publish it; it might have been of such kind as to be inadmissible in evidence."[14] And the Justice added that English courts were determined not to substitute "trial by newspaper" for trial by jury.

A newspaper was held in contempt for publishing articles describing as a "crank" and a person regarded by the police as a "harmless lunatic nursing a grievance" one Hutchison, who, close to a Royal procession, was arrested for the unlawful possession of firearms.[15] Mr. Justice Swift stressed that it was essential when a criminal charge was made against a person, that there be no tampering of any sort or kind with those who would ultimately have to decide the matter.

The editor of the *Daily Worker* was convicted of contempt for alleging that the forthcoming trial of a defendant was a "frameup" and that he was "a class-war prisoner."[16] An English newspaper may be held in contempt for publishing before trial what is said to be the defense of the accused.[17] A prejudicial cartoon may constitute a contempt of court.[18] A newspaper may be guilty of contempt for publishing a photograph of an accused, if identification becomes an issue in the case, and if there is any possibility of the photo influencing the minds of witnesses. Edgar William Smith had been charged with the attempted murder of a policeman. On the day he was to stand in the police line-up for identification, the *Daily Mirror* and the *Daily Mail* published photographs of him, and referred to him as the man accused of shooting the policeman. The only witness to identify him had a copy of the *Daily Mail* in his pocket. In his opinion for the court, Lord Chief Justice Hewart noted that, "The phrase 'contempt of Court,'

. . . consists not in some attitude or supposed attitude to the Court itself, but the prejudice to an accused person. It is not something which affects the status of the Court, but something which may profoundly affect the rights of citizens." Lord Hewart felt that the newspapers should have anticipated the question of identity arising.[19]

The *Daily Herald* was convicted of contempt in 1931 for displaying a promotional poster containing the words "Another Blazing Car Murder" which, although relating to another case, came at a time when an accused stood committed for trial on the charge of murdering a man in a car and then burning the vehicle to destroy the evidence.[20]

English courts have been particularly sensitive to newspapers which employ amateur detectives or their own reporters to investigate the facts of a crime and publish their results. In the first notable case of this kind, the *Evening Standard* hired detectives to investigate the murder and dismemberment of a young girl in Eastbourne. The results were published in a series of articles and photographs which included an account of the married life of the accused. The newspaper also interviewed a prospective witness who had been warned by police not to make a statement.

In citing the editor for contempt, the court noted that it would not have been possible even for the most ingenious mind to have anticipated with certainty what were to be the real issues in the case, to say nothing of the more difficult question of what was to be the relative importance of different issues in the trial which was about to take place.[21] Lord Hewart sternly rejected the notion that it was the duty of newspapers to elucidate the facts in criminal cases. The *Evening Standard* was fined 1000 pounds. The *Daily Express* and the *Manchester Guardian,* which had also printed the story—the *Guardian* because the victim was a Manchester girl—each paid 300 pounds and costs. During the 50-year editorship of the distinguished C. P. Scott of the *Guardian,* this was the only contempt of court citation brought against his newspaper.

English judges on occasion have had as much difficulty as American judges in deciding what may or may not be prejudicial. In 1943, the Court of Criminal Appeals quashed a conviction for larceny where a list of prior convictions had been read before the magistrates to enable them to decide how to deal with the case, and a local newspaper, in its report of the preliminary proceedings, had published the list.[22]

On the other hand, in 1951, where a defendant had been sentenced at Surrey Quarter Sessions to four years' corrective training for larceny and his previous convictions had been recounted before trial in the Surrey newspapers, the same court declined to infer either that the jury had read the report, or, if they had, that they were biased.[23]

A speedy trial seems to rank high among English judicial values. English judges are hesitant to use such procedural remedies as change of venue, continuance or mistrial, which American judges use with alacrity. However, on November 6, 1957, at Exeter City Assizes, Mr. Justice Salmon stopped the trial of John Henry Walter Oliver, who had pleaded not guilty to a charge of murdering his wife. On the first day of the trial, three newspapers and the Press Association, a wire service which carried the story, published reports which the court believed might have been grossly prejudicial to a fair trial. Humble apologies were tendered and the media admitted the inaccuracy of one report which a reporter had obtained second hand. In the story what was supposedly part of the opening speech of the Crown counsel at the trial was actually part of the speech made by the prosecutor at the preliminary hearing in Magistrate's court.[24]

Justice Salmon deplored the fact that two witnesses would have to undergo the harrowing experience of giving their evidence all over again, and much public time and money would be wasted.

Inaccuracy can be expensive for English journalists. In a 1954 case, the *Evening Standard* was fined 1000 pounds and costs for a story which appeared under the headline, "Trunk Trial Story of Marriage Offer—Husband is Accused." During the course of the trial—in which the accused was charged with the murder of his wife whose body had been found in a trunk—the reporter left the courtroom to telephone his newspaper. He thereby missed a crucial point of evidence. The result was an inaccurate story which the court said might have interfered with the course of justice. Since neither the reporter nor the editor appeared to have intentionally misrepresented the court proceedings, no separate penalties were imposed upon them. The accused was subsequently acquitted. Lord Chief Justice Goddard considered this a "disastrous interference with justice."[25]

PRELIMINARY HEARINGS AND IN CAMERA PROCEEDINGS

There has been a good deal of debate in England and the United States as to whether preliminary proceedings should be held in secret to protect the defendant from prejudiced jurymen. Proceedings in a police court or in petty sessions preliminary to a committal for trial deal only with the evidence of the prosecution, not all of which may be admissible at the trial itself.

As far back as 1865, Chief Justice Lefroy ruled that a fair and accurate report of such proceedings did not constitute a contempt of court for, he said, "it is of the utmost importance for the public to know that the magistrates do their duty impartially and without influence of any sort, and that they exercise their duty fairly and correctly according to the evidence brought before them—not only to prevent them from making unfair orders against the prisoners, but also to prevent them from undue influence which might be ascribed to them as officers appointed by the Crown."[26] Similarly, in a 1925 case, it was decided that a fair and accurate report of a Recorder's charge to the grand jury was privileged and publications based on it were immune from contempt proceedings.[27]

Long-standing doubts as to the wisdom of these judgments came into sharp focus, as we have noted, during the murder trial of Dr. Adams. Details concerning the deaths of a number of his patients, presented at the preliminary hearing to illustrate a pattern of criminal action, were vividly reported in the press. Adams' counsel had asked that such evidence be given in a closed hearing, but the request was refused. At the trial itself, the prosecution restricted itself to one act of alleged murder.

In summing up at the Old Bailey, Lord Devlin urged that proceedings in the magistrate's court in such cases be held in private in the future, since it seemed impossible that an unprejudiced jury could be assembled after such a "disgraceful" and "scandalous" performance by the press. This was clearly "trial by newspaper," said Lord Devlin. To counteract these potential evils, the English jurist advocated that magistrates have the power, while sitting in open court, to prohibit the press from publishing reports in whole or in part which would prejudice a man even before a charge had been made.

Early in the celebrated case of John Profumo and Christine Keeler, the tabloid London *Mirror* had somehow obtained an amorous letter from the War Minister to the prostitute—"trafficking in scandal," Lord Denning called it in his subsequent Report to the Prime Minister. The newspaper did not bring the letter to the attention of the government nor did it publish it for fear of a whiplash punitive libel action. With the assistance of the inevitable grapevine, French and Italian magazines had made references to the allegations pending against Profumo, and he had brought libel actions against two of them. Their British distributors had publicly apologized in court and had made settlements with Profumo in lieu of libel damages that might have been assessed had the cases come to trial—a most unusual procedure by American standards. There was also the contempt power to reckon with. Two reporters had gone to jail for refusing to divulge their sources of information in the Vassall spy case shortly before. Only after Profumo's resignation did the *Mirror* print the celebrated letter, opening the door to a cascade of press commentary on the sordid affair. But English newsmen had already "sat" on this explosive story for nearly six months.

Ludovic Kennedy, in his book *The Trial of Stephen Ward*, is convinced that the conviction of Ward, the Profumo-Keeler intermediary, and his later suicide were dictated by the wide publicity given to the lower court proceedings. At that point, the testimony of many of the principals in the affair was being recorded in all its titillating detail. But it is difficult to ignore the legitimate public interest in matters of this kind.

As a result of Devlin's remarks on the Adams trial, the Home Secretary in June, 1957 appointed the Tucker Committee to review the question of preliminary hearings. Press reaction was immediate, condemning strongly anything suggestive of secret court hearings and questioning the qualifications of judges to decide what should and should not be open to the public.

The Institute of Journalists, pointing to the time lag between committal and trial, recommended that there be no general ban on press reporting but that magistrates have the power to direct that certain parts of preliminary testimony not be published.

The Press Council also opposed secret hearings for the following reasons: (1) the injustice of gossip and rumor would be a poor substitute for publicity; (2) witnesses are sometimes prompted by publicity to come forward—and not necessarily for the defense—with valuable evidence, and the accused learns at least in outline the charges he has to face; (3) if the general public is admitted to preliminary hearings but press reports are prohibited, inadequate and misleading, reporting by word of mouth will take their place; (4) faith in trial by jury rests upon the "proved" ability of juries to respond to the directions of the judge and come to their verdict on the evidence they have heard, and that evidence alone, disregarding what they have heard or read elsewhere; (5) it is important that the work of Justices of the Peace be done with the full knowledge of the public; and (6) magistrates should have no more power than they possess already to hear in private evidence relating to indictable offenses.[28]

Not so, said L. C. B. Gower, a noted legal scholar. Gossip and rumor, he said, based on the one-sided account of the prosecution, would be given much wider distribution and stimulation by the press. There are better ways of gathering witnesses than by advertising for them in the press. The grapevine, said Gower, does not travel as far as a press report, and unless a report is verbatim, it may be no less inadequate and therefore misleading. The assumed "proved ability" of jurors to reach verdicts dispassionately has been pretty conclusively disproved. Investigation of the behavior of juries, Gower added, shows that the one way of ensuring that a piece of evidence is indelibly imprinted on their minds is for the judge to direct them to forget it. Since the work of Justices of the Peace is subject to review by a higher court, it is not important that their work be scrutinized by the public.[29]

The Howard League for Penal Reform thought that committal proceedings should receive no publicity except at the request of the defense counsel or where no case had been found.

The Tucker Committee viewed preliminary hearings as primarily for the benefit of the accused in safeguarding him against the inconvenience of a trial based on frivolous or malicious prosecution. But the committee did not favor a more extensive use of secret proceedings. It did recommend that newspapers be restricted to publishing only the bare essentials of the charge and the committal court's decision, the full account waiting until the trial itself had been concluded. So far the recommendations of the Tucker Committee have not been implemented.

Neither British practice nor precedent is clear on this issue. More lawyers are asking for and more courts are granting closed preliminary hearings. But the matter is far from settled in either England or the United States. Lord Denning suggests that "the importance of having all judicial proceedings in public outweighs . . . all the suggested disadvantages," for the press is "the watchdog of justice."[30]

In the leading case on the question, the highest British court, the House of Lords, made it clear that, apart from statutory authority, a judge can only order a trial to be held behind closed doors to prohibit the publication of reports when, owing to the special circumstances of the case, justice could not be done if the trial was a public one. The mere fact that a case involves evidence of an indecent nature does not justify an order for a private hearing. "Courts of justice in this country," Lord Loreburn explained, "must administer justice in public. To justify an order for a hearing in camera it must be shown that the paramount object of securing that justice should be done would be rendered doubtful of attainment if such order were not made. It cannot be dealt with by the presiding Judge as a matter resting in his individual discretion as to what is expedient."[31]

If proceedings have been properly heard in camera, and an order has been made that no report be published, it will be a contempt to disobey the order by reporting the hearing, although the general conclusion can be announced. The one settled rule of law in this area would seem to be that in cases involving wards of the court—infants and persons of unsound mind—the judge has a complete discretion to allow or to forbid the publication of the proceedings.

Again, Lord Devlin proposes that defense counsel be permitted to decide what is too objectionable to the cause of his client to be publishable: "In an important case of public interest, the jury is bound to have some preconceived notions based upon the opening statement made by the prosecution in the preliminary proceedings and upon the evidence which, in such a case, is normally reported with great particularity. The defendant normally reserving his defence, inevitably the report becomes one-sided. Is it not contrary to human nature to expect that each member of the jury—even after a strong and clear direction—will be able effectively and entirely to divest his mind or hers of every memory of that opening statement? That the opening statement before the magistrate should not be reported, seems obviously right."[32]

The inevitable outcome of such thinking was the proposal in April 1965 of legislation which would exclude newsmen from preliminary hearings. Although a specific bill has not yet been introduced in Parliament, the old arguments, pro and con, are being revived. If such legislation is accepted, it will mean that unless the accused is discharged, or until his case reaches the trial court, the reporting of committal proceedings will be restricted to his name, the charge, and the decision.

The Magistrates Association favors the proposal. The National Union of Journalists has indicated it will contest any restriction on the right of access of journalists to courts of law. Proclaiming that "publicity is the best guardian of the rights of the individual," the *Daily Express* said the idea of secret courts was "regarded as alien" and that the Government's proposal would undermine that principle. That reports of proceedings before an examining magistrate might prejudice an accused's trial before a jury later was only supposition, and the *Express* added, "Experience shows the opposite: that juries are made up of reasonable people who will decide cases solely on the facts presented to them at the trial. . . . In many cases newspaper reports of preliminary hearings have helped secure a just verdict. Key witnesses for the defence have come forward as a result of the publicity."

Lord Chief Justice Parker would seem to agree for he has been quoted as advocating the greatest publicity for committal proceedings. "The idea," he says, "that the jury at the trial is influenced by what it reads in the papers is overdone."

Sir Linton Andrews, former editor of the *Yorkshire Post* and former chairman of the Press Council, has noted that publicity is useful in letting the public know the charge an accused has to face; witnesses come forward, and gossip is quelled."[33]

The Tucker Committee may yet have the last word, but it will not be without a fight.

Some segments of the legal profession, and the press in general, are disturbed by the fact that a great many proceedings in chambers are final and never result in a court trial. "Only a fraction of civil proceedings," said *The Times*, "now ever sees the light of day, yet, if one constitutional principle has been firmly established in the past, it is that there should be no undue secrecy about any judicial proceedings—whether heard in public or in private, publication of them may occasionally be delayed but never entirely suppressed."

A THIRD LINE OF DEFENSE

Fair trial in England is further bulwarked by the hypersensitivity of English judges to criticism—a doctrine which has become alien to the American experience. Theoretically anyone can criticize a judge after a case has been concluded and no appeal is pending, providing that the criticism is framed in respectful terms and does not imply that the judge was motivated by partiality or corruption. But English editors must approach this judicial compromise with the utmost caution.

In the Birmingham Spring Assizes of 1900, Justice Darling warned the press not to give a detailed account of an obscenity trial since there could be no protection for the publication of objectionable, obscene and indecent matter. The editor of the *Daily Argus* criticized the judge for his "defense of decency." Such publication, said the court in a subsequent contempt action, was scurrilous personal abuse of a judge and a contempt of court punishable on summary process—even though the attack came after the termination of the judicial proceeding.[34]

In *R. v. New Statesman (Editor), Ex parte Director of Public Prosecutions*,[35] an editor was held liable for publishing criticism of a judge who presided in a libel case involving an apostle of birth control. An excerpt from the offending article follows: "We cannot help regarding the verdict given this week in the libel action brought by the Editor of the *Morning Post* against Dr. Marie Stopes as a substantial miscarriage of justice. We are not at all in sympathy with Dr. Stopes' work or aims, but prejudice against those aims ought not to be allowed to influence a court of justice in the manner in which they appeared to influence Mr. Justice Avory in his summing up. . . . The serious point in this case, however, is that an individual owning to such views as those of Dr. Stopes cannot apparently hope for a fair hearing in a Court presided over by Mr. Justice Avory—and there are so many Avorys."

The Attorney-General argued that to say a judge was so steeped in prejudice and bias that he could not try a case of a certain kind was worse than to say that on a particular occasion he had deliberately allowed his private views to influence him. Lord Chief Justice Hewart accepted this argument and only the most effusive apologies by the editor and his counsel prevented the respondent from paying more than the costs of the proceeding.

Thomas Colsey, editor of *Truth,* in commenting upon an earlier decision of the Court of Appeals having to do with the setting up of a Trade Board for the catering business, wrote the following sentence: "Lord Justice Slesser, who can hardly be altogether unbiased about legislation of this type, maintained that really it was a very nice provisional order or as good a one as can be expected in this vale of tears." In spite of an expression of deep regret and the acceptance by the court of a plea of lack of intention, the authority of the judge had been lowered and the editor paid a fine of 100 pounds and costs.[36]

In 1930 the Communist *Daily Worker* criticized Mr. Justice Swift for the sentence he imposed upon a Communist Party member and alleged that the jurist was animated by a "strong class bias—the bewigged puppet and former Tory M. P. chosen to put Communists away in 1926." The comment was held by the court to be a "gross and outrageous contempt" and those responsible for the article were sentenced to terms of from five to nine months imprisonment.[37]

The rationale for this seemingly unlimited judicial power has been stated succinctly by a jurist noted for his liberalism: "The judges must of course be impartial," says Lord Denning, "but it is equally important that they should be known by all people to be impartial. If they should be libelled by traducers, so that people lose faith in them, the whole administration of justice would suffer."[38]

Dissenting from this rationale would appear to be members of the Privy Council of the House of Lords who from their high places have seemed singularly unimpressed with the rationalizations of scandalized judges, and have reversed judgments brought to them on appeal from colonial and dominion courts. In one notable 1936 case,[39] Lord Atkin made the following significant statement: "But whether the authority and position of an individual judge, or the due of administration of justice, is concerned, no wrong is committed by any member of the public who exercises the ordinary right of criticizing, in good faith, in private or public, the public act done in the seat of justice. The path of criticism is a public way: the wrong headed are permitted to err therein: provided that members of the public abstain from imputing improper motives to those taking part in the administration of justice, and are genuinely exercising a right of criticism, and not acting in malice or attempting to impair the administration of justice, they are immune. Justice is not a cloistered virtue: she must be allowed to suffer the scrutiny and respectful, even though outspoken, comments of ordinary men."

But the question remains: where can the criticism of a judge or his judicial acts begin? And if his competence can be questioned with impunity, how can an editor, or anyone else, distinguish between innocent imputation and dangerous allegations of partiality or corruption? This whole method of procedure is calculated to deter, and does deter, newspapers from offering reasonable criticism of the administration of justice when that criticism is deserved. Surely judges must be independent and secure, but should they be made secure from just criticism?

SUMMARY

The English solution to the free press-fair trial conflict is the law of contempt. The law is set in motion by out-of-court publications having a "reasonable tendency" to obstruct or impair the proper administration of justice, whether before a judge or a jury, or to influence or prejudice either litigants or witnesses to a cause; by violation of the rules with respect to pendency, which may begin before a suspect is arrested and continue until all possibilities of appeal have been exhausted; by the illegal coverage of preliminary examinations; and by criticism of a judge which may "lower his authority."

English journalists complain that the law is so ill-defined that it is capricious and arbitrary. The penalties are so severe that they are intimidating—the maximum punishment being life imprisonment, and unlimited fine, or both. The court is at the same time the aggrieved victim, judge and jury. The following editorial excerpt from *The*

Times reflects the reactions of some newsmen: "The pattern of case after case today is as familiar as it is squalid. The dominating consideration for the defense is to keep the editor who is alleged to have erred out of prison. With this object the case begins with an abject apology by him. The point of law is then put rather than pressed—the wrath of the court must be averted at all costs; *a man already grovelling is hardly in the best position to defend a constitutional principle.*"[40] (Emphasis added.)

This brief survey of landmark English contempt cases is necessitated by those American lawyers and judges—with the late Justice Felix Frankfurter in the vanguard—who would prescribe the English system for the United States. The chief difficulty with their proposal is the First Amendment to the Constitution, interposed as it is between the rights of the people and their legislatures. The sovereign Parliament is challenged by no such barrier, and it can act vigorously, as it did in the 1960 Administration of Justice Act, to redress what it assumes to be an imbalance between free press and fair trial.

There are other relevant societal differences. The London daily newspapers are for the most part national newspapers delivered the same day they are published. Not even the *New York Times* can have the broad daily impact of the London press.

The Court of Criminal Appeals—highest appellate court short of the House of Lords—never orders a new trial. The judgment of the court of original jurisdiction is either affirmed or reversed. American appellate courts frequently direct a new trial in criminal cases, especially where there is substantial error in the judge's charge to the jury, or where the defendant has been materially prejudiced in some other way, for example, by newspaper comment. So British justice does not always get its second chance.

Another factor is the rigidity of precedent—what the lawyers call *stare decisis*—in English law. Courts seldom reverse themselves or overrule prior decisions, unless they are decisions of a lower court. If this rule is based on the proposition that it is better for the law to be certain than to be right, it is based on a questionable social policy. But the relative stability of English court rulings, in contempt for example, give a clear mandate to English judges to use the contempt power—except where statutes have intervened.

There is no such certainty in the American system. Although the judicial power theoretically belongs to the courts, the fine line between legislative and judicial power is not unbroken. In a number of cases[41] it has been clearly assumed by the courts that the power to punish summarily for contempt committed out of court is a judicial prerogative; yet the federal contempt Act of 1831 limited the court's power to punish for out-of-court contempt. This congressional "infringement" was challenged by a Supreme Court judge in 1835,[42] was acknowledged by the Supreme Court as being within the authority of Congress in 1874,[43] was challenged again in 1844[44] and in 1918,[45] and was finally accepted by the federal courts in 1941.[46]

Complicating the picture is the power of state courts to declare state legislation repugnant to either state or federal constitutions; and the power of the United States Supreme Court to hold both state and federal laws unconstitutional.

There is a better defined "separation of powers" between legislature and judiciary in the British system; and British courts enjoy an almost unique independence from political or other interferences. Judges ordinarily possess life tenure and can be removed only by action of both Houses of Parliament. Notable also is the comparative efficiency of English justice, its speed, its undramatic quality, the rigid legal training of court officers, and their divorcement from political aspiration. Prosecuting is not a path to political office in England.

In vivid contrast to American court procedure is the disuse of *voir dire* in England. Barristers are content to leave the selection of the jury to chance, confident that they can lay their case successfully before an impersonal jury about whose prejudices and predispositions they have no knowledge. English judges take pains to define and delimit the issues the jury must decide. This leads to a certain uniformity in the administration of English justice, and a well-settledness that affords the Englishman an unusual amount of guidance as to the legal rules of behavior. Certainly some of these qualities reflect the English character, the cultural and geographic unity of the English society, and could not be simply transplanted into an alien constitutional system.

The administration of law is more complex in America. While only precedents of a state jurisdiction in which a dispute arises, and precedents of the federal courts, are binding upon U.S. attorneys, decisions in all 51 jurisdictions, as well as those of English and Dominion courts, may have persuasive authority. Precedent appears to be less important in the American system. The Supreme Court, for example, will turn sharp corners in overruling its past decisions when, in its opinion, the general welfare requires it.

But where the rights of free press and fair trial collide, the English have failed to weigh in the balance the interest of the nation in free discussion. There is no "trial by newspaper" in England; but, as *The Guardian* has said, the greater freedom of criminal news reporting in the United States, while sometimes abused, is on the whole healthier than the repressions to which in the last 50 years the British press has become subject. The English contempt remedy for curing the free press-fair trial sore is not appealing to or consonant with American constitutional tradition.

CHAPTER 13

PROPOSALS FOR RESOLVING THE CONFLICT

"Some of the cleansing of ancient plague spots, the judges ought to do themselves. To the extent that they are unwilling or unable, there must be resort to legislation."—Justice Benjamin Cardozo.[1]

H. L. Mencken, as has been noted, said a long time ago that journalistic codes of ethics were all moonshine. This is true of all codes to the extent that expediency rather than conviction dictates their writing. Few codes, with perhaps the exception of the Comic Book Code, have been successful in elevating their signers to a higher plane of responsible performance. And we are obligated to note that 24 of the original 29 Comic Code subscribers were out of business three years after signing it. We would seem to have an adequate supply of codes; the trick is to get people to live by them.

In 1923 the American Society of Newspaper Editors adopted its Canons of Journalism, one of which condemned publication of "unofficial charges affecting reputation or moral character without opportunity given to the accused to be heard," and of "details of crime and vice, publication of which is not demonstrably for the general good."

A joint committee of leading editors, publishers and members of the bar met in 1937 to explore the problem of prejudicial publicity, and recommended the formation of a permanent national committee and local committees to seek voluntary compliance with recommendations for self-restraint.

In 1953, under the direction of Edwin M. Otterbourg, the New York County Lawyers Association drew up a Fair Trial-Free Press Code intended to prohibit press comment tending to influence a judge or jury, to anticipate the outcome of a case or to recommend punishment, or to speculate on the evidence or on the credibility of witnesses. In addition, the Code proscribed sensational headlines, news reports which tended to impair public morals or corrupt the young, confessions and prior records, and pre-trial statements by attorneys. The press would also be prohibited from polling jurors.[2]

At the same time, the New York State Bar Association's Committee on Civil Rights proposed legislation to make it unlawful for prosecutor, defense counsel or law enforcement officials to discuss the evidence in a criminal case before the trial. Louis Waldman, chairman of the Committee, denied that the proposal would in any way gag the press; the two constitutional rights did not belong exclusively to press and bar but to the people as a whole. The Committee report went on: "Largely as a result of the tremendous growth of mass media of communication, the Bar, the Bench and responsible members of the community generally have become disturbed and alarmed over a situation which places in jeopardy, in some cases, our ancient and valued tradition of fair trial. The danger arises primarily from the fact that however scrupulously fairness is maintained in the courtroom, publications outside the courtroom may seriously prejudice the parties and the outcome. . . . These practices have been aptly called 'trial by newspaper,' and have been roundly condemned in many quarters. They smack of that gross departure from our conception of fair trial, represented by such institutions as the People's Courts in Communist totalitarian countries. Trial and conviction by public clamor on questionable or inadmissible evidence is the very antithesis of our system of justice."[3]

If this was to be the tenor of press-bar cooperation, the press would have none of it. The resolution was seen in some press quarters as a "vicious attempt to interfere with the traditional spirit of open justice," and its implications were strongly resented. In an angry telegram, the Newspaper Reporters Association of New York City reminded lawyers that newsmen, unlike attorneys, who are rarely subject to libel or slander when spoken in the courtroom, are at all times susceptible to contempt, libel and slander proceedings. "Therefore," said the Association, "we are doubly careful of what facts we report, especially those given by certain lawyers outside the courtroom."[4]

Otterbourg joined newsmen in challenging the legislative intent of the resolution, calling instead for lawyers to clean their own house. The New York State Bar Association eventually rejected the idea of legislation, substituting a plan to amend Canon 20—which, in the final analysis, would have nearly the same effect.

But the Otterbourg proposals were also generally unacceptable to the press. The *New York Times*, however, saw merit in a voluntary code and with its customary aloofness suggested that "freedom of the press implies an obligation of responsibility on the part of the press. It is the individual newspaper and not the judiciary that ought to shoulder the responsibility of deciding, within the limits of national security, what it will or will not publish in court cases, and no newspaper can dodge its individual responsibility for good taste and fair play. The clash between free press and fair trial is not inevitable if a sense of fairness and of restraint is coupled with recognition both of the public's right to factual information and of the individual's right to impartial justice."[5]

The reaction of James Russell Wiggins, executive editor of the *Washington Post and Times Herald*, was perhaps more typical of the news fraternity. He saw in the code proposals an attempt to emulate the restrictive British system. And he doubted that the much maligned press was responsible for very many unfair trials or wrong convictions; otherwise the United States Supreme Court would have reversed them. Few newspapers would suppress factual statements, said Wiggins, simply on the presumption that they would impair public morals. Juries would be polled as long as such polls disclosed attempts to bribe or corrupt juries. And Wiggins saw some advantage in keeping the plight of an accused person constantly before the public mind after arrest and before trial.[6]

Bilateral code discussions in this country got off to a bad start. Too much of the exchange between bar and press has depended upon invective and cliché. The press is accused of engaging in reckless competition for news copy, of putting circulation and advertising revenue above morality, of seeking to administer justice by its own standards, and of bringing political pressure to bear upon judges and prosecutors. Then it is threatened with news blackouts, with the contempt power, with federal legislation or regulation. It has even been suggested that if the press does not discontinue its policy of "trial by newspaper" it will *indefinitely lose (its) license to publish.*"[7] (Emphasis added.)

On the other side of the controversy, news media sanctimoniously deny any responsibility for the impairment of fair trial. Rather, they raise the cry that the courts belong to the people; that bar association codes of ethics are an outright abridgement of the absolute constitutional rights of free speech and press; that lawyers seek to subvert the constitutional principle of open justice; and that lawyer-dominated legislatures conspire to pass bills which will handcuff the press.

The 1958 Report of the Advancement of Freedom of Information

Committee of Sigma Delta Chi, journalistic society, offered this conciliatory description of the legal profession: ". . . (M)ore and more lawyers retreat from their once great position in American society; remove themselves from the people; spurn the sacrifices of public service; cloister themselves in fine offices; and make the collection of fat fees an end in life."

In such an acrid atmosphere the outlook for bilateral codes of conduct is indeed dim. But the debate, futile as it may seem in getting either side to accept primary responsibility for originating prejudicial information, may not be in vain. The few bilateral and unilateral codes adopted recently by bar and press associations alike, and the preoccupation of newsmen and lawyers with the subject itself, may portend an emerging norm, a higher level of self-restraint on both sides in the handling of criminal cases.

The Oregon Bar-Press Joint Statement of Principles directs the editor, in the exercise of his judgment, to consider an accused person innocent until proved guilty; to consider that readers and listeners are potential jurors; and to bear in mind that no person's reputation should be injured needlessly.

The American Bar Association's Committee on Fair Trial and Free Press is planning a "summit" meeting with a special committee of the American Newspaper Publishers Association. And in his recent address before UPI editors and publishers, Edward W. Kuhn, newly elected ABA president, suggested that bar associations and news media organizations across the land establish continuing liaison committees for joint discussions and mutual enlightenment as to each other's views and problems in the fair trial-free press area. Moreover, the bar appears to be taking steps to enforce its Canons of Ethics and to impose greater professional discipline upon lawyers in the protection of fair trial—a stricture that has had little effect in the past.

DISCIPLINING OF LAWYERS

"A big murder trial," wrote Damon Runyon, "possesses some of the elements of a sporting event. I find the same popular interest in the murder trial that I find . . . on the eve of a big football game, or a pugilistic encounter, or a baseball series. There is the same conversational speculation on the probable result only more of it. . . . The trial is a sort of game, the players on the one side the attorneys for the defense, and on the other side the attorneys for the State. The defendant figures in it merely as the prize. . . . And the players must be men well-schooled in their play. They must be crafty men. . . . The game of murder trial is played according to very strict rules, with stern umpires, called judges, to prevent any deviations from these rules.[8] In such an atmosphere, a well-devised publicity campaign can make the difference between victory and defeat.

Professional zeal is sometimes carried to a dangerous extreme. In 1953, a Chicagoan, Vincent Ciucci, shot and killed his wife and three children, then set fire to his home in order to cover up the crime. He was first tried for the murder of wife, convicted, and sentenced to 20 years in prison. The prosecutor, dissatisfied with the sentence, arranged to have Ciucci tried again, this time for the murder of one of his own children. Again convicted, he received a sentence of 45 years. Still not satisfied, the prosecutor is alleged to have announced to the press that Ciucci would be tried until a jury could be found that would recommend a death sentence. In a third trial, the jury gratified the desires of the prosecutor.

In an appeal to the United States Supreme Court,[9] Ciucci appended a number of articles which had appeared in Chicago newspapers, confirming the prosecutor's sinister objectives. Since the articles had not been included in the record certified to the High Court from the Illinois Supreme Court, the U.S. Supreme Court declined to consider them, and the lower court judgment was confirmed. Justice Douglas said in a dissenting opinion, joined by Chief Justice Warren and Justice Brennan, that the case presented an example of a prosecutor being allowed to harass an accused with repeated trials and convictions on the same evidence, until he achieved the desired result —a capital verdict. Ciucci was executed on March 23, 1962.

The legal profession recognizes that lawyers, particularly prosecuting attorneys, bear a large share of the responsibility for the release to the press of pre-trial and trial publicity. But it has been peculiarly unsuccessful in abating these activities.

In an attempt to meet this threat, the New York State Bar Association in 1954 adopted a resolution urging amendment of its own and the ABA's Canon 20 which labelled "unprofessional" the giving of statements on pending trials to the press. The amendment would prohibit such conduct under penalty of a contempt citation and possible disbarment. The rationale of the amendment was that, until the Supreme Court decides what is to be the power of the state and of Congress in safeguarding the fair administration of justice, it is incumbent upon the bar to restrain its own members from contributing to "trial by newspaper."

The substance of the proposed amendment follows: "That no

attorney in any pending or anticipated criminal or matrimonial litigation shall make any public statement or furnish any information to any media of publicity which may interfere with a fair trial or otherwise prejudice the due administration of justice, irrespective of whether such statement is published under the name of the attorney or anonymously. Such a rule will prohibit the furnishing of information as to what an attorney expects to prove in a litigation, or as to the names of any witnesses he proposes to call. It is proposed that if an attorney violates the rule during a trial, he may be summarily dealt with by the trial judge. If he does so prior to a trial, or subsequent thereto, then any organized bar association, or any aggrieved party can institute a special proceeding to have him punished for a contempt and the court may give other appropriate relief."

Three years later the Association extracted the teeth of the proposal by adopting a revised version of Canon 20 which omitted the penalties and added the proviso that "this canon shall not be so construed as to limit the right of an attorney in good faith to divulge information for publication in reply to any public statement which adversely affects the interests of his client, provided that the information is supported by fact and does no more than contradict or mitigate the effect of said statement." Defensive publicity was to be condoned.

More recently the Standing Committee on Professional Ethics of the American Bar Association recommended an amendment to Canon 5 of its Canons of Professional Ethics which includes the following paragraph: "It is the duty of a lawyer engaged either in the protection or the defense of a person accused of a crime to refrain from any action which might interfere with the right of either the accused or the prosecuting governmental entity to a fair trial. To that end it is improper and professionally reprehensible for a lawyer so engaged to express to the public or in any manner extrajudicially any opinion or prediction as to the guilt or innocence of the accused, the weight of evidence against him or the likelihood that he will be either convicted or acquitted."

As early as 1937 the ABA recommended disbarment for such behavior, although no disbarment proceedings have ever been reported. The federal courts have also raised the possibility of disbarment for irresponsible trial tactics.

In the notorious *Rosenberg* treason trial, the court assumed that the prosecutor, early in the trial, had made public a sealed indictment, deliberately timed to be maximally prejudicial to the defendants. Such tactics, said the court, cannot be too severely condemned, and are not beyond the reach of disbarment.[10]

The failure of the bar to enforce its own Canons has fortified the view of some elements of the press that the Canons *per se*, and their proposed amendments, are manifestations of the desire of lawyers to muzzle the press. *Editor & Publisher* has questioned whether prosecutors should be responsible to bar associations at all. The courts belong to the people and the prosecution of criminals is conducted in the name of the people who have every right to know what is being done for them, said the trade publication. And it added, with an air of sanctity defying reality: "The Bar Association is battling windmills in its attack upon so-called 'trial by newspaper,' which does not and never has existed."[11]

Commenting upon the action of the State Bar Association, the *New York Times*, in a more enlightened vein, suggested that "There is no interference with the constitutional guarantee of freedom of press in this injunction, but there is a strengthening of another constitutional guarantee—the right to a fair trial. . . . We think the press does have a responsibility to treat pretrial information with restraint. But the best way to protect the defendant from unfair and prejudicial press statements by lawyers or prosecutors is to stop this abuse at the source; and that is what the new Canon 20 attempts to do. If it doesn't succeed, it should be strengthened again."[12]

Canon 20 is bland: "Newspaper publications by a lawyer as to pending or anticipated litigation may interfere with a fair trial in the courts and otherwise prejudice the due administration of justice. Generally they are to be condemned. If the extreme circumstances of a particular case justify a statement to the public, it is unprofessional to make it anonymously. An *ex parte* reference to the facts should not go beyond quotation from the records and papers on file in the court; but even in extreme cases it is better to avoid any *ex parte statement*." Canon 20 has been approved either as a statute or court or bar association rule in all states except Alabama, California and Oregon.

The American College of Trial Lawyers has adopted a slightly stronger and more specific rule regarding pending litigation. Whatever the wording of the Canon, its effectiveness will depend upon enforcement by the courts; and until the courts translate concern into action, newsmen are going to look upon the bar ethics with a jaundiced eye and greet lawyers' pronouncements on violations of justice with characteristic cynicism.

Dean Erwin N. Griswold of the Harvard Law School has forthrightly urged the Standing Committee on Professional Ethics of the American Bar Association to adopt an "absolute prohibition" on the release by any lawyer of material relating to the trial prior to a verdict. His proscription would include appearances on radio or television, the release of statements bearing on confessions and alibis, or evidence of any kind. He would invoke the rule-making and contempt powers of the courts to enforce these strictures upon both attorneys and law enforcement officials. In states where the courts are reluctant to accept the responsibility of setting guidelines, legislation would be sought.

"If the lawyers and courts will thus put their house in order," Griswold concludes, "there will be far less basis for complaint about the news media."

Edward J. Ennis, general counsel of the American Civil Liberties Union, recommends a court rule under which the court, upon complaint of either side that improper information had been divulged, would immediately hold a summary hearing and publicly rebuke lawyers responsible for such a leak and also refer the matter to the appropriate bar association grievance committee. "The advantage of such summary procedure over a criminal statute," says Ennis, "is that its curative effect can be applied immediately and not await another criminal trial." An obvious objection to this procedure, of course, is the difficulty of ascertaining the responsibility for a leak in the face of a denial.

While the press may justifiably reject strict codes of conduct for itself, it can hardly object to the bar's striving for a higher plane of conduct for its own membership. Bench and bar have every right to determine their own ethical standards, and their professional concern for a purer justice deserves the respect of the press. Elisha Hanson, former attorney for the American Newspaper Publishers Association, declared back in 1955 that there would be no such problem as "trial by newspaper" if judges presiding at trials, lawyers representing parties to the proceedings, and public officials charged with the prevention of crime would take proper steps to insure a fair trial.

EXCLUSION OF PRESS AND PUBLIC FROM THE COURTROOM

The concept of public trial stands in marked contrast to the secrecy and despotism of the Star Chamber. In 1768, the illustrious Blackstone wrote that "This open examination of witnesses *viva voce*, in the presence of all mankind, is much more conducive to the clearing of the truth, than the private and secret examination taken down in writing before an officer or his clerk. . . ."[13]

Jeremy Bentham favored open trials and said that the "establishment of publicity (and without any limits to the degree of it, but what are set by consideration of the collateral inconveniences of delay, vexation, and expense) will stand recommended by the general rule, as being, in most cases, conducive to the direct ends of justice. . . . Without publicity, all other checks are insufficient: in comparison of publicity, all other checks are of small account." The spirit of Anglo-American jurisprudence would hold with Bentham that "the evil attached to secret judicature strikes against the whole body of the community; deprives the public of an indispensable security for good judicature; runs counter to the ends of justice."[14]

Public trials encourage witnesses to be truthful, open up new avenues of evidence, move officers of the court toward strict conscientiousness in the performance of their duties, protect the judge from the imputation of wrong doing, educate citizens as to the law, and serve as a deterrent upon those who might be inclined to commit offenses against the law.[15]

Although neither Blackstone nor Bentham could have foreseen the growth and ubiquity of the modern mass media, their precept has survived, and 40 state constitutions and the Sixth Amendment guarantee fair and *public* trials.

In 1948, the U.S. Supreme Court held that Michigan had denied a witness, appearing before a one-man grand jury behind closed doors, due process of law in convicting him of contempt in a trial from which the public was excluded. The Court justified open trials as (1) a safeguard against attempts to use the courts as an instrument of persecution; (2) a notice to witnesses who will thereby be encouraged to give pertinent and truthful evidence; and (3) a means of extending public confidence in judicial remedies through observation of the courts in action.[16]

Courts have disagreed on the precise meaning of "open trial." Is a public trial the right of the accused only, the right of the public, or the right of both? In a number of cases,[17] courts have ruled that a defendant may waive a public trial, just as he may waive trial by jury. But if a defendant has neither had nor waived a public trial, prejudice is presumed and his conviction will likely be reversed. The majority view would seem to be that the accused must not be deprived of his right to have representatives of the public attend his trial, unless it is demonstrated that granting of the right will seriously interfere with the administration of justice.[18]

An accepable definition of "open trial" would be the admission of all members of the public within the physical limitations of the courtroom, that is, in the ordinary common sense acceptance of the term, with due regard to the size of the courtroom, the convenience of the court, the right to exclude objectionable characters and youth of tender years, and to do whatever else is necessary for the proper conduct of the trial. Some courts have qualified the right by declaring that "public" means simply that the trial cannot be "secret" and that the judge may exclude certain members of the public as long as a reasonable cross section of the community remains.[19]

A difficulty here is that many courtrooms have an uncommonly limited seating capacity, and it may be questioned whether a reasonable cross section of the public is ever present.

In the notorious *Jelke* trial, in which the scion of an oleomargarine fortune was charged with pandering, Judge Valente ordered the general public and the press excluded from the courtroom in "the interest of good morals." Only friends and relatives were permitted to remain to protect the accused's interests. The United Press brought an action to restrain the judge from enforcing his ruling, but the highest New York court refused to accede to the demand, contending that no state statute conferred any enforceable right upon the public to attend trials. And if the right was statutory, said the court, it would be conferred on the public-at-large and not on any individual member of the public. The rationale seemed to be that a ruling in favor of United Press would deprive Jelke of all power to waive his right to a public trial and thereby deprive him of following a course which he thought to be in his own best interests.

"The public's interest," said the court, "is adequately safeguarded as long as the accused himself is given the opportunity to assert on his own behalf, in an available judicial forum, his right to a trial that is fair and public."[20]

Jelke did assert his right to a public trial and was granted a new trial.[21] A trial is not *public*, said the same court, if only a certain privileged class of people are permitted to attend, and there is no member of the press among them.

Two years before the Jelke trial, a federal court had reached a similar conclusion: The rights of an accused should take clear precedence over freedom of the press; the right to a public trial is the defendant's right and not the right of the media.[22]

More in harmony with journalistic elan was the opinion of the Ohio Court of Appeals that newspapermen and the public have a right to attend trials which cannot be defeated by the accused signing a waiver of that right. In other words, the defendant may not insist upon a secret trial.[23]

However, in few cases have the courts vested newspapers with any absolute right to attend trials, and only as members of the general public has the right generally been extended. Most juvenile proceedings are closed to the public and thereby the press, and in a few states statutes close court cases dealing with rape, sodomy, adultery, fornication and divorce to protect public morals and the individual interests of witnesses and defendant.

It is doubtful that any broad policy of excluding the press in an attempt to thwart "trial by newspaper" will succeed. Where such attempts have been made, they may reflect the frustrations of judges who, shorn of the contempt power, have no other means of punishing a recalcitrant press.

MODIFICATIONS IN THE JURY SYSTEM

It is frequently suggested that special panels of jurors be assembled for celebrated criminal cases. One jurisdiction, New York, provides a special list of talesmen—chosen largely on the basis of education—to either side when "the subject matter of the indictment or the issue to be tried has been so widely commented upon that the court is satisfied that any ordinary jury cannot without delay and difficulty be obtained."[24] The underlying assumption would seem to be that the threat of prejudicial pre-trial publication is essentially a threat to the ordinary jury process. It would be useful to know what particular qualifications are looked for in those jurors conscripted to hear a widely publicized criminal case.

The jury system itself has its critics. Some believe that this uniquely Anglo-American institution bases its decisions on mere suppositions of what the law is or ought to be; that it ignores or misapplies judicial instructions, thus subverting not only the proper authority of the judge, but that of the legislator as well; and that juries arrive at their verdicts by the most circuitous and illogical routes.

The late Judge Jerome Frank doubted whether juries understood either the law as it is declared by the judge or the facts as they are presented by contesting lawyers. There is no better instrument, said Frank, than the usual jury trial for achieving uncertainty, lack of uniformity, capriciousness, disregard of legal rules, and unpredictable decisions. The emotional component of the deliberative process is substantial. "We tell jurors to do—have them take an oath to do—what we do not at all expect them to do." Because the jury system is captive to the fight-theory which, in turn, inhibits courtroom fact-finding, Frank would restrict its use in most kinds of civil actions, as has been done in Great Britain.[25]

Justice Benjamin Cardozo, Judge Learned Hand, Carl Lotus Becker, and others, have also had serious reservations about the jury. William Willoughby perceived the jury as a "body of laymen, selected almost at random, regarding whose ability to perform the delicate function of weighing evidence free from sentimental and emotional influences nothing is known, and who perform their duties under no sense of continuing responsibility."[26]

Judge Frank objected to the excluding of hearsay evidence. He felt that most of the evidence on which men act out of court, in business and industry, consisted of the equivalent of hearsay. Yet, because we distrust juries and question their competence to make allowances for the second-hand character of hearsay evidence, it is barred in jury trials—evidence which would be accepted by an administrative agency, a juvenile court, or a legislative committee. As a consequence, frequently a jury does not know what it should know to lead it to an intelligent conclusion.

We cannot be certain of Frank's definition of hearsay, for in the *Leviton* case he attacked the press for the influence its reports can have on a jury; and yet press reports would on occasion at least seem to qualify as hearsay evidence.

We are reminded again, however, of the fruitless search for the unbiased jury and the antiseptic jury chamber. Carried to its logical extreme, our insistence upon jurors without knowledge or feelings would tend to insure that only the least alert and sensitive among us would ever see jury duty. Perhaps, in the final analysis, it is one's estimate of human nature that determines the degree of confidence one will place in the individual juror.

Critics of the jury system place more reliance upon the pure rationality of judges than many would care to risk. And in the absence of more reliable knowledge about juries, favorable speculation about the jury is no less persuasive. A former New York prosecutor and judge, George DeLuca, rejects the assumption that prior disclosure of evidence in the newspapers is necessarily prejudicial, because it does not give adequate consideration to the human desire to be fair and just and to the independence of opinion of most jurors. It does not recognize the fact that the human mind is complex, that reactions to a given set of facts and circumstances will vary with different individuals and cannot be predicated as falling into a set of rigid patterns.[27]

The English jurist, Lord Devlin, observes that "hard cases make bad law; the jury is sometimes too frightened of the hard case and the judge of the bad law. This is the eternal conflict between law in the abstract and the justice of the case—how to do what is best in the individual case and yet preserve the rule. At its best it comes from the coalition of the lay mind with the legal; but if there is conflict, it is the lay mind that predominates. That is what is meant by trial by jury."[28] Devlin feels that the more limited the jury's function the greater the chance of uniformity in the administration of justice.

If uniformity and fairness are synonymous—and this may be doubted—one might suggest that American judges exert greater control over juries by limiting and defining the specific questions with which they will have to deal. The suggestion may be particularly pertinent where the issue is complex or where the case contains a multitude of variables.

The jury may be a hardier institution than we imagine, and it is unlikely that its demise is near. More factual knowledge is needed about this deeply ingrained Anglo-American judicial instrument.

In the meantime, courts would do well to place greater reliance upon social scientific evidence when faced with the problem of drawing a jury from a public believed to have been prejudiced by inflammatory publicity. Also, where a court is faced with the problem of deciding whether or not a motion for a procedural remedy should be granted, the expert evidence of the public opinion analyst, or other behavioral scientists, might greatly assist in measuring the depth and bitterness of community passion.

Consideration should also be given to requests to record, under proper safeguards, jury deliberations so that we may learn more about this crucial decision-making process, even though recent court opinions indicate that prejudice may be found as a matter of law, and that it is unnecessary to show actual prejudice in individual jurors in order to win a reversal of a criminal conviction.

It is here submitted that whatever improvements are made in the jury system, they may have the tangential effect of alleviating the conflict between free press and fair trial.

LEGISLATION

It is inevitable in a democratic society that new laws will be proposed in an effort to resolve social dilemmas. It has been recommended that legislatures, through narrowly drawn contempt or criminal statutes, ban specific press practices which appear to create a serious danger of improperly influencing jury verdicts.

Such laws would make the press liable for reporting, (a) the criminal record of an accused, (b) alleged confessions, (c) statements speculating on the guilt or innocence of an accused, (d) comments on the credibility of witnesses, and (e) evidence likely to be inadmissible and highly prejudicial to a defendant.[29] And they would have a deterrent effect on the press that reversing unfairly obtained convictions does not have.

It has also been proposed that publication of all evidence introduced at a preliminary hearing be delayed until it is admitted at the trial, and that such news accounts be limited to the nature of the charge, the decision of the court, and information merely descriptive of the proceeding itself.

Justice Bernard S. Meyer of the Supreme Court of the State of New York advocates a law which would interdict any publication threatening the parties in a case, their counsel or witnesses, grand or petit jurors, or the court, but would not extend to the criticism of judges, in line with earlier Supreme Court rulings.

Justice Meyer envisions two categories of prejudicial matter. The first would include material which as a matter of law is assumed to present a serious and imminent danger of substantial prejudice: confessions, criminal records, and opinions about the credibility of witnesses or the guilt of the accused. The second category would include such material as interviews with the family of a victim of a crime, statements as to how a witness will testify, publication of the names and addresses of jurors, and appeals to racial, political and economic biases. The prejudicial character of material in the second category would depend upon the circumstances of the case, and would be determined by a jury. Such factors as the stage of the case at which publication occurs, the context in which it is published, whether the proceeding is civil or criminal, and the specific topic involved would have to be considered.

The New York jurist would base provisions of the law on scientific evidence wherever such evidence was relevant; but legislation should not have to wait upon scientific findings. Meyer is proposing a delaying statute only. He would not seek to prevent publication any longer than is essential to fair trial. Premature publication would constitute a misdemeanor for which specific punishments would be provided. Since officers of the court and their employees, as well as editors, would be liable, his proposal would have the effect of enforcing Canon 20. The usual rules of criminal procedure would apply to offenders: indictment or attachment, trial by jury, and the right of appeal and reversal upon a showing that the publication was not in fact a clear and present danger to the administration of justice. These traditional protections are not available in contempt proceedings.[30]

The question of constitutionality may be inherent in fair trial legislation. If the penalties invoked were to have a substantial deterrent effect on free expression, these laws might also be construed as having the effect of prior restraint—and would be struck down by the Supreme Court. At the same time, legislation vague enough to escape the charge of prior restraint might be challenged on constitutional grounds as being too indefinite and obscure to provide an ascertainable standard of guilt. The problem would be to draw a statute broad enough to satisfy the requirement of the "clear and present danger" test and still stay within the boundaries of constitutionality.

The presumption of constitutionality has been withdrawn by the Supreme Court from many laws restrictive of free speech and press. And frequently the Court construes such statutes not in terms of the validity of their purpose, but in terms of the mischief possible in their names. To say the least, such legislation would have to be flexible.

But all of this is speculative. The Supreme Court has not yet dealt with contempt convictions of newspapers or their editors for bringing publicity pressure to bear upon jurors; cases such as *Bridges, Pennekamp, Craig,* and more recently, *Wood* v. *Georgia,* all have involved judges or a grand jury. No individual was on trial. So the full power of the state to protect the administration of justice by its courts has not been appraised, as Justice Douglas noted in *Craig.* And in the *Bridges* case, Justice Black implied that the Court would give much weight to a legislative appraisal by the state that a "specific danger" justified restricting a "particular kind of utterance." Legislative direction from California would have been welcome.

Justice Meyer also finds language in a 1965 case, *Cox* v. *Louisiana,*[31] supporting his view that a carefully drawn statute could be constitutional. Although that case concerned picketing near a courthouse rather than press publicity, Justice Arthur Goldberg, in his opinion for the court, said that a state "may adopt safeguards necessary and appropriate to assure that the administration of justice at all stages is free from outside control and influence. A narrowly drawn statute . . . is obviously a safeguard both necessary and appropriate to vindicate the State's interest in assuring justice under law." But Goldberg does distinguish the case from one concerned with "such a pure form of expression as newspaper comment."

The question remains: would statutes explicitly condemning specific, enumerated mass media practices, and restricting both divulgence and dissemination of prejudicial matter, be viewed as a prior restraint?

Proponents of laws which would set some upper limits on press performance in criminal cases—perhaps those implied in the *Irvin* case—feel that these laws would have a dissuasive influence on irresponsible editors and officers of the court which mere disapprobation by the court does not have. Moreover, they would provide a more economic and efficient way of preserving private rights. The *Irvin* case, for example, was in the courts for six years. It is also argued that the suppression of out-of-court comment does not deny the citizen information vital to the democratic process, as long as the trial itself can be fully covered.

So far legislation has met with only moderate success. The Morse Bill (S. 290), introduced for a second time in the 1965 session of Congress, met strong opposition in hearings before the Subcommittees on Constitutional Rights and Improvements in Judicial Machinery of the Senate Judiciary Committee.[32] The Bill, designed to punish officers of the court for any disclosure which "might affect the outcome of any pending criminal litigation," was opposed by the Department of Justice, United Press International and the Associated Press, the three broadcasting networks, the American Newspaper Publishers Association, the National Association of Broadcasters, the Radio and Television News Directors Association, Sigma Delta Chi, professional journalistic society, the American Civil Libertes Union, and individual lawyers and law professors. It was challenged on grounds of vagueness, ambiguity, inflexibility, prematurity and constitutionality. Although its purpose of preventing inflammatory and self-serving statements that might impair a fair trial is laudable, the bill poses a number of difficult questions. Would a defendant face a contempt citation for complaining of police brutality or misconduct on the part of judge or prosecutor? Would an attorney face punishment for making a statement outside the courtroom even though the defendant's or the public's interest demanded it?

"Silencing the accused and his spokesman," said Dr. Frank Stanton in his testimony for CBS, "in cases involving oppressive police tactics, improper detention, unsubstantiated charges, and whimsical arrests, might compound rather than relieve the violation of his rights . . . The bill is an oversimplified way of solving a complex problem. It offers a cure to human failings in a form that may carry more potential for injury both to individuals and to the Nation than an ailment that has not yet been fully diagnosed."[33]

Fred W. Vinson, Jr., assistant attorney general in the Justice Department's Criminal Division, testified that "The standard 'might affect the outcome' of a criminal case would be very difficult to apply. The phrase 'criminal litigation' leaves unclear whether this covers a period of time beginning with an arrest or whether it contemplates the filing of an indictment or information, or even whether it contemplates the period commencing with the impaneling of the jury." "In any event," Vinson continued, "I think it is undesirable to apply at this time the broad contempt power, without a jury trial, to the entire period from the beginning to the end of a criminal proceeding."[34]

"I do not have the the the foggiest notion of what 290 does," declared Ronald Goldfarb, Washington, D. C. attorney, in his testimony before the Subcommittee: "I question whether or not it is appropriate to statutorily inhibit a defendant or his attorney from furnishing or making available in the words of the statute 'information not already properly filed with the court.' It strikes me that such an inhibition might violate the first amendment's guarantee of freedom of speech and freedom of petition, and the sixth amendment's right to counsel. Aside from these constitutional questions, as a practical matter I question whether or not it is wise to prevent a defendant from making certain comments about the case against him during the pendency of the case. For example, an indictment may accuse and hurt a defendant severely. Would this statute stop him from, at the least, denying the charge against him? Indictments frequently include more than technical legal charges against a person. They accuse (often in detail) defendants of a course of conduct of an anti-social and embarrassing nature. To punish an individual or his attorney for speaking out in self-defense at such times seems to me to be unreasonable, if not unconstitutional."[35]

Although the preponderance of testimony against the Bill may have diminished its chances of passage, it is probably not dead. The 1965 session of the Judicial Conference of the United States approved S. 290, and its Committee on the Administration of Criminal Law decided to "recommend a further change in language which may serve to strengthen the measure against attack on constitutional grounds but without impairing its effectiveness." The objective is to give Canon 20 legislative status.

Much to the consternation of newsmen, Massachusetts lawyers did not appear to be satisfied with a 1963 "Guide for the Bar and News Media," a voluntary statement of standards ratified by bar, newspaper and broadcasting groups, and have since sought repressive legislation. Early in 1965, a third unsuccessful attempt was made in the Massachusetts House to win approval for a bill to protect trial by jury.

The bill would prohibit all news media from reporting confessions, criminal records, inferring guilt, or discussing evidence on pain of a $1,000 fine and a 30-day jail sentence. Truth, lack of prejudicial effect, and lack of intent to prejudice would be no defense. A 1964 bill provided for the designation of a special assistant attorney general and staff who would "check the publication of all news media operating throughout the Commonwealth, day by day, week by week, thoroughly and methodically, and cite for contempt those news media breaking the existing laws of the Commonwealth regarding the reporting of court and criminal news." Such "voluntarism" reflects an uncommon lack of good faith, in the opinion of newsmen.

In 1961, the Association of Florida Circuit Judges recommended a bill which would make it unlawful for news media to refer to pretrial confessions of incriminating admissions by those accused of crime. The bill did not pass.

But not all legislative attempts have failed. In 1965, Texas approved a "Revised Code of Criminal Procedure" which brought that state's handling of criminal cases much closer to the procedures followed in the federal courts. For example, law enforcemnt officers are admonished not to prejudice a defendant's case by the pre-trial release of a confession—a common practice in the past. Prior to the new laws, prosecutors would freely discuss evidence with newspaper reporters. When James Cross, Jr., convicted in February 1966 of first degree murder, was arrested in connection with the strangling deaths of University of Texas co-eds, Shirley Ann Stark and Susan Rigsby, Justice of the Peace Frank McBee chatted with reporters about the suspect's alleged confession until his secretary, who appeared better versed in the revised law, intervened to warn: "If that's a newsman, you had better keep still." McBee did not continue.[36] Police officers and attorneys, scrupulously followed the pre-trial strictures of the new code, and did not discuss the case with reporters prior to the beginning of the trial on Feb. 7.

In December 1965 the Wisconsin House of Representatives passed a bill which would prohibit attorneys and law enforcement officials from making "public statements relative to the guilt or innocence of the defendant," or disclosing "the existence of a statement or confession of the accused, or a statement of a witness. . . ." An amendment which would have included all news media in the ban was defeated. The assembly majority said: "Newspapers can speculate all they want to. If they have the facility and the interest to dig up the facts, that's their prerogative, but it's not the business of the police or district attorney to try their cases in the newspapers."

In late November 1965, Tucson Superior Court Judge Richard Roylston isued a temporary injunction forbidding law enforcement officials to give further information to the press in the case of Charles Schmid, Jr., charged with the murder of two teen-age sisters and a 15-year-old girl, and the secret burial of their bodies in the Arizona desert.

A closed-door preliminary hearing was held in an atmosphere electric with rumors of teen-age sex and drinking clubs in Tucson. The sisters, 13-year-old Wendy and 17-year-old Gretchen Fritz, were daughters of a prominent Tucson heart surgeon.

Headlines in the Tucson *Daily Citizen* such as "Threat to Gretchen Revealed" and "Charlie Said He'd Kill Her" led Judge Roylston to believe that a fair trial for Schmid was becoming impossible. The Judge relied on a recent Arizona Court of Appeals decision in a child-beating case which turned partly on the pre-trial publicity issue. That court said: "We hereby inform both press and bar alike that should the situation arise in the future, this court will stand ready to support a courageous bench which can and should unhesitatingly step in to prohibit pre-trial publicity . . . which, by its quantity and quality is prejudicial to the rights of the defendants, and which is calculated to inflame the public to such an extent that fair and impartial administration of justice is impaired."[37] In response, the *Daily Citizen*, in a front page editorial headed "What the Judge Did To YOU," charged Judge Roylston with imposing a ban on legitimate information. On March 1 a jury found Schmid guilty of murder and recommended the death penalty.

When reporters attended an open Superior Court hearing on a defense petition to dismiss a murder charge because of insufficient evidence, Phoenix Judge E. R. Thurman threatened them with contempt charges if their newspapers published details. The judge dismissed a petition by Donald Chambers who was charged with the murder and robbery of an auto supply dealer. On a request from the defense attorney, the Judge ordered a reporter from the Phoenix *Gazette* to withhold information introduced at the hearing and to report only that the request for a writ of habeas corpus had been denied. All Phoenix news media ignored the Judge's threat and carried the story in detail. There were no repercussions.

What are the objections to proposals for new laws? First of all, many newsmen see in these legislative proposals giant steps toward censorship and the drying up of traditional news sources. What right does the judicial branch of government have to shield itself from journalistic, and thereby public, scrutiny by instigating the passage of secrecy laws? Secondly, the bills go too far in admitting of no exceptions and in assuming that every criminal case follows a rigid and similar pattern. Can pre-trial publicity *never* serve the ends of justice? Hardly. And it would certainly be a perversion of justice if defense attorneys, and news media, were to be punished for attempting to protect defendants from harassment and persecution. There are cases enough to support this contention.

And yet there can be rigidity on the other side. Irwin Ross, writing in *The Atlantic*,[38] decries the dissemination of pre-trial publicity by police and prosecutor, but would permit a defendant who thought he was being framed to take his case to the press. But this does not solve the problem. In some jurisdictions—those in which defendants are charged with the murder of civil rights workers or Negroes—this procedure might very well jeopardize the state's case and therefore the public interest in a just result.

The attractiveness of Attorney General Katzenbach's recent statement of policy concerning the release of information to the press lies in its flexibility, in its admitting of exceptions. Katzenbach recognizes a legitimate public interest in certain factual aspects of a criminal case— a defendant's prior record or the fact that he is a fugitive from justice. At the same time, he appreciates the potential danger of angry speculation by policemen and prosecutor. He believes also that newsmen have a share in the proper administration of justice, and that "news is when news happens; it is not something held in suspension."

A third and more concrete objection to legislation—one expressed by Dr. Frank Stanton—is that under the kinds of laws that have been proposed, the courts would have to sit in continuous judgment over the press, and there would be an endless parade of indictments, trials, appeals, heaped upon already overburdened dockets. The costs would be astronomical. But, more important, the courts and the media would be at bitter odds, and the public would suffer. For in such an atmosphere, court reporting might be avoided and we would lose much news of legislation, court rulings, appointments and court proceedings in general.

Finally, a vocal segment of the press feels that it is being convicted by theory, by the unsupported hypothesis of a direct cause-effect relationship between news reports and jury verdicts. It is to this crucial question—a question of evidence—that we must now direct our attention.

CHAPTER 14

PUBLICITY AND JURY VERDICTS

"I don't think we can solve our problem by shouting 'free speech' and 'fair trial' at each other. I think what we need is an impartial scientific investigation of this subject by an impartial agency, an agency of such stature that both the Bar and the media would respect it."—Richard P. Tinkham.[1]

Court opinion bearing upon the collision of the competing constitutional rights, free press and fair trial, tells us what the law is and what it ought to be, but leaves unanswered the essential question: what *is* the effect of trial and pre-trial publicity on jurors?

The legal profession has built its case against "trial by newspaper" without testing its premise that there is a direct cause-effect relationship between press reports and jury verdicts. Not even the most positivistic school of jurisprudence, with its insistence upon the application of scientific method to problems of law, has taken steps toward anchoring this particular problem on the solid foundation of empirical fact and defining it within an adequate conceptual framework.

Under the influence of such thinkers as Max Weber and Roscoe Pound, legal research no longer enjoys that majestic isolation of a half century ago; and Lord Coke's "special logic" of the law is today hardly a sufficient analytical tool. In fact, the more recent work of Herman Pritchett and Glendon Schubert may portend a revolution in legal research which will push the law well beyond the logical limits now set by its own postulates, assimilate the objective realities of the present, and further loosen the bonds of *stare decisis*.[2] One behavioral scientist suggests that rule-logicians—and there are such in the legal as in most other disciplines—seek to reduce law to a kind of dehumanized legal geometry.[3] Law must not be allowed to degenerate to the point where it ignores human variables. "The life of the law

197

[is] experience," said Oliver Wendell Holmes, and that experience is inevitably human.

The late Jerome Frank recounts in his coruscating book, *Courts on Trial*, how the dead hand of precedent may stunt the growth of the law: In 1947 two enterprising law students sought to study how jurors decide cases. At the conclusion of jury trials they planned to have judges ask jurors to voluntarily complete a carefully worded questionnaire and be interviewed by the students. The proposal was made without success to nine judges of several different jurisdictions. One federal judge said he did not approve of a "holier-than-thou attitude toward juries." Another, in refusing to cooperate, said he had never made such a study when he was in law school. Still another said, "How they decide is their business." One state judge, enthusiastic about the study, submitted the questionnaire to jurors and returned the answers to the students. He also granted permission to conduct informal interviews, but reneged when he received adverse criticism from some of his colleagues.

In the great reform movement which swept the common law in the nineteenth century, the utilitarians sought to illuminate judicial processes. Rules, once thought to be pronouncements from on high, were traced to their operational origins. How the law works (the "living" law) rather than what it is (the positive law) became the primary consideration. In one of his most important books, Jeremy Bentham presented a realistic appraisal of the probable influence of extraneous publication on judge and jury:[4]

"In England, publications of the cases of litigant parties are altogether unusual, and if distributed for any such purposes as that of influencing the decision of the jury, would be liable to be treated on the footing of an offence against justice. . . . In England, the ground for the prohibition put upon these *ex parte* publications, is the danger of their exercising an undue influence on the minds of the jury. . . . On professional and cultivated minds, engaged by the necessity of office to procure the whole mass of evidence and argument, the premature exhibition of a part would rather be turned aside from as useless, than apprehended by anybody as dangerous. It was to the eye of the public at large, and not to the eye of . . . a judge that these statements were addressed. In what way could the probity of the judge be endangered by receiving at one time a part of those documents, the whole of which would come before him of course? Even in England, the reason on which the prohibition relies for its support has more of surface than of substance in it. The representations given by publications of this sort will of course be partial ones: the color given to them will be apt to be deceived, and their affections engaged on the wrong side. Partial? Yes: but can anything in these printed arguments be more partial than the *viva voce* oratory of the advocates on the same side will be sure to be? The dead letter cannot avoid allowing full time for reflection: the *viva voce* declamation allows of none. The written arguments may contain allegations without proofs, true: but is not the spoken argument just as apt to do the same? When, of the previous statement given by the leading advocate, any part remains unsupported by evidence, the judge of course points out the failure: whatever effect this indication has on the jury, in the way of guarding them against that source of delusion in spoken arguments, would it have less efficacy in the case of written ones?"

Compare this with the verbiage of less cautious commentators. Earlier, an English jurist had declared:[5] "It is the pride of the constitution of this country that all causes should be decided by jurors, *who are chosen in a manner which excludes all possibility of bias.*" (Emphasis added.) And Justice Felix Frankfurter dissenting in the *Stroble* case[6] noted that: "Science with all its advances has not given us instruments for determining when the impact of such newspaper exploitation has spent itself or *whether the powerful impression bound to be made by such inflaming articles* as here preceded the trial can be dissipated in the mind of the average juror by the tame and often pedestrian proceedings in court." (Emphasis added.) Adherence to such conclusions would obviate the necessity of applying scientific methods to the examination of social and constitutional conflicts.

Another judge has admitted that when a decision was difficult he would rely primarily on "the hunch—that intuitive flash of understanding which makes the jump-spark connection between question and decision, and at the point where the path is darkest for the judicial feet, sheds its light along the way."[7] If "hunch" is the mental mechanism by which judges reach decisions, can we expect legally untrained jurors to bring any degree of objectivity to their deliberations?

If, with Dean Pound, we accept the view that there is much in the law which is social engineering, it would seem to follow that the accumulated knowledge and methodology of the social sciences would be helpful in solving legal problems. Much of the substance of law is drawn from sources outside the law itself, and few valid conclusions with regard to the function of law can be reached by depending solely upon legal theory. Moreover, "the basis of any significant critique of the law must be how successfully the law actually works to achieve social ends which are desired for reasons not found in the law itself."[8]

It should be recognized, of course, that the goal of judicial processes is not always knowledge, and that the search for "truth" is frequently suppressed by the need for victory in an adversary system. In making decisions, says Sidney Ulmer, the judge recognizes (1) that the case must be decided one way or another, even when the evidence is not sufficient for a "scientific" conclusion; (2) that judicial factfinders are not bound by rules of consistency, and (3) that facts may be bent by the judicial process to serve an ulterior purpose.

This is not to suggest that all members of the legal profession are blind to the judicial value of the scientific method or that lawyers conspire to subvert "truth." It does suggest that the conventional logic of the law, with its dependence upon analogy, is inadequate when the law reaches out to other disciplines to justify legislation or legal reform. One lawyer has admonished his profession by pointing out that the law may better boast of its maturity and sophistication when it seeks the counsel of sociologists and psychologists in solving problems of publicity, the *cause celebre*, and the jury.[9] Until it does, the free press-fair trial conflict will remain simply an issue of passionate speculation.

To what extent do juries have prior knowledge of the cases on which they sit, and what proportion of such knowledge is derived from news coverage? If the media do impinge upon the trial process, what is their degree of influence and at what point in a trial is prejudicial publicity most likely to be operative? What is the effect upon jurors of news reports of (a) confessions; (b) prior criminal records; (c) expressions of opinions concerning the guilt or innocence of the accused; (d) interviews with the family of a victim; (e) the anticipated testimony of witnesses; and (f) statements that appeal to racial, religious, political or economic bias? Is the juror conscious of any effect of such reports upon him, and do his own composite predispositions override any amount of press comment? How effective are judicial instructions to a jury? Do such procedural remedies as change of venue, change of venire, continuance and mistrial serve to diminish prejudice? Does locking up a juror until the termination of a trial prejudice him against a defendant? Are there positive effects of publicity which may counterbalance possible negative effects? To what extent do rumor and gossip take over when the press is censored or restricted? Finally, do we accept Wigmore's view that "to equate the stamina of judges and jurors runs counter to one of the basic assumptions of the law of evidence—that jurors must be protected from the undue prejudice of improper evidence upon which, however, the judge may safely pass"; or shall we agree with the appellate court opinion in the *Baltimore Radio* case [10] that there are citizens possessing the same firmness and impartiality as judges?

Because of its dramatic role and its central importance in the trial process, the American jury has been the focal point of a number of pioneering social-scientific investigations. By far the most significant of these was the University of Chicago Law School Jury Project.[11] The project was directed by Harry Kalven, Jr., Hans Zeisel and Fred Strodtbeck, and sponsored by the Ford Foundation.

Jury Project collected basic data on jury behavior through statistical analysis and refinement of existing court records, post-deliberation interviews, simulated cases before experimental juries, and the recording of a limited number of actual jury deliberations. Public opinion surveys were used to determine population attitudes toward the jury system. Other phases of the study sought to analyze the methods and results of jury selection. Trained observers were assigned to a series of jury trials to witness the trial, interview the judge and counsel, and interview the jury panel at the end of the trial. With the approval of the court and counsel for both sides, six actual jury deliberations were tape recorded, primarily to validate the other investigative methods.

Among the over-all purposes of the study were: (a) to determine if the jury perceives its function the same way the law conceives it; (b) to determine if the jury understands the judge's instructions; (c) to see if the jury's criteria for a verdict are consistent with those laid down by the law; (d) to see if the jury comprehends the evidence; and (e) to determine if the jury is moved by "rational" or by emotional factors.

As part of the study, 1,500 jurors who had served in 213 different criminal cases were subjected to intensive interviewing. Among the findings: juries were unanimous on the first ballot in 30 per cent of the cases; in the remaining 70 per cent there was a lack of unanimity on the first ballot. But in 90 per cent of these cases the majority on the first ballot ultimately won its point. The broad conclusion is that most criminal cases are decided during the trial, not during jury deliberations.

Similar conclusions were reached in a study by Weld and Danzig at Cornell University.[12] A simulated trial designed to create the real atmosphere of a court room was divided into stages, with jury members at each stage indicating their belief in guilt or innocence—and recording their opinions before all of the evidence was heard. Judgments fluctuated considerably during the proceedings as individuals reacted differently to the same testimony. Judgment was often affected by admiration for or antagonism toward the counselors. Even these jurors, above average in intelligence and education, did not seem to reach decisions through a logical analysis of the case, and apparently no juror attempted to maintain an attitude of doubt until he had heard all of the evidence.

Early in the trial at least 25 per cent of the jurors reached a fairly definite decision, but later testimony seemed to change this certainty. In this regard, the opening and closing statements of the attorneys were important.

In another segment of Jury Project, 500 trial judges filled out questionnaires—one for each jury trial over which they had presided. Fifteen hundred criminal-case questionnaires were returned. In 83 per cent of these cases the judges and jury had agreed on the verdict and in 17 per cent there was disagreement. Judges appeared more prone to convict than did jurors. If all defendants in the 1,500 cases had been tried by a judge, the number of acquittals would have been cut in half.[13]

In a detailed study of the decision differences of juries and judges in personal-injury suits, it was found that the percentage of agreement between judge and jury remained almost constant whether or not the judge summarized the evidence, whether or not written instructions were given the jury, and whether or not the judge commented on the weight of the evidence. There is a strong suggestion here that at least in personal-injury suits these procedural controls make the jury neither more nor less like the judge.

Edwin Schur observes that theoretically the selection of jurors is geared to finding value-free persons, and any opinion on the case or type of problem involved may serve to disqualify the prospective juror. But he adds: "Actually, of course, we know that the selection proceeds on radically different grounds, each attorney scrupulously dedicated to the selection of those jurors whose value systems will most favor his client's cause."[14] Jury Project noted that 60 per cent of the lawyers' *voir dire* time was spent in indoctrinating jurors and only 40 per cent in asking questions designed to separate favorable from unfavorable jurors.

Strodtbeck sought to evaluate the importance of three variables in jury deliberations: differentiation between the roles of men and women; social status; and physical position at the jury table.[15] In the sex-role differentiation study, jurors drawn by lot from regular jury pools were exposed to recorded trials, then asked to deliberate under customary discipline and return their verdicts. The deliberations were recorded by hidden microphones. Twelve sessions of an original set of 30 were scored in terms of group interaction categories. Analysis indicated that men dominate jury deliberations—they initiate long bursts of talking directed at the achievement of a verdict. Women were found to be more likely to react emotionally to the contributions of others.

In the social status study, jurors were drawn at random from voting registration lists. The professions and the very low education and occupation groups were slightly under-represented in the sample because the usual jury-list bias was taken into account.

The latent premise of the study was that high-participation in deliberations is an indication of ability to influence others. The study also assumed at the outset that there is a high degree of presumption of equality among jury members—a presumption which is heightened by the requirement that the verdict be unanimous.

The findings indicated that men and high-status persons had higher participation, influence, satisfaction and perceived competence for the jury task than did women and persons of lower status. Jurors with high participation rates in deliberations were perceived to be more competent—respondents, should they be on trial, would choose such persons as jurors.

Finally, using data accumulated during Jury Project, Strodtbeck attempted to define the impact on participation of physical position at the jury table. A multidimensional scaling technique showed that table width and length and the visual accessibility of each of the jurors to his fellows contributed to the concept of "social distance." This social distance was found to affect the participation of individual jury members, and jurors perceived those closer to them as being more like-minded and dependable than those physically farther away. This esoteric approach may seem to offer little in terms of practicality, but it is such small bits of brick and mortar which contribute to building a strong foundation for future research.

A group of Georgia investigators attempted to determine the effect of the jury foreman's prestige and method of leadership on the behavior of the jury.[16] Eleven members of a moot-court jury in a fabricated personal-injury suit were "guinea pigs" whereas the twelfth was a confederate of the investigators.

In each of the juries the twelfth man was the foreman—"typed" to exert different kinds of leadership. The other jurors were not aware of the subterfuge. Although characteristics of the jurors had been matched to insure equivalent groups, the mode of leadership had no consistent effect on jury behavior. The study also showed that although the foremen were generally able to change the opinions of individual jurors regarding what constitutes equitable damages, the juries reached their decisions on damages through a deliberate, arithmetic averaging of individual opinions. Members of the jury, realizing that a consensus had to be attained, in some cases voted against their personal convictions.

An interesting question arises at this point. The Strodtbeck study of seating at the jury table showed that in a statistically significant number of cases the foreman was chosen from one of two jurors sitting at the end positions of the table. One might profitably investigate the type of person motivated to choose this position of prominence in the jury room to determine if he had the personality attributes manipulated in the Georgia study.

Using the Strodtbeck sex and status study as a baseline, Hawkins further analyzed the interaction of juries to determine activity rates for jurors aligned in factions.[17] He found that the smaller the faction size, the greater the participation of each member of the faction. Two possible explanations were advanced: (1) personality factors causing active talking might also relate to a tendency on the part of these "talkers" to avoid hearing other persuasive arguments by pressing their own; and (2) factional splits might cause changes in how jurors participate. Zeisel offers a third explanation.[18] He feels that three factors may determine the amount of participation by members of a faction: (1) If both sides argue for equal periods of time, the smaller faction must have more talking per person; (2) every additional member will add new arguments or new versions of old ones, thus adding to total time; and (3) the greater the size disparity between factions, the greater the tendency of the minority to hold out and the greater the pressure applied by the majority.

James found that participation during deliberations varied directly with the amount of the individual's education. The more highly educated jurors gave more emphasis to procedural matters and instructions from the judge, while the less well educated tended to pay more attention to trial testimony, personal experience and opinion.[19] Education, however, did not influence persuasiveness or persuasability. James also found that 50 per cent of the deliberation time was spent exchanging personal experiences, 25 per cent was spent on procedural matters, 15 per cent on reviewing facts and 8 per cent on discussing the instructions.

Another type of jury study is that concerned with the *a priori* bias injected into juries by the manner in which jurors are chosen. Robinson found a great discrepancy in the occupational makeup of grand jury venires compared with what would be expected from a probability sample of the community as a whole.[20] In a 13-year period he found 894 professionals, semi-professionals, proprietors, managers and officials when, judging by their numbers in the community, there should have been only 299—an over-representation of 595. In the same period only 26 craftsmen, foremen and kindred workers were selected (instead of 167) and only two unskilled workers (instead of 200). "In view of the well-known correlations between socio-economic status and political and economic attitudes," Robinson concludes, "there is a strong presumption that the occupational bias will result in political and economic bias as well."

What was to become the most controversial aspect of Jury Project was the tape recording of an actual jury deliberation in a 1954 federal civil case in Wichita, Kansas. With full knowledge and consent of judge and attorneys, but unknown to the jury, a microphone was concealed in the jury chamber. A year later the recordings thus obtained were played before an audience of 200 members of the bar at the annual Judicial Conference of the Tenth Circuit at Estes Park, Colorado.

Although there were no protests at that time, a story on the "bugging" in the Los Angeles *Times* three months later ignited a nationwide outcry. Jury Project was condemned by editors, columnists and radio commentators. The Senate Subcommittee on Internal Security, led by James O. Eastland of Mississippi and William O. Jenner of Indiana, conducted an investigation with the avowed intention of showing the need of legislation to prevent the use of concealed microphones. Some members of the subcommittee even called for legal action against everyone involved in the project, including the Ford Foundation, the consenting judge and attorneys, and, of course, the researchers. "The fact that the persons who made the recordings were competent social scientists pursuing a serious study of an important American institution appeared to make no difference to critics."[21]

Few lawyers appeared to be disturbed by the research—in fact some prominent legal figures publicly endorsed it—but the courts seem to have mixed feelings about this practice. In one federal case, the court said:[22] "If jurors are conscious that they will be subjected to interrogation or searching hostile inquiry as to what occurred in the jury room and why, they are almost inescapably influenced to some extent by that anticipated annoyance. The courts will not permit that potential influence to invade the jury room. *He who makes studied enquiries of jurors as to what occurred* there acts at his peril, lest he be held as acting in obstruction of the administration of justice." (Emphasis added.)

Other federal courts have affirmed this position, and the American Civil Liberties Union also favors tightly closed jury rooms.

Noting that there was no state law or constitutional provision establishing the inviolability of the jury room, a Michigan court took the opposite view:[23] "Just as physicians observe a living patient for research purposes, the improvement of the administration of justice necessitates the limited use of direct observation. . . . If the general practice of medicine and surgery is to progress, there must be a certain amount of experimentation carried on; but such experiments must be done with the knowledge and consent of the patient or those responsible for him, and must not vary too radically from the accepted method of procedure."

Another judge has recommended making a stenographic record of jury deliberations to enable the trial judge to determine whether the verdict was reached by improper means; if so he would set aside the verdict.[24]

It should be noted that few social scientists came to the defense of their colleagues, nor was there much public support for the project. But after polling 300 sociologists, political scientists and lawyers, Burchard found that most political scientists and sociologists would approve the use of concealed devices in jury research. Lawyers were evenly divided in approving and disapproving.

Jury Project did not deal with the impact of newspaper publicity on the jury. In a letter to Judge Herbert F. Goodrich, director of the American Law Institute, Jury Project coordinator Kalven assessed that problem:[25]

"Our materials as to the impact of newspaper publicity on the jury are even less satisfactory. *As a matter of prudence we decided not to interview in major criminal cases where there was trial by newspaper. And we have been unable to think of a way of importing the stimulus of the news to our experimental jury routine.* As a result the vast majority of the cases we have studied simply do not present the problem of the newspaper. We do, however, have evidence that the jurors take with surprising seriousness the admonition not to read the paper or to discuss the case with other people. . . . Our over-all impression . . . is that the jury is a pretty stubborn, healthy institution not likely to be overwhelmed either by a remark of counsel or a remark in the press. The chief reason for this is that in most cases the jurors are initially in some disagreement and there are champions for both sides of the case in the jury room. Thus a prejudicial remark which is likely to please one side is equally likely to irritate the other and would be offset by counter-argument. But this is unfortunately only a general impression. . . ." (Emphasis added.)

Since this letter was written, at least one attempt has been made to assess the possible impact of pre-trial publicity. Kline and Jess used eight 6-man juries in mock trial situations at the University of Minnesota.[26] Control and experimental juries were assigned to each of four trials. Prior to the trial, the jurors were exposed to two kinds of material. The experimental groups received information designed to be prejudicial about the case they were deliberating. The control group received an "unbiased" version of the story. The information was "planted" in a newspaper and radio news tapes purported to have been recorded off the air. Each jury was told by the judge to disregard any evidence obtained outside the courtroom or that was not admitted into evidence.

All jury deliberations were tape recorded. The experimental groups were also observed through one-way glass and their discussions recorded using a modified Bales interaction analysis technique.[27] This technique utilized trained observers who classified statements into three categories: orientation statements, or attempts to attain a common definition of the problem; evaluation statements, or those indicating differing values and interests and providing ways for common resolution; and control statements, or those made by jurors who were trying to influence fellow jurors. Each juror was also given a set of questions to answer after deliberations. These included a scale designed to measure authoritarianism, and one to measure dogmatism.[28]

In each of the four trials at least one member in each of the experimental juries made reference to the information contained in the news stories. In the control juries no such references were made. This could be explained by the fact that in the experimental juries "new" information was provided by the news accounts, whereas in the control-jury situation the material in the news stories was similar to that offered as evidence.

In three of the four cases the experimental juries decided not to use the extraneous "prejudicial" evidence due to internal group pressures. In these three cases both the control and experimental juries found for the defendant—despite the outward appearance of it being a plaintiff's case. In the fourth case, both experimental and control juries found for the plaintiff. It was in this case that the experimental jury based a portion of its rationale for decision on the "prejudicial" material presented in the news stories.

The finding that all four experimental juries made reference to the "prejudicial" evidence in their deliberations points up the possibility of the prejudicial impact of publicity and the need for further research in this sensitive area.

A second hypothesis investigated in this study was that a juror who brings a "closed" mind or an "authoritarian" frame of reference to a jury room might also bring to the deliberations preconceived notions which would be unaffected by the logical argumentation that is supposed to prevail in a court of law. It was thought that these traits, along with balanced or offsetting lawyer presentations, might also cause extended deliberations and tend to produce hung juries. In this study one jury returned a split decision.

In general, the Kline and Jess study supported the findings of Weld and Danzig and the Jury Project to the effect that jurors decide how they will vote prior to deliberations. Of the 42 jurors who returned questionnaires, 35 indicated that they had made up their minds prior to deliberations. In this experiment, contrary to what was found in Jury Project, the judge's instructions apparently had the desired effect on three of the four experimental juries, but it's at least possible that students would be more responsive than non-students to such a legal admonition.

In another recent study of the effect of newspaper publicity on prospective jurors, Simon suggests that jurors take seriously the judge's instructions that they lay aside opinion formed prior to the presentation of evidence.[26a] Using an experimental design similar to Kline and Jess, but with tape-recorded trials, she found that prior to the presentation of evidence the effect of "prejudicial" publicity caused the jurors to think the defendant more guilty. This difference dissipated upon hearing the evidence in the case. She concludes that these results suggest that the dangers to fair trial by pre-trial publicity are yet to be proven.

A few tangential field studies have been made in recent years.[29] A report on a public opinion survey by Cornelius Du Bois, Inc., a New York public relations firm, was attached to the Alger Hiss motion for a change of venue on the grounds of newspaper-fostered prejudice in New York City. Of the New Yorkers questioned, 45.1 per cent said they had formed opinions on the guilt or innocence of Hiss, compared to only 33.8 per cent of those questioned in Rutland,

Vermont, to which city Hiss sought to have his second trial removed. But there were unexpected results. In New York, 21.8 per cent of the interview sample believed Hiss to be guilty and 12.1 per cent thought him innocent. In Rutland, 23.1 per cent thought him guilty and only 5.9 per cent thought him innocent. The fact that less coverage of the case and more anti-Hiss sentiment occurred in Rutland did not support the asserted conclusion that trial there would be fairer. The effect of inflammatory reporting in large, metropolitan communities, where it is most likely to occur, is especially open to question. Some judges in these communities believe that the continuous succession of sensational reporting tends to produce no impression.[30]

In 1953, Elmo Roper applied scientific principles to a legal issue. He was engaged by the NAACP to determine by public opinion poll whether prejudice against a Negro, accused of the rape of a white woman, was higher in the Florida county in which the trial was scheduled than it was in three surrounding counties. Roper concluded that the atmosphere would be more temperate in the other counties and his findings were submitted with an application for a change of venue. But the court refused to consider this "newfangled" approach to legal questions, characterizing the results of the survey as "hearsay."[31]

A different approach to the problem of "trial by newspaper" is suggested by a content analysis which sought to measure press performance in the 1948 Condon controversy.[32] Dr. Edward U. Condon, director of the National Bureau of Standards, had been denounced by the House Committee on Un-American Activities. Almost simultaneously he was cleared by the Department of Commerce, under which his agency was established. Soon, however, he was the center of a tempest involving other Congressional committees, two executive departments, the FBI, learned, scientific, and juristic societies, and eminent personages including the President of the United States. Subsequently the Atomic Energy Commission attested to Condon's loyalty and he was cleared.

The study focused on the press of New York City for an eight-month period covering the time from the original denunciation to the final clearance. Without attempting to interpret their findings, the researchers concluded that, taking the New York press as a whole, there was a preponderance of statements favorable to Condon. There was a wide variation among the nine newspapers in treatment of the case—four appeared to be favorable to him and five were unfavorable. Background material revived for use in the running news stories seemed to have had the effect of building up the case against him by restating the original charges. All newspapers reported the House Committee's promise to give the accused scientist a hearing far more often than they reported its subsequent failure to do so.

And a recent study of pre-trial coverage by North Carolina newspapers[32a] showed that of 568 crime stories in 330 issues of the papers examined, 60 included confessions and admissions of guilt and 45 carried references to prior criminal records. Sixty-three per cent of the stories contained no such details at all; in the 37 per cent that did, lawyers were the source in less than two per cent of the cases while slightly more than 18 per cent of such references were attributed to police, sheriffs or other investigators. Another 15 per cent were attributed to "others," usually witnesses. The investigators, John B. Adams and John Jennrich, felt that the statements credited to police officers were probably quoted from privileged documents such as warrants for arrest. But these sources were not cited specifically in news stories. A noteworthy finding was that lawyers were not the primary source of prejudicial pre-trial statements they are presumed to be. Adams and Jennrich conclude that newspapers should be more specific in their use of attributions.

The free press-fair trial conflict can also be examined in the context of research into the effects of mass communication. The limited knowledge available suggests that mass communication ordinarily does not serve as a necessary and sufficient cause of audience effects, but rather functions among and through "a nexus of mediating factors and influences."[33] Seldom, if ever, is mass communication a sole cause, but often it is a contributory agent which serves to reinforce pre-existing attitudes. The effects of mass communication, whether direct or indirect, are determined by the characteristics of the media and their messages, the communication situation, the nature of the sources and medium, and the existing climate of public opinion. This suggests that we could profitably examine such variables as the emotional tone of crime reports, the circulation of the medium, the depth of its readership or listenership, and the nature of the crime itself.

Reinforcement may be abetted, according to Klapper, by (1) predispositions and the related processes of selective exposure, selective perception and selective retention; (2) the groups, and the norms of the groups to which the audience members belong; (3) interpersonal dissemination of the content of communications; (4) the exercise of opinion leadership; and (5) the nature of mass media in a "free enterprise" society.

Related findings of communication effects studies show that: Susceptibility toward an attitude change may be inversely proportional to the intensity of the initial attitude.[34] Communication content may be more effective in influencing public opinion on new or relatively unstructured issues, or issues on which the audience is unlikely to have prior opinions.[35] Communications may be capable of "inoculating" persons—rendering them more resistant to later communications which are contrary in view.[36] Fear appeals may readily influence opinions.[37] A prestige source may greatly facilitate persuasion, and the media may confer status on a source.[38] An attitude frequently changes from a subordinate to a dominant position when it is justified by the authority of print.[39] Persuasive communication which states explicit conclusions is more likely to be effective than is communication which allows the audience to draw its own conclusions. Communications suggesting specific actions also seem more likely to be followed because they are specific.[40]

There is also evidence that in critical social situations the mass media may play a more crucial role.[41]

Wilbur Schramm suggests that the mass media place our broad social environment in perspective, correlate society's responses to this environment, and transmit the social heritage from one generation to another. They also affect the social mores by contributing heroes and myths to the culture, and, by their power either to mention or ignore, serve as arbiters of social status. And the media assist the larger community in achieving some degree of consensus.[42]

The sociological concept of a two-step flow of communication, although it has been substantially refined and modified, postulates an indirect flow of information via opinion leaders who expose themselves more frequently and more intensely than others to the mass media. The concept implies a network of individuals socially interconnected in functional groups and reference groups through which mass communication messages move in a patterned way; it rejects the notion of an audience of discrete, unorganized individuals linked directly to the media.

At the very least, communication studies suggest that there is probably no simple and direct cause-effect relationship between publicity and jury verdicts—although the converse has been held as a "law" by most Anglo-American courts. The courts have looked "too much for the messages the media bear and too little for the ways in which the audience actively participates and shapes its experience of the media."[43] At the same time, Klapper warns that there is a danger in blindly minimizing the effects and potentialities of mass communications:[44] "In reaping the fruits of discovery that mass media function amid a nexus of other influences, we must not forget that the influences nevertheless differ. Mass media of communication possess various characteristics and capabilities distinct from those of peer groups or opinion leaders. They are, after all, media of *mass* communication, which daily address tremendous cross-sections of the population with a single voice."

So it should be kept in mind that the mass media may be responsible for extensive, dramatic and even dangerous effects.

Particularly, press comment appears to make its strongest impression when conforming to stereotypes already in the public mind. For this reason, such comment may *follow* community bias as often as it *instigates* it. This would suggest that the press is particularly obligated to exercise self-restraint and moral judgment in cases involving atrocious sex crimes, especially where children are the victims; in cases of espionage or treason; and in cases where members of minority groups are before the court. Here the newspaper may act as a catalytic agent in a situation where there is already an acute sensitivity and where community prejudices are already apparent. The reinforcement function of the mass media is the effect most frequently cited by mass media theorists.

As a minimum, responsible segments of the press ask for a systematic study of the free press-fair trial complex before the imposition of either legislation or an angry revival of the contempt power. And it is doubtful whether the courts, the press and the legislatures in concert can do much to neutralize prejudicial predispositions of jurors to the point of making the criminal trial completely antiseptic.

As first steps in shedding light on the vexing problem of "trial by newspaper," exploratory studies are needed to formulate relevant hypotheses consonant with social theory. The basic issue is whether the right to a fair trial can be prejudiced by news reports. Apart from what lawyers and judges may have concluded on this matter, it is by no means a settled question in the social sciences. Prejudice is said to occur when a juror's partiality is disturbed, when his judgment of the issues before him is affected either for or against any party to a trial by the intrusion of material that would not otherwise reach him.[45] An impartial jury is one which knows nothing about a case aside from what has been presented in evidence; or one which, though it has been buffeted by outside information, is able to disregard it and decide the case as if no such extraneous knowledge were available.

There are many approaches to the study of the relationships in the intricate interaction of publicity and jury deliberations. Among these are: experimentation, similar to that described above; interviews with real jurors upon completion of their deliberations, or with judges, attorneys and other officers of the court; participant observation with trained researchers involving themselves with the actual flow of information they disseminate; or the use of survey techniques and content analysis to ascertain how segments of the public are affected by what they read, see or listen to in the media. The social scientist has a range of tools at his disposal. What is needed is a bridge over the gap which now exists between press and bar. Empirical evidence seems to be the logical material with which such a structure could be solidly built.

Within the last year or so, tentative moves have been made to span this abyss in our understanding of how legal processes operate and the effect upon them of outside institutions. An extensive study under conditions of jury simulation has been proposed by Columbia University.[46] And a proposal for an exhaustive study of press coverage of governmental processes has been submitted to the Brookings Institution. The latter contains a "real life" study of pre-trial publicity and its impact on juries.[47] When these two studies are completed, a great deal more will be known about the effects of mass media coverage on jury trials.

The problem remains, however, of relating these large-scale efforts to the attitudes of both parties toward this type of research. The media have long used social science research techniques to assess their products, to boost advertising revenue, and to determine audience uses of the total product. One would expect the media, then, to draw upon this experience and to feel confident that an accumulation of evidence on influence of the media on jury trials would provide them with answers. This does not appear to be the case. Rather they rely upon intuitive speculation.

Prior to the 1956 presidential election, the Council for Communication Research, an affiliate of the Association for Education in Journalism, comprised of research-oriented faculty members of the major journalism schools in the United States, attempted to get approval of publishers for a study of press performance during the campaign. Financial support was to come from the Ford Foundation. Sigma Delta Chi, a professional journalistic society, acting in conjunction with the research group, polled a cross section of newspaper publishers for reaction to such a study. The study was rejected. Indicative of the publishers' position was an editorial in *Editor & Publisher*, the industry's trade magazine, which said support for the study by journalism educators and some editors and publishers was "out of a desire to prove some preconceived notions about the press" and that such a study would be of little value *no matter what its conclusions*.[48] The *Chicago Tribune* called the proposal "remarkable for its silliness."[49]

This reaction to a systematic analysis of the press—despite reliance upon this kind of investigative technique as it relates to the profit motive—reflects how at least a part of the industry looks upon social scientific analysis. That a segment of the press would take the same position when it comes to investigating the possible impact of publicity upon juries does not seem unlikely. It is paradoxical that society's "critic" is so shy of criticism itself.

The bar, on the other hand, has had a rather uneven set of experiences which may hinder its ability to accept this type of evidence. It has relied on deductive approaches for most of its decision-making process. Robert and Theodore Sorenson state:[50] "The future of opinion research evidence in the courts lies with lawyers and social scientists. . . . to the extent that they recognize the need for familiarizing themselves with opinion research methods and presenting them to illuminate rational pathways of decision-making. Without question, the path is open to them."

This type of data most often has been used in business law cases, but some other areas have also been touched upon and discussed. In *Repouille* v. *United States*[51] Judges Learned Hand and Jerome Frank disagreed on how one should determine what is "good moral character." In the majority opinion, Judge Hand allowed that in the absence of a Gallup Poll on the topic he did not know what exactly the prevailing opinion of "good moral character" is—but nevertheless made a decision based on what he thought it was. Justice Frank, dissenting, indicated that the case should be sent back to the lower courts with instructions that further evidence—public opinion evidence—be gathered so that a proper evaluation of the concept could be made. Another argument for a "jural law"—that is scientific generalities to be derived from examination of laws in society—has been presented by Beutel. He says:[52] "Medieval conceptions can no longer be allowed to govern those who live in a modern scientific era." Such arguments, however, seem to be the exception in legal circles. It does seem reasonable that if the courts are willing to predicate decisions upon evidence gathered using scientific tools, they should be willing to appreciate the use of this same kind of data in evaluating legal institutions.

Beyond this kind of research loom these two questions: How effective are existing procedural remedies? And is there evidence enough to support legislation which would restrict crime news and court reporting or otherwise limit the freedom of the press? Since the assassination in Dallas there has been a new ring of urgency to these questions.

CHAPTER 15

A FINAL WORD

"But our belief in absolutes has been shaken in all directions. There is a presumption that all of these defined rights are subject to certain conditions about which we are not yet quite clear. But it seems to us that one of the conditions under which any man ought to hold his rights is *his own good-will* toward his fellow citizens and the public welfare."—William Ernest Hocking[1]

This review of the major tenets of the free press-fair trial debate has perhaps fortified the notion of Mr. Justice Holmes that we live in an intricate web of public and private interests, all of which tend to declare themselves absolute when taken to their logical extreme.

Conflict, impasse, dilemma are words used to characterize the press-bar dialogue. Free press has been pitted against fair trial. Free press has been placed above fair trial and fair trial above free press in our hierarchy of constitutional values. Voluntary codes, judicial remedies, secrecy, the contempt power, legislation, and good judgment have been proposed as ways to balance better the two constitutional rights. The legislatures appear to be waiting for a definitive Supreme Court ruling; the Supreme Court seems receptive to legislative guidance. Certainly there are good and reasonable men on both sides of the question; but somehow professional dogmas emerge from the fray tattered but reinforced; and neither press nor bar will accept primary responsibility for the dissemination of possibly prejudicial information.

Throughout the dialogue a major question remains unexamined and unanswered: what *is* the effect of news reports on jury verdicts? Even though the United States Supreme Court has dismissed the question as being either hypothetical or irrelevant, and has relied instead upon a standard of implied bias, elements of both press and bar have called for a scientific study of the relationship.

216

Lawyer Richard Tinkham has stated that we need a scientific investigation of the subject by an impartial agency of such stature that both the bar and media will respect it. A Washington attorney, Ronald Goldfarb, has observed that "unless the prejudicial effects of press coverage can be clearly shown to exist, the protection of fair trial at the expense of press freedom may be a loss of liberty without corresponding gain." The American Society of Newspaper Editors' Bar-Press Committee reported recently: "We hope that various current proposals for making scientific studies of the effect of news coverage on jurors' attitudes will be undertaken promptly, so that some of the alleged facts supporting the theory that confronts us can be either documented or discounted."

Without such a study the debate will never end, short of a complete alienation of press from bar. The problem is one of human behavior, and only through a systematic examination of the relevant factors of such behavior will the effects of the press on the administration of justice be understood.

To begin with, of course, it must be agreed that valid evidence concerning this relationship will be considered admissible, and that the bar will reappraise its assumptions if need be; and that the press will accept corrective legislation if from such a study it appears to be called for. If the evidence is prejudged, discounted for its abstractness, or if there is a lack of sincerity in its pursuit, the results of these studies will make no impression and will have no effect on the problem. Cumulation of evidence will require time and will tax the patience of press critics.

Impractical as a recommendation for scientific research may sound, the alternative is not attractive: a perpetuation of the now redundant arguments of a 35-year-old debate between press and bar.

We have endorsed the watchdog function of the American press. Under a British system, the Bobby Baker story might have been suppressed beyond the point of social safety. That case, which casts a shadow over the highest levels of government by its disclosures of influence peddling, grew out of the filing of a civil suit against Baker, then Senate Democratic Majority secretary. A perceptive and persistent press simply made a cover-up impossible. The facts emerged, and the informed public's threshold of naivete was raised.

We must not look for solutions in a British context. The immemorial power to smite publication is alien to American tradition; our constitutional system has followed a different route. The contempt power may have taught the British press the rules of evidence, but it has subtracted from the total freedom of Englishmen, and some segments of the English press and bar are concerned. If a judge is of such moral frailty that he must be insulated from criticism and extraneous pressures, society runs a fearful risk in freeing him from public surveillance. To adjust social values so as to throw "a blaze of glory around the courts" is to give the courts the right to a false reputation and to provide them with a mantle which may cover ugliness and sordidness. When free press preempts fair trial in America, balance must be restored within an American value system.

We know, too, that the American judicial system is closely woven into the fabric of politics, and that there can be substantial political rewards for certain kinds of legal performance. Moreover, judicial officers are sometimes well integrated into the power structures of closed communities where justice can be aggrieved even in the full glare of publicity. And experience teaches that there are frame-ups, that the arrest of an underling may relieve pressure on or detract attention from a king-pin, and that police, prosecutor and defense may suppress legitimate evidence to serve an authority other than the law. It is better to hazard some of the abuses which attend the exercise of free speech than to run the risks inevitable when that fundamental right is suppressed. A press properly representing the public will bring social infections to public attention. When it fails, it violates its First Amendment trust. The courts are the people's business; they are not the private preserve of either press or bar.

Lawyers frequently confess their culpability in impairing jury verdicts; the press would seem to be less willing to admit its role in violating basic principles of justice. It is reasonable to assume that freedom of press, fundamental as it is to the well-being of society, was never meant to prevent a man on trial for his life from receiving a fair trial. Segments of the press are simply oblivious to private rights. Jack Ruby's desolate ex-girl friend, Alice Nichols, had testified in his behalf in Dallas. "Just as she left the courtroom," John Kaplan and Jon Waltz relate in their book *The Trial of Jack Ruby,* "the flashbulbs began exploding before her face, and this additional stress was enough to destroy her brittle composure. She broke into tears and struggled to get away from the pursuing photographers. She ran out of the courthouse and down the steps, followed by a shouting mob of some twenty photographers snapping pictures all the way. They had been told to get a picture of Ruby's girl friend and this they intended to do. Finally, about a half a block from the courthouse, the strange procession ended when Miss Nichols, out of breath, permitted herself to be surrounded by her pursuers, who snapped picture after picture as she sobbed and shouted incoherently."[2]

The ideal is a press both free and fair. It is estimated that only about eight per cent of criminal cases come to jury trials, and only a fraction of these are covered by the press. Even though these figures suggest the improbability of fair trial being diminished for more than a handful of defendants each year, we should take no comfort. One such human tragedy in a decade is moral grounds for concrete corrective measures in the absence of overriding opposing rights.

Recent huge libel judgments are pointed to by some newsmen as an adequate deterrent to irresponsibility. They may be. But truth and fair comment protect the press against libel. What may be true and fair for legal purposes, may, when published, be severely prejudicial to an accused.

Former Justice Arthur Goldberg has recommended a joint standing committee of press and bar to provide continuing answers to recurring problems of crime reporting. Such a press-bar council could be useful. As long as there is consultation and a sincere and constructive exchange of opinion, a higher level of performance on both sides is possible. Lawyers and newsmen may become increasingly aware of the fact that some kinds of pre-verdict comment are socially unacceptable. Furthermore, the flexible Katzenbach rules and the bilateral press-bar codes should be given some opportunity to prove their worth.

But until evidence has been collected to show or to deny a causal relationship between pre-verdict information and impaired jury verdicts, a moratorium should be declared on all attempts at restrictive legislation, a revival of the arbitrary contempt power, or unilateral codes designed to inhibit or interfere with press coverage, without corresponding gains to the fair administration of justice.

It is urgent that recent proposals made by the Brookings Institution and Columbia University for a scientific study of press coverage of judicial and legislative proceedings, with emphasis on pre-trial reporting, find financial backing. An unconditional grant from CBS has been declined by Brookings since it was not thought wise to accept funds for such a project from a news organization. But if such a study is permitted to die in embryo, the free press-fair trial dilemma will persist, and impatient, ill-considered laws may be the consequence. As long as these two constitutional rights remain on a collision course, legislation, applying to both newsmen and lawyers is inevitable, for this is the manner in which we customarily seek social equilibrium. And the business of government would be greatly impeded if all power were withheld simply because of a possibility of abuse.

Jurors are probably hardier souls than we have imagined, and the search for the unbiased juror is as futile as the search for the Holy

Grail. But there are antipathetic situations in which community predispositions are already aligned against an accused. Press comment makes its strongest impression when reinforcing stereotypes already in the public mind and reflecting community prejudice; and the editor who is insensitive to individual rights or to the presumption of innocence can be a catalytic agent in an already explosive situation. Under such pressures, our judicial system is also put to the test. It is the environing atmosphere which may determine the tone and texture of justice.

Until more reliable evidence concerning the influence of inflammatory press publicity upon judges and jurors has been gathered and incorporated into legal thinking, the press has an obligation to evaluate concomitant private and public rights in deciding what to print; and, in this regard, two assumptions will have to be considered: (1) the public interest sometimes demands that information violative of private rights be published; and (2) on occasion the mass media are capable of impairing the rights of an accused without any overriding social interest being served. It follows that the American editor, being relatively exempt from judicial or other governmental restraints, has a moral question to face in deciding whether or not to publish facts in his file. He has no moral right and therefore should have no legal right to be deliberately in error. Considerations of a professional or commercial nature are secondary to questions having to do with the life or reputation of a defendant. Although rights are interdependent and none is purely private or wholly public, social rights are ultimately the sum total of individual rights. We therefore deliberately destroy an individual right at our peril. But in those instances when public and private rights appear to be irreconcilable, a choice may have to be made. A civilized society respects human life, liberty and happiness: it also recognizes that freedom of speech and press is close to the central core of all freedoms. Neither can be held lightly. Where a choice must be made, it must be made in the clear conscience that, in the particular circumstances, either the individual or social right is overriding.

Any attempt to assess the influence of publicity in creating "a community pattern of deep and bitter prejudice"—the lower limit in the *Irvin* case—would necessarily take into account the level of public interest in the case, the initial attitudes of the community, the question of pendency, whether or not the speech at issue legitimately strengthens the spirit of inquiry, the probable effect of the publication on witnesses, whether the case is civil or criminal, and the nature of the crime itself. At the focal point of the analysis would lie such questions as: to what extent do the mass media create community attitudes; and to what extent do community attitudes prevail upon the minds of jurors? Public opinion surveys and other behavioral research would assist in providing reliable answers to these questions.

The courts will continue to use their procedural remedies to protect fair trial, for, as Justice Douglas has observed, "Our remedy for excessive comment by the press is not the punishment of editors, but the granting of new trials, changes in venue, or continuances to the parties who are prejudiced." In its dedication to due process of law, the Supreme Court is recommending to the states a fairly liberal standard of proof of prejudice in the use of these judicial devices. Moreover, the granting of mistrials and new trials may also serve to reprove editors who, though they have no personal stake in a trial, may reconsider their policy when they find that publications of confessions and criminal records, serving no substantial public interest, have resulted in the reversal of otherwise valid convictions. The press, of course, must be vigilant in its cooperation.

The prosecution in the Appalachin conspiracy case was anxious to guard against a prejudiced jury being used as grounds for a dismissal or mistrial. Twenty gangland defendants were on trial for having conspired to commit perjury and obstruct justice in connection with the November 14, 1957 "crime convention." Pre-trial publicity had been so extensive that Federal District Judge Irving R. Kaufman took steps to protect the trial from further public comment by delaying certain publicity-provoking indictments until after a verdict; related criminal and civil trials and hearings were adjourned; and arrangements were made to conduct some arguments in camera.

Milton R. Wessel, a special assistant to the Attorney-General, wrote letters to all New York newspapers, radio and television stations requesting cooperation in postponing further public comment until evidence was introduced at the trial. The press generally complied; but unfortunately for the future of such voluntary agreements, the convictions were overturned by an appellate court as being based on "bad law."[3] It is extremely doubtful that a soundproof curtain between arrest and trial will invariably serve the cause of justice.

As soon as the bar begins enforcing its own ethical canons and modifying the adversary system so as to take the one-upmanship out of the trial process, the press will be under great pressure to adopt similar forms of institutional self-restraint. If it fails to do so, restrictive legislation should come as no surprise. And the Supreme Court may not stand in the way of such legislation, for, as has been noted, the court has shown a deep concern in recent terms with fairness in criminal procedure. There is no reason to believe that it will turn its back on the publicity issue.

Journalism—in newsroom and classroom—is being challenged as never before to reflect a new spirit of professional maturity. As the coholder of both freedom and responsibility under the Bill of Rights, the press has much at stake in the final solution to the vexing free press-fair trial problem. The higher the right the greater the responsibility for its moral exercise. Ideally, free press and fair trial must be like two themes in a symphony, simulated, balanced and in harmony: realistically, the relationship between the two constitutional values is ripe for research and well within the boundaries of human comprehension.

In the meantime, let us observe the admonition of Zechariah Chafee, Jr., that "the only direct cure for these evils lies in the internal ideals of the enterprises . . . It is mainly a question of revising professional standards . . . The law can take us only a little way toward the ideal of fairness to all. What we desire from the instrumentalities of communication which citizens see or hear, where personality becomes a vital factor, is responsibility to different elements in the community; and this is largely beyond the reach of the law."[4]

REFERENCES

CHAPTER 1

1 *Editor & Publisher,* August 21, 1954.
2 *Newsweek,* January 3, 1955.
3 *Ibid.*
4 *Editor & Publisher,* October 30, 1954.
5 *Ibid.,* January 8, 1955.
6 *Sheppard* v. *Ohio,* 135 N.E. 2d 342 (1956).
7 *Sheppard* v. *Maxwell,* 231 F. Supp. 37 (S.D. Ohio 1964).
8 Paul Holmes in *The Sheppard Murder Case* (New York: David McKay & Co., 1961) develops an interesting argument for Sheppard's innocence, and cites press, prosecutor and court for violating the defendant's rights. Holmes covered the case for the *Chicago Tribune.*
8a 346 F. 2d 707 (1965)
9 After veniremen are sworn, a defendant is allowed an unlimited number of challenges for cause during the *voir dire* (literally "to speak the truth") examination in which prospective jurors are questioned to ascertain whether they are incompetent to serve by reason of having an interest in the cause or of having prejudice which might affect their impartiality with respect to the case. When a jury has been sworn, the defendant still has a stipulated number of preemptory challenges—usually from 15 to 20 in a criminal case.
10 *Irvin* v. *State,* 139 N.E. 2d 898 (1957).
11 *Irvin* v. *Dowd,* 153 F. Supp. 531 (1957); *Irvin* v. *Dowd,* 251 F. 2d 548 (1958).
12 *Irvin* v. *Dowd,* 359 U.S. 394 (1959).
13 *Irvin* v. *Dowd,* 366 U.S. 717 (1961).
14 *Ibid.,* 723.
15 *Ibid.,* 727-28.
16 366 U.S. 716 (1961).
17 *Irvin* v. *Dowd,* 366 U.S. 717, 730 (1961).
18 *People* v. *Van Duyne,* 204 A.2d 841 (1964).
19 Barbara Spector and Marilyn Van Saun, "New Interpretation of Crime News Curbs Keeps Newsmen Hopping—and Guessing," *News Workshop* (Department of Journalism, New York University, March 1965) p. 1 and *passim.*

CHAPTER 2

1 Statement of the American Civil Liberties Union, "Civil Liberties Aspects of the Lee Harvey Oswald Case, and Developments Arising Out of the Assassination of President Kennedy," December 6, 1963, *passim.*
2 *Report of the President's Commission on the Assassination of President John F. Kennedy* (1964), pp. 201-42 and *passim.*
3 Bradley S. Greenberg and Edwin B. Parker (eds.), *The Kennedy Assassination and the American Public: Social Communication* (Stanford: Stanford University Press, 1965).

CHAPTER 3

[1] "Televising Parts of a Criminal Trial Over the Objection of the Accused in a Trial of Widespread Public Interest Is a Violation of Due Process of Law Even When No Prejudice Is Shown," 43 *Texas Law Review* 992-95 (July 1965).

[2] William O. Douglas, "The Public Trial and the Free Press," 46 *American Bar Association Journal* 842-43 (August 1960).

[3] *Estes* v. *Texas*, 380 U.S. 532 (1965).

[4] 373 U.S. 723 (1963).

[5] Fred Rodell, "TV or No TV in Court?" *New York Times Magazine*, April 12, 1964.

[6] *In re Hearings Concerning Canon 35*, 296 P. 2d 465 (Col. 1956). Don Brod, "First Step in an Unplowed Field: The Billie Sol Estes Case," (unpublished seminar paper, University of Minnesota, 1966), p. 14 and *passim*.

[7] *Graham* v. *People*, 302 P. 2d 737 (Col. 1956).

[8] The Special Committee on Radio and Television of the Association of the Bar of the City of New York, *Radio, Television, and the Administration of Justice* (New York: Columbia University Press, 1965).

[9] *Ibid.*, p. 70-72. *United States* v. *Rees*, 193 F. Supp. 864 (D.Md. 1961).

[10]

[11] *New York Times*, September 25, 1962.

[12] *Saturday Review*, July 10, 1965.

[13] *Broadcasting*, June 14, 1965.

[14] *Lyles* v. *State of Oklahoma*, 330 P. 2d 734(1958).

[15] *Okla. Stat. 1961*, Title 5, at 384-85.

[16] June 9, 1965.

[17] June 13, 1965.

[18] June 8, 1965.

[19] Peacock and Teague, *op. cit.*

[20] *Editor & Publisher*, June 12, 1965.

[21] *Editor & Publisher*, December 11, 1965.

CHAPTER 4

[1] CBS Reports, "The Press and the Law," January 18, 1965.

[2] *New York Times*, March 20, 1965.

[3] A survey conducted by Clifton Daniel, managing editor of the *New York Times*, showed that while there were 11,724 felonies committed in New York City in January 1965, only 41 of them were even mentioned in the *Daily News*, the newspaper which publishes the most crime news.

CHAPTER 5

[1] "Justice and the Press, Communication Inside and Outside the Courtroom," 6 *St. Louis University Law Journal* 487 (1961).

[2] Oscar Hallam, "Some Object Lessons on Publicity in Criminal Trials," 24 *Minnesota Law Review* 435 (1940); Walter Lippmann, *Problems of Journalism* (proceedings of the American Society of Newspaper Editors), 1936, pp. 154-56.

[3] Harold W. Sullivan, *Trial by Newspaper* (Hyannis, Mass.: The Patriot Press, 1961). A collection of recent cases also assuming a direct cause-effect relationship between publicity and jury verdicts is Howard Felsher and Michael Rosen, *The Press in the Jury Box* (New York: The Macmillan Company, 1966).

[4] *United States* v. *Accardo*, 298 F. 2d 133 (1962).

[5] "Did the Press Kill Caryl Chessman?" *The Progressive,* December 1960.

[6] *Geagan* v. *Gavin,* 292 F. 2d 244 (1st Cir. 1961), cert. denied, 370 U.S. 903 (1962).

[7] D. M. Treuhaft, "Trial by Headline," *Nation,* October 26, 1957.

[8] Gene Marine, "The Jury Said 'Death'," *Nation,* May 19, 1956.

[9] "Newspapers and the Pursuit of Justice," *Saturday Review,* April 3, 1954.

[10] Harold W. Sullivan, *Trial by Newspaper, op. cit.*

CHAPTER 6

[*] Research and writing for this chapter was done partly by Donald Brod, assistant professor of journalism at Wisconsin State University (River Falls).

[1] *Secrecy and Publicity* (Baltimore: The Johns Hopkins Press, 1961), p. vii.

[2] Leonard W. Levy, *Jefferson & Civil Liberties: The Darker Side* (Cambridge, Mass.: The Belknap Press of Harvard University Press, 1963), pp. 70-71.

[3] *New York Times,* March 27, 1965.

[4] *Richmond* (Va.) *Times-Dispatch,* April 5, 1965.

[5] *Free Press and Fair Trial,* Hearings before the Subcommittee on Constitutional Rights and Subcommittee on Improvements in Judicial Machinery of the Committee on the Judiciary, United States Senate, Eighty-Ninth Congress, First Session, on S. 290, Washington, D.C., 1966, p. 42

[6] *Ibid.,* p. 70.   [7] *Congressional Record—Senate,* June 27, 1963, p. 11259.

[8] Sidney Lens, "The Pursuit of Jimmy Hoffa," *Progressive,* February, 1963.

[9] Hearings on S. 290, p. 467.

[10] *Coleman* v. *Newark Morning Ledger Co.,* 140 A.2d 193 (N.J., 1959).

[11] Rourke, *op. cit.,* p. 136 and *passim.*   [12] *Ibid.,* p. 203.

[13] *Campbell* v. *New York Evening Post,* 137 N.E. 153 (N.Y., 1927).

[14] Harold L. Nelson, *Libel in News of Congressional Investigating Committees* (Minneapolis: The University of Minnesota Press, 1961), Chapter VIII.

[15] *Congressional Record—House,* Feb. 18, 1965, pp. 2950-2953.

[16] Hearings on S. 290, p. 469.

[17] *Culombe* v. *Connecticut,* 367 U.S. 568 (1961).

[18] Gerald Stern, "The Two Forums of a Criminal Trial: The Courtroom and the Press," 14 *Syracuse Law Review,* (Spring 1963).

[19] Hearings on S. 290, p. 365.

[20] *New York Times,* Dec. 12, 17, 18, and 19, 1948.

[21] A. J. Liebling, *The Press* (New York: Ballantine Books, Inc., 1961), pp. 143-157.

[22] *Ibid.,* p. 157.   [23] *New York Times,* June 27 and 28, 1958.

[24] *Congressional Record—House,* Aug. 13, 1958, p. 17365.   [25] *Ibid.,* pp. 17373

[26] *Beck* v. *Washington,* 369 U.S. 541 (1962).   [27] Hearings on S. 290, p. 171.

[28] Edward Bennett Williams, *One Man's Freedom* (New York: Atheneum, 1962). Williams appeals for the protection of individual rights against the power of the state, i.e., the public, whatever the circumstances.

[29] Lens, *op. cit.*   [30] Hearings on S. 290, p. 176.   [31] Lens, *op. cit.*

[32] Hearings on S. 290, pp. 172-173.   [33] *Time,* Jan. 11, 1963.

[34] *Congressional Record—Senate,* June 27, 1963, pp. 11245-11247.

[35] *New York Times,* March 3, 1965.   [36] Hearings on S. 290, pp. 174-175.

[37] *New York Times,* March 3 and 5, 1965.

[38] Hearings on S. 290, pp. 213-214.

[39] *Minneapolis Star,* Jan. 31, 1966, and *Time,* Feb. 11, 1966.

CHAPTER 7

[1] James L. High (ed.), *Speeches of Lord Erskine* (Chicago: Callaghan & Company, 1876), p. 525.

[2] Robert Steele, *Tudor and Stuart Proclamations* (Oxford, 1910), No. 2847, cited in Fredrick S. Siebert, *Freedom of the Press in England, 1476–1776* (Urbana: University of Illinois Press, 1952), p. 201.

[3] *People* v. *Croswell*, 3 Johns. Cas. 337 (1804).

[4] Leonard W. Levy, *Legacy of Suppression* (Cambridge: Harvard University Press, 1960), p. 263 ff.

[5] *Smith* v. *California*, 361 U.S. 147, 157–59 (1959).

[6] *Free Speech and Its Relation to Self-Government* (New York: Harper and Brothers, 1948).

[7] *Dennis* v. *United States*, 341 U.S. 494, 523 (1951).

[8] Roscoe Pound, "A Survey of Social Interests," 57 *Harvard Law Review* 2 (1943).

[9] Peter Bachrach, "Balance of Interest Doctrine," 14 *Western Political Quarterly* 391 (June 1961).

[10] *Kovacs* v. *Cooper*, 336 U.S. 77, 95 (1949).

[11] *Roth* v. *United States*, 354 U.S. 476, 484 (1957).

[12] *Ullman* v. *United States*, 350 U.S. 422 (1956).

[13] *West Virginia State Board of Education* v. *Barnette*, 319 U.S. 624, 648 (1943).

[14] *Schenck* v. *United States*, 249 U.S. 47 (1919).

[15] *Abrams* v. *United States*, 250 U.S. 616 (1919).

[16] *Schaefer* v. *United States*, 251 U.S. 466 (1920).

[17] Paul A. Freund, *The Supreme Court of the United States.* (New York: The World Book Publishing Company, 1962), p. 44.

[18] Wallace Mendelson, "Clear and Present Danger—From Schenck to Dennis," 52 *Columbia Law Review* 313–33 (1952). The case reference is *West Virginia State Board of Education* v. *Barnette, op. cit.*

[19] *Dennis* v. *United States*, 314 U.S. 494 (1951).

[20] *Gitlow* v. *New York*, 268 U.S. 652 (1925).

[21] *Near* v. *Minnesota*, 283 U.S. 697 (1931); *Lovell* v. *City of Griffin*, 303 U.S. 444 (1938); *Grosjean* v. *American Press Company*, 297 U.S. 233 (1936); *Yates* v. *United States*, 345 U.S. 298 (1957).

[22] *Winters* v. *New York*, 333 U.S. 507 (1948).

[23] *Speiser* v. *Randall*, 357 U.S. 513, 526 (1958).

[24] *NAACP* v. *Alabama ex rel. Patterson*, 357 U.S. 449 (1958).

[25] Jay W. Jensen, "Freedom of the Press: A Concept in Search of a Philosophy," in *Social Responsibility of the Newspress.* (Marquette University College of Journalism, 1962).

[26] The Commission On Freedom of the Press, *A Free and Responsible Press.* (Chicago: University of Chicago Press, 1947), p. 131.

CHAPTER 8

[1] F. H. Heller, *The Sixth Amendment.* (Lawrence: The University of Kansas Press, 1951), p. 46.

[2] *Snyder* v. *Massachusetts*, 291 U.S. 97, 137 (1934). See also *Cox* v. *Louisiana* 379 U.S. 559, 562 (1965); *Jackson* v. *Denno,* 378 U.S. 368, 377 (1964).

[3] *Hurtado* v. *California*, 110 U.S. 516 (1884).

[4] William J. Brennan, Jr., *The Bill of Rights and the States* (Santa Barbara: Center for the Study of Democratic Institutions, 1961), p. 11 and *passim*. Justice Black, dissenting in *Adamson* v. *California,* 332 U.S. 46, 68 (1947), and in subsequent cases, contends that the Fourteenth Amendment did indeed make all of the federal Bill of Rights binding upon the states. But this opinion has yet to command the support of a majority of the Court.

[5] *Gitlow* v. *New York,* 268 U.S. 652 (1925).

[6] *Patterson* v. *Colorado,* 205 U.S. 454 (1907).

[7] *Gilbert* v. *Minnesota,* 254 U.S. 325 (1920).

[8] *Dorr* v. *United States,* 195 U.S. 138 (1904).

[9] *Frank* v. *Magnum,* 237 U.S. 309 (1915).

[10] *Moore* v. *Dempsey,* 261 U.S. 86 (1923).

[11] 287 U.S. 45 (1932).

[12] *Tumey* v. *Ohio,* 273 U.S. 510 (1927).

[13] *Pierre* v. *Louisiana,* 306 U.S. 354 (1939).

[14] *Upshaw* v. *United States,* 335 U.S. 410 (1948); *Ashcraft* v. *Tennessee,* 322 U.S. 143 (1944); *McNabb* v. *United States,* 318 U.S. 332 (1943).

[15] *Chambers* v. *Florida,* 309 U.S. 227 (1940).

[16] *Brown* v. *Mississippi,* 297 U.S. 278 (1936). See also *Lyons* v. *Oklahoma,* 322 U.S. 596 (1943); *Payne* v. *Arkansas,* 356 U.S. 560, 568 (1958).

[17] *Mooney* v. *Holohan,* 294 U.S. 103 (1935).

[18] *Rochin* v. *California,* 342 U.S. 165 (1952).

[19] *Robinson* v. *California,* 370 U.S. 660 (1962).

[20] *Griffin* v. *Illinois,* 351 U.S. 12 (1956).

[21] *Gideon* v. *Wainwright,* 372 U.S. 335 (1963). See Anthony Lewis, *Gideon's Trumpet* (New York: Random House, 1964).

[22] 378 U.S. 478 (1964).

[23] *Mallory* v. *United States,* 354 U.S. 449 (1957).

[24] *Colombe* v. *Connecticut,* 367 U.S. 568 (1961); *Rogers* v. *Richmond,* 365 U.S. 534 (1961); *Haynes* v. *Washington,* 373 U.S. 503 (1963).

[25] *Mapp* v. *Ohio,* 367 U.S. 643 (1961).

[26] *Nardone* v. *United States,* 302 U.S. 379 (1937).

[27] *Malloy* v. *Hogan,* 378 U.S. 1 (1964).

[28] *Pointer* v. *Texas,* 380 U.S. 400 (1965). The Court also held that a pretrial hearing can have a profound effect on the trial itself and effectively prevent an accused from having a fair trial.

[29] *Murphy* v. *Waterfront Commission of New York Harbor,* 378 U.S. 52 (1964).

[30] *Turner* v. *Louisiana,* 85 S.Ct. 546 (1965).

[31] *Convicting the Innocent* (New Haven: Yale University Press, 1932), p. 371.

[32] Harold Burtt, *Legal Psychology* (New York: Prentice-Hall, Inc., 1931), cited in Jerome H. Spingarn, "Newspapers and the Pursuit of Justice," *Saturday Review,* April 3, 1954. See also Theodore Reik, *The Compulsion to Confess* (New York: Farrar, Straus & Cudahy, 1959).

[33] Lloyd Paul Stryker, *The Art of Advocacy* (New York: Simon and Schuster, 1954), pp. 212-13.

[34] James A. Wechsler, "New York County Lawyer's Association Conference on Fair Trial-Free Press," 11 *Bar Bulletin* 25 (May 1953).

[35] *West Chicago Ry.* v. *Grenfell,* 90 Ill. App. 30 (1900). See also *United States* v. *Borelli,* 336 F. 2d 376 (2d Cir. 1964).

[36] *Beck* v. *United States,* 298 F. 2d 622 (1962).

37 *United States* v. *Rees,* 193 F. Supp. 861, 864 (1961).

38 *Craig* v. *Harney,* 331 U.S. 367, 394-5 (1947).

39 Simon H. Rifkind, "New York County Lawyers Association Conference on Fair Trial-Free Press," 11 *Bar Bulletin* 7 (May 1953).

CHAPTER 9

1 *Abrams* v. *United States,* 250 U.S. 628 (1919); *Patterson* v. *Colorado,* 205 U.S. 462 (1907).

2 *Pennekamp* v. *Florida,* 328 U.S. 331 (1946).

3 William O. Douglas, "The Public Trial and the Free Press," 46 *American Bar Association Journal* 844 (August 1960); and *The Right of the People* (Garden City, N. Y.: Doubleday & Company, Inc., 1958), p. 52.

4 *In re Murchison,* 349 U.S. 133 (1955).

5 *Cox* v. *Louisiana,* 379 U.S. 559, 583 (1965).

6 Fred E. Inbau (ed.), *Free Press—Fair Trial: A Report of the Proceedings of a Conference on Prejudicial News Reporting in Criminal Cases* (Chicago: Northwestern University School of Law and the Medill School of Journalism, 1964), p. 83.

7 Claude R. Sowle, "Press-Created Prejudice in Criminal Trials—A Mirage?" *Nieman Reports,* September 1964.

8 J. Skelly Wright, "What the Newsman Can Contribute to Criminal Justice—A Judge's View," address before the Section on Judicial Administration of the American Bar Association Seminar on "The Right of Fair Trial," New York, August 11, 1964.

9 Louis L. Jaffe, "Trial By Newspaper," 40 *New York Law Review* 504 (May 1965).

10 Erwin Griswold, "When Newsmen Become Newsmakers," *Saturday Review,* October 24, 1964.

11 Milton R. Wessel, "Controlling Prejudicial Publicity in Criminal Trials," 48 *Journal of the American Judicature Society* 105 (October 1964).

12 *United States* v. *Milanovich,* 303 F. 2d 626 (C.A. 4th 1962).

13 246 F. 2d 190 (C.A. 5th 1957).

14 George Thiem, *The Hodge Scandal* (New York: St. Martin's Press, 1963).

15 Edward T. Folliard, "A Dramatic Case in Point," *The Bulletin* of the American Society of Newspaper Editors, February 1, 1965.

16 Richard D. Peters, "In New York: Alert Journalism Prevents Two Serious Miscarriages of Justice," *The Bulletin* of the American Society of Newspaper Editors, March 1, 1965.

17 Emmett Dedmon, "Three Citations from the Chicago Sun-Times," *The Bulletin* of the American Society of Newspaper Editors, March 1, 1965.

18 Hugh R. Dillon, "Pre-Trial Publicity—A View from Behind the Bars," *Editor & Publisher,* May 8, 1965.

19 Inbau (ed.), *Free Press-Fair Trial, op. cit.,* p. 96 ff.

20 Percy Hoskins, "The Press and the Administration of Justice," *Federal Probation,* June 1958, pp. 31-35.

21 Herbert Brucker, "Freedom of the Press in Crime News Reporting," in Inbau, *Free Press-Free Trial, op. cit.,* p. 96 and *passim.*

22 Gerald Stern, "The Two Forums of a Criminal Trial: The Courtroom and the Press," 14 *Syracuse Law Review* 450 (1963).

23 Clifton Daniel, "Pre-trial Publicity," *Nieman Reports,* September 1965.

24 Edward Bennett Williams, "On Trial: Jimmy Hoffa and Adam Clayton Powell," *Saturday Evening Post,* June 16, 1962.

25 Jerome Frank, *Courts on Trial* (Princeton, N. J.: Princeton University Press, 1949), p. 92; David Dressler, "Trial by Combat in American Courts," *Harper's,* April 1961.

26 Anthony Lewis, "The Case of 'Trial By Press'," *New York Times Magazine,* October 18, 1964.

27 *Near* v. *Minnesota,* 283 U.S. 697 (1931).

28 *The Liberty of the Press, Speech, and Public Worship* (London: Macmillan and Company, 1880), p. 41.

CHAPTER 10

1 *Shepherd* v. *Florida,* 341 U.S. 50 (1951).

2 Walter Gellhorn, *American Rights: The Constitution in Action* (New York: The Macmillan Company, 1960), p. 39.

3 *People* v. *Stroble,* 226 P. 2d 330 (1951).

4 *Stroble* v. *California,* 343 U.S. 181 (1952).

5 *Beck* v. *Washington,* 369 U.S. 541 (1962).

6 *Rideau* v. *Louisiana,* 373 U.S. 723 (1963).

7 *Marshall* v. *United States,* 360 U.S. 310 (1959).

8 *Briggs* v. *United States,* 221 F. 2d 636 (1955).

9 *United States* v. *Powell,* 171 F. Supp. 202 (1959).

10 *Coppedge* v. *United States,* 272 F. 2d 504 (1959).

11 *United States ex rel. Bloeth* v. *Denno,* 313 F. 2d 364 (2d Cir.) cert. denied 372 U.S. 978 (1963).

12 200 F. Supp. 885 (1962).   13 *Singer* v. *State,* 109 S. 2d 7 (1959).

14 *People* v. *Genovese,* 180 N.E. 2d 419 (1962).

15 William O. Douglas, "The Public Trial and the Free Press," 46 *American Bar Association Journal* 841 (August 1960).

16 *United States* v. *Florio,* 13 F.R.D. 296 (1952).

17 *For Prejudice in the District or Division.* The court upon motion of the defendant shall transfer the proceeding as to him to another district or division if the court is satisfied that there exists in the district or division where the prosecution is pending so great a prejudice against the defendant that he cannot obtain a fair and impartial trial in that district or division.

18 *Jones* v. *State,* 45 A. 2d 350 (Md. 1946). In Maryland, a defendant in a capital case can have a change of venue by merely suggesting that he cannot get a fair trial (Maryland Code, Art. 75 § 109 (Flack's Annotated Code, 1939), (Md. Const. Arts. VII, VIII). Other states have statutes permitting a change of venue generally at the discretion of the trial judge.

19 *Powell* v. *Alabama,* 286 U.S. 540 (1931); *Hopkins* v. *People,* 1 P. 2d 937 (Col. 1931); *State* v. *Bigler,* 23 P. 2d 598 (Kans. 1933); *People* v. *Connors,* 230 N. W. 931 (Mich. 1930); *United States* v. *Dioguardi,* 147 F. Supp. 421 (1956); *People* v. *Lyon,* 288 P. 2d 57 (Calif. 1955); *People* v. *Broady,* 90 N.Y.S. 2d 864 (1949); *Commonwealth* v. *Bonomi,* 140 N.E. 2d 140 (Mass. 1957); *Sorber* v. *State,* 76 So. 2d 234 (Miss. 1954), cert. denied, 350 U.S. 876 (1955); *Shockley* v. *United States,* 166 F. 2d 704, cert. denied 334 U.S. 850 (1947).

In *People* v. *Brindell,* 185 N.Y.S. 533 (1921) the court said that "if newspaper articles furnished grounds for removal, no defendant could ever be tried in this county for a spectacular crime."

In *State* v. *Gordon,* 155 N.W. 59 (1915), the Supreme Court of North Dakota, in a typical reaction to a request for a change of venue, said proof that prejudice exists or that a derogatory article has been published in one of the cities of the county is not proof that a fair trial cannot be had in the county at large, or that such county as a whole is prejudiced. "In order to justify a change of venue on account of the excitement or public prejudice," said the court, "it must be shown that its natural tendency will be to intimidate or swerve the jury."

[20] 20 Conn. Sup. 242, 131 A. 2d 337 (1957), aff'd 147 Conn. Sup. 242, 131 A. 2d 239 (1960).

[21] *Culombe* v. *Connecticut,* 367 U.S. 568 (1961).

[22] Note, "Controlling Press and Radio Influences On Trials," 63 *Harvard Law Review* 840–43, (1950).

[23] *Ibid.,* p. 846.

[24] *United States* v. *Feldman,* 299 F. 2d 914, 919 (CA 2d 1962); *Dranow* v. *United States,* 307 F. 2d 545 (CA 8th 1962); *United States* v. *Carruthers,* 152 F. 2d 512 (CA 7th 1945); *Rowley* v. *United States,* 185 F. 2d 523 (CA 8th 1950).

[25] *United States* v. *Crosby,* 294 F. 2d 928, 949–50 (CA 2d 1961); *Cohen* v. *United States,* 297 F. 2d 760, 763–64 (CA 2d 1962); *United States* v. *Vita,* 294 F. 2d 524 (CA 2d 1961).

[26] *People* v. *Sandgren,* 75 N.Y.S. 2d 753 (1947); *United States* v. *Hoffa* 156 F. Supp. 495 (1957).

[27] *Reynolds* v. *United States,* 98 U.S. 145 (1879).

[28] Hurd. Rev. St. Ill., 1885, p. 752, c. 78, 14.

[29] *Wilson* v. *People,* 94 Ill. 324 (1880).

[30] *Spies and Others* v. *People,* 12 N.E. 865, 991 (1887).

[31] *Spies* v. *Illinois,* 123 U.S. 131 (1887).

[32] *Holt* v. *United States,* 218 U.S. 245 (1910).

[33] *Commonwealth* v. *Crehan,* 345 Mass. 609, 188 N.E. 2d 923 (1963).

[34] *United States* v. *Weber,* 197 F. 2d 237 (1952).

[35] *United States* v. *Carruthers, op. cit.; United States ex rel. Darcy* v. *Handy,* 351 U.S. 462 (1955).

[36] 193 F. 2d 355 (1951).   [37] *State* v. *Snowden,* 5 So. 2d 355 (1941).

[38] 102 F. Supp. 824 (D.C. Pa. 1952). See G. H. Fischer, "Jurors Reading of Newspaper Account of Trial in Criminal Cases During Its Progress as Ground for Mistrial, New Trial or Reversal," 31 *American Law Reports Annotated,* 2nd series, pp. 417-36.

[39] *Shushan* v. *United States,* 117 F. 2d 110 (1941), cert. denied 313 U.S. 574 (1941); *Richardson* v. *Commonwealth,* 312 S.W. 2d 470 (Ky. 1958).

[40] *Commonweath* v. *Dougherty,* 32 *Erie Co. L. J.* 126 (1948).

[41] *Quinn* v. *State,* 16 P. 591 (Okla. 1932).

[42] *State* v. *Lilja,* 193 N.W. 178 (Minn. 1923).

[43] *Miller* v. *Kentucky,* 40 F. 2d 820 (1930); *Gicinto* v. *United States,* 212 F. 2d 8, cert. denied, 348 U.S. 884 (1954); *Ferrari* v. *United States,* 244 F. 2d 138, cert. denied 355 U.S. 873 (1957).

[44] *State* v. *Cunningham,* 144 P. 2d 303 (Ore. 1943). Walter J. Kennedy, "Trial Practice—Mistrial—Juror's Reading of Newspaper Account of Trial in Criminal Cases," 4 *Kansas Law Review* 131 (1955).

[45] *Reining* v. *United States,* 167 F. 2d 362 (1948); *Howell* v. *State,* 247 S.W. 2d 952 (Ark. 1952).

[46] *Weer* v. *State,* 37 N.E. 2d 537 (Ind. 1941).

[47] *Tinkoff* v. *United States*, 86 F. 2d 868 (1937); *State* v. *Soltau*, 2 N.W. 2d 155 (Minn. 1942).

[48] 200 F. 2d 666 (2d Cir. 1952). cert. denied, 345 U.S. 965 (1953).

[49] *Grammer* v. *State*, 100 A. 2d 257 (1953).

[50] *Baltimore Radio Show* v. *Maryland*, 67 A. 2d 497 (1949).

[51] *Meyer et al.* v. *Cadwalader*, 49 Fed. 32 (1891).

[52] 105 Fed. 371 (1900). [53] 295 Fed. 437 (1924).

[54] *Mattox* v. *United States*, 146 U.S. 140 (1892).

[55] *People* v. *Hryciuk*, 122 N.E. 2d 532 (1954).

[56] *Wiley* v. *State*, 332 S.W. 2d 725 (1960).

[57] *Ball* v. *State*, 163 P. 259 (Ariz. 1918).

[58] *Capps* v. *State*, 159 S.W. 193 (Ark. 1913).

[59] *People* v. *Stokes*, 37 P. 207 (Calif. 1894).

[60] *Perry* v. *People*, 163 P. 844 (Col. 1917).

[61] *State* v. *Tilden*, 147 P. 1056 (Idaho 1915).

[62] *People* v. *Murawski*, 68 N.E. 2d 272 (Ill. 1946).

[63] *Sprinkle* v. *State*, 102 S. 844 (Miss. 1925). [64] *Ball* v. *State, op. cit.*

[65] *State* v. *Claypool*, 237 P. 730 (Wash. 1925).

[66] *Editor & Publisher*, February 23, 1957.

[67] *United States* v. *Grieco*, 161 F. Supp. 683, aff'd 261 F. 2d 414 (1958), cert. denied, 359 U.S. 907 (1959).

[68] *McDonald* v. *Pless*, 238 U.S. 264 (1915).

[69] *Brown* v. *United States*, 69 App. D.C. 96, 99 F. 2d 131 (1938), cert. denied 305 U.S. 562; reaff'd in *Carter* v. *United States*, 252 F. 2d 608, 612 (1957).

[70] *Welch* v. *United States*, 135 F. 2d 465 (1943).

[71] Linza B. Inabnit, "Trial Jury—The Possible Prejudicial Effects of Newspaper Articles on Juries in Criminal Cases," 47 *Kentucky Law Journal* 232 (Winter 1959).

[72] Francis X. Busch, *Law and Tactics in Jury Trials*, Vol. I (Indianapolis: The Bobbs-Merrill Company, Inc., 1959), pp. 732-82.

[73] 5 Cush 295, 52 Am. Dec. 711, (1850).

[74] 33 N.E. 1 (1893).

[75] *United States* v. *Holt*, 218 U.S. 245 (1910); *Medley* v. *United States*, 155 F. 2d 857 (1946); *United States* v. *Titus*, 210 F. 2d 210 (1954); *Finnegan* v. *United States*, 204 F. 2d 105 (1953); *People* v. *Daugherty*, 256 P. 2d 911 (Calif. 1953); *People* v. *Schneider*, 14 N.W. 2d 819 (Mich. 1944); *State* v. *Johnson*, 245 S.W. 2d 43 (Mo. 1952); *State* v. *Fuller*, 93 S.E. 2d 463 (S.C. 1956); *Parsons* v. *State*, 271 S.W. 2d 643 (Tex. 1954).

[76] *Busch, op. cit.*, pp. 781-84.

[77] John D. Lawson and Edwin R. Keedy, "Criminal Procedure in England," 1 *Journal of Criminal Law and Criminology* 609 (1911).

[78] *Commonwealth* v. *Jacques*, 1 Pa. Dist. 287 (1892).

[79] 111 N.W. 443 (Iowa 1907).

[80] *Juelich* v. *United States*, 214 F. 2d 950 (1954).

[81] Jim Thompson, "The Law of Prejudicial Newspaper Publicity," (unpublished manuscript distributed at Short Course for Prosecutors, Defense Lawyers, Newsment, etc., Northwestern University School of Law, March 1960), p. 6.

[82] *Commonwealth* v. *Geagan*, 339 Mass. 487, 159 N.E. 2d 870, cert. denied, 361 U.S. 895 (1959).

[83] *Ciucci* v. *People*, 21 Ill. 2d 86 (1960).

84 *Delaney* v. *United States,* 199 F. 2d 107 (1922).   85 Nov. 19, 1951.

86 *United States* v. *Dennis,* 183 F. 2d 201 (1950).

87 *Leviton et al.* v. *United States,* 193 F. 2d 848 (1951), cert. denied, 343 U.S. 946 (1952).

88 *Krulevitch* v. *United States,* 336 U.S. 440, 453 (1949).

89 Harry Kalven, Jr., "The Work of the Illinois Supreme Court Committee on Jury Instructions—the Elimination of Instructions," 9 *The University of Chicago Law School Record* 21 (December 1960); Alexander Holtzoff, "The Relation Between the Right to a Fair Trial and the Right of Freedom of the Press," 1 *Syracuse Law Review* 369, 371 (1950).

90 *United States* v. *Wolf,* 102 F. Supp. 824 (1952); *United States* v. *Weber,* 197 F. 2d 237 (1952).

91 *People* v. *Murawski,* 68 N.E. 2d 272 (Ill. 1946).   92 281 U.S. 276 (1930).

93 *Johnson* v. *Zerbst,* 304 U.S. 458 (1938); *Shepherd* v. *United States,* 163 F. 2d 974 (1947); *United States* v. *Sorrentino,* 175 F. 2d 721, cert. denied 338 U.S. 868 (1949).

94 "Public Information, Criminal Trials and the Cause Celebre." 36 *New York University Law Review* 832 (April 1961).

95 Dale W. Broeder, "The University of Chicago Jury Project," 38 *Nebraska Law Review* 750 (1959).

CHAPTER 11

1 "Freedom of Speech and Contempt of Court," 36 *Illinois Law Review* 615 (1942).

2 Sir John Fox, *The History of Contempt of Court* (Oxford: Clarendon Press, 1927), p. 1.

3 *Re Read and Huggonson (Roach* v. *Garvan),* 2 Atk. 469 (1742).

4 Wilm. 243 at 254 (1765).

5 *United States* v. *Barnett,* 376 U.S. 681 (1964).

6 *Respublica* v. *Oswald,* 1 Dallas 319 (Pa. 1788), was the first American case of constructive contempt. Chief Justice McKean justified the summary procedure, but on appeal to the House of Representatives, the House questioned the pertinence of English precedent, presaging the Pennsylvania statute of 1809 which curtailed the summary process.

7 *Respublica* v. *Passmore,* 3 Yeates 441 (1802).

8 Walter Nelles and Carol Weiss King, "Contempt by Publication in the United States," 28 *Columbia Law Review* 401-31 and 525-62 (April and May 1928). This is a comprehensive and authoritative account of the evolvement of the contempt power in America in both its legal and political contexts. The discussion assumes a conflict between judicial power and the liberal tradition.

9 *United States Code Annotated,* Title 28, § 385.

10 16 Ark. 384 (1855).   11 205 U.S. 454 (1907).

12 *Toledo Newspaper Company* v. *United States,* 247 U.S. 402 (1918).

13 *Ibid.,* 425.   14 263 U.S. 255, 278 (1923).   15 356 U.S. 165 (1958).

16 *Ex parte Shuler,* 292 P. 481 (1930).   17 313 U.S. 33 (1941).

18 314 U.S. 252 (1941).   19 Max Radin, *op. cit.,* 603.

20 *Times-Mirror Co.* v. *Superior Court,* 15 Cal. 2d 99 (1940).

21 *Bridges* v. *California, op. cit.,* at 260, 263.

22 *Ibid.,* 263.   23 *Ibid.,* 268.   24 *Ibid.,* 290-92.

25 328 U.S. 331 (1946).   26 331 U.S. 368 (1947).

[27] Zechariah Chafee, Jr., *Government and Mass Communications* (Chicago: University of Chicago Press, 1947), Vol. II, p. 433.

[28] *Ex parte Craig,* 150 Tex. Crim. App. 598, 193 S.W. 2d 178, 186–88 (1946).

[29] *Craig* v. *Harney, op. cit.,* 377.

[30] *The Constitution and the Supreme Court* (New York: Dodd, Mead & Company, Inc., 1959), p. 363.

[31] *Abrams* v. *United States,* 250 U.S. 628 (1919).

[32] William O. Douglas, *The Right of the People* (Garden City, N. Y.: Doubleday and Company, Inc., 1958), p. 41.

[33] The opinion of the Baltimore City Criminal Court is abstracted under the title *In re Maryland Broadcasting Company* in 17 *U.S. Law Week* 2381 (February 18, 1949); the decision of the Maryland Court of Appeals, under the title *Baltimore Radio Show* v. *State* is reported at 67 A. 2d 497 (1949).

[34] *Maryland* v. *Baltimore Radio Show, Inc.,* 338 U.S. 912 (1950).

[35] *Baltimore Radio Show* v. *State, op. cit.,* p. 507. The "rules" refers to Rule 904.

[36] *Ibid.,* p. 511. [37] *Ibid.,* p. 512. [38] *Ibid.,* p. 521.

[39] *People* v. *Goss,* 141 N.E. 2d 385 (1957). [40] *Ibid.,* p. 389.

[41] *Atlanta Journal,* June 6, 1959.

[42] *Atlanta Newspapers Inc.* v. *Georgia,* 113 S.E. 2d 148 (1960).

[43] *McGill* v. *Davis,* 74 S.E. 2d 78 (Ga. 1953); *Weston* v. *Commonwealth,* 195 Va. 175 (1953).

[44] 108 So. 2d 33 (Fla. 1959). [45] *Wood* v. *Georgia,* 370 U.S. 375 (1962).

CHAPTER 12

[1] British Section of the International Commission of Jurists, (JUSTICE), *Contempt of Court* 34 (1959).

[2] *Newsweek,* April 1 and 8, 1957.

[3] *R.* v. *Griffiths, Ex parte Attorney-General* (1957) 2 All E.R. 379.

[4] Sybille Bedford, *The Trial of Dr. Adams* (New York: Grove Press, Inc., 1958), pp. 209–10. This is a fascinating, day-by-day account of the trial, suggesting the service journalism could preform for its readers by the same kind of coverage.

[5] (1945) 2 All E.R. 167 (D.C.).

[6] *R.* v. *Duffy* (1960) 2 Q.B. 188 at 197-98. [7] *Ibid.*

[8] *R.* v. *Daily Mail, Ex parte Farnsworth* (1921) 2 K.B. 733 .

[9] *R.* v. *Bolam, Ex parte Haigh* (1949) 93 Sol. J. 220 (D.C.).

[10] *R.* v. *Odhams Press Ltd., Ex parte Attorney-General* (1956) 3 All E.R. 494.

[11] January 17, 1958. [12] JUSTICE, *op. cit.* p. 9.

[13] *Administration of Justice Act,* 1960, 8 & 9 Eliz. 2, c. 65 § 11(1).

[14] *R.* v. *Clarke, Ex parte Crippen* (1910) 103 L.T. 636.

[15] *R.* v. *Editor, Printers and Publishers of the Evening News,* The Times, July 30, 1936 (K.B.).

[16] *R.* v. *Mason,* The Times, December 7, 1932 (K.B.).

[17] *R.* v. *News of the World; Ex parte Kitchin* (1932) 48 T.L.R. 234.

[18] *R.* v. *Editor of the Evening News,* The Times, October 27, 1925.

[19] *R.* v. *Daily Mirror, Ex parte Smith* (1927) 1 K.B. 845.

[20] *R.* v. *Editor, Printers and Publishers of the Daily Herald* (1931) 75 Sol. J. 119 (K.B.).

[21] *R.* v. *Evening Standard (Editor); Manchester Guardian (Editor); Daily Express (Editor), Ex parte Director of Public Prosecution* (1924) 40 T.L.R. 833, 835.

[22] *R.* v. *Dyson* (1943) 169 L.T. 237.

[23] *R.* v. *Armstrong* (1951) 2 All E.R. 219.

[24] *The Times,* November 6 and 7, 1957.

[25] *R.* v. *Evening Standard Co., Ltd.* (1954) 1 Q.B. 584.

[26] *R.* v. *Gray* (1865) 10 Cox C.C. 184 (Q.B.).

[27] *R.* v. *Editor and Publisher of the Evening News, Ex parte Hobbs* (1925) 2 K.B. 158.

[28] *The Times,* May 2, 1957.

[29] L. B. C. Gower, "Publicity in Judicial Proceedings," 20 *Modern Law Review* 388 passim (1957).

[30] Sir Alfred Denning, *The Road to Justice* (London: Stevens & Son Limited, 1955), p. 73.

[31] *Scott* v. *Scott* (1913) 82 L.J.R. 75.

[32] Sir Patrick Devlin, *Trial By Jury.* (London: Stevens & Sons Limited, 1956), quoted in George J. Webber, "Trial by Newspaper," in Keeton and Schwarzenberger (eds.) 11 *Current Legal Problems* 60 (1958).

[33] *Editor & Publisher,* April 17, 1965.

[34] *R.* v. *Gray* (1900) 2 Q.B. 36.   [35] (1928) 44 T.L.R. 301.

[36] *R.* v. *Colsey, Ex parte Director of Public Prosecutions,* The Times, May 9, 1931.

[37] *R.* v. *Wilkinson and Others, Ex parte The Attorney-General,* The Times, July 16, 1930.

[38] Denning, *The Road to Justice, op. cit.,* p. 73.

[39] *Ambard* v. *Attorney-General for Trinidad and Tobago* (1936) A.C. 322, 335.

[40] June 17, 1958.

[41] *Gompers* v. *Buck's Stove & Range Co.,* 221 U.S. 418 (1911); *In re Debs,* 158 U.S. 564 (1895).

[42] Mr. Justice Baldwin in *Ex parte Paulson,* 19 Fed. Cas. 1205, No. 11, 350 (E.D. Pa. 1835).

[43] *Ex parte Robinson,* 19 Wall. 505 (1874).

[44] *United States* v. *Anonymous,* 21 F. 761 (W.D. Tenn. 1884).

[45] *Toledo Newspaper Company* v. *United States,* 247 U.S. 402 (1918).

[46] *Nye* v. *United States,* 313 U.S. 33 (1941).

CHAPTER 13

[1] *The Growth of the Law* (New Haven: Yale University Press, 1924), p. 120.

[2] Edwin M. Otterbourg, "Fair Trial and Free Press: A Subject Vital to the Existence of Democracy," 39 *American Bar Association Journal* 979 (November 1953).

[3] "Pre-Trial Secrecy Law Advocated," *Editor & Publisher,* January 30, 1954.

[4] *Ibid.*   [5] "Trial By Newspaper," *New York Times,* August 26, 1953.

[6] James Russell Wiggins, *Freedom or Secrecy* (New York: Oxford University Press, 1956), pp. 50-52.

[7] John Newton Baker, "The Press and Crime," 33 *Journal of Criminal Law and Criminology* 463-67 (March–April 1943).

[8] Quoted in Jerome Frank, *Courts on Trial* (Princeton, N. J.: Princeton University Press, 1949), p. 92,

[9] *Ciucci* v. *Illinois,* 356 U.S. 571 (1958).

[10] *United States* v. *Rosenberg,* 200 F. 2d 666, 670 (1952), *cert. denied,* 345 U.S. 965 (1953).

[11] "Law or Canon?" *Editor & Publisher,* July 3, 1954.

[12] "Trial By Newspaper," *New York Times,* March 29, 1957.

[13] Blackstone's *Commentaries* (Kerr ed. 1876), pp. 373–74.

[14] Jeremy Bentham, *Rationale of Judicial Evidence* (London: Hunt and Clarke, 1827), p. 513.

[15] James Russell Wiggins, *Freedom or Secrecy op. cit.,* pp. 26–28.

[16] *In re Oliver,* 333 U.S. 257 (1948).

[17] *United States* v. *Sorrentino,* 175 F. 2d 721 (1949); *United States* v. *Kobli,* 172 F. 2d 919 (1949); *People* v. *Miller,* 177 N.E. 306 (N. Y. 1931).

[18] "Exclusion of Public During Criminal Trials," 156 *American Law Reports* 265 (1945).

[19] *People* v. *Hartman,* 103 Calif. 1, 242 (1894). See Warren Freedman, "News Media Coverage of Criminal Cases and the Right to a Fair Trial," 40 *Nebraska Law Review* 393 (April 1961).

[20] *United Press Ass'n* v. *Valente,* 123 N.E. 2d 777 (N. Y. 1954).

[21] *People* v. *Jelke,* 123 N.E. 2d 769 (N. Y. 1954).

[22] *United States* v. *Kleinman,* 107 F. Supp. 407 (1952).

[23] *E. W. Scripps Co.* v. *Fulton,* 125 N.E. 2d 896 (Ohio 1955).

[24] *New York Judiciary Law,* § 749 - aa (4).

[25] Jerome Frank, *Courts On Trial* (Princeton: Princeton University Press, 1949) p. 118 ff.

[26] William F. Willoughby, *Principles of Judicial Administration* (Washington, D.C.: Brookings Institution, 1929), pp. 489–90.

[27] George B. DeLuca, "Fair Trial-Free Press: A Panel Discussion," *New York State Bar Bulletin,* July 1954, p. 214.

[28] Sir Patrick Devlin, *Trial By Jury* (London: Stevens & Sons Limited, 1955).

[29] Comment, "The Case Against Trial By Newspaper," 57 *Northwestern University Law Review* 250 (May–June 1962). A model statute is outlined.

[30] Bernard S. Meyer, "Are Additional Remedies Needed in the United States to Implement the Constitutional Guarantee of Fair Trial?" An address to the National Conference of State Trial Judges, San Francisco, August 4, 1962.

———, "First Amendment vs. Sixth Amendment: Is Reporting Prejudicial to Fair Trials," An address to Associated Press Managing Editors, Minneapolis, September 28, 1962.

———, "Free Press v. Fair Trial: The Judge's View," 41 *North Dakota Law Review* 14 (November 1964).

[31] 85 S. Ct. 476 (1965).

[32] S. 290: "It shall constitute a contempt of court for any employee of the United States, or for any defendant or his attorney or the agent of either, to furnish or make available for publication information not already properly filed with the court which might affect the outcome of any pending criminal litigation, except evidence that has already been admitted at the trial. Such contempt shall be punished by a fine of not more than $1,000."

Free Press and Fair Trial, Hearings before the Subcommittee on Constitutional Rights and the Subcommittee on Improvements in Judicial Machinery of the Committee on the Judiciary, United States Senate, Eighty-Ninth Congress, First Session on S. 290, Washington, D. C., 1966.

The two-volume Subcommittee hearings constitute a useful handbook on the free press-fair trial question.

[33] *Ibid.,* pp. 454, 457.   [34] *Ibid.,* p. 43.   [35] *Ibid.,* p. 117.

[36] *Houston Chronicle,* August 8, 1965.   [37] *Newsweek,* December 13, 1965.

[38] Irwin Ross, "Trial By Newspaper," *The Atlantic,* September 1965.

CHAPTER 14

[1] "Fair Trial and Freedom of the Press," 19 *Federal Rules Decisions* 16, 25 (1957).

[2] See articles by Ralph S. Brown Jr., Theodore L. Becker, Vilhelm Aubert, S. Sidney Ulmer, and Charles Winick in "Frontiers of Legal Research," *The American Behavioral Scientist,* December 1963.

[3] Edwin M. Schur, "Scientific Method and the Criminal Trial Decision," 25 *Social Research* 175 (1958).

[4] Jeremy Bentham, *Rationale of Judicial Evidence* (London: Hunt and Clarke, 1827), p. 604.

[5] *R.* v. *Jolliffe,* 4 T.R. 285, 100 Eng. Rep. 1022 (K.B. 1787).

[6] *Stroble* v. *California,* 343 U.S. 181, 201 (1952).

[7] J. C. Hutcheson Jr., "The Judgment Initiative: The Function of the 'Hunch' in Judicial Decisions," 14 *Cornell Law Quarterly* 274, 278 (1949).

[8] Sidney Post Simpson and Ruth Field, "Law and the Social Sciences," 32 *Virginia Law Review* 855, 862 (1946).

[9] Ronald Goldfarb, "Public Information, Criminal Trials and the Cause Celebre," 36 *New York University Law Review* 810, 838 (1961).

[10] *Baltimore Radio Show, Inc.* v. *State,* 193 Md. 300, 67 A. 2d 497 (1949).

[11] Dale Broeder, "The University of Chicago Jury Project," 38 *Nebraska Law Review* 744 (1959). See also Glenn W. Ferguson, "Legal Research on Trial," 39 *Journal of the American Judicature Society* 78 (1955).

[12] H. P. Weld and E. R. Danzig, "A Study of the Way in Which a Verdict is Reached by a Jury," 53 *American Journal of Psychology* 518 (1940).

[13] Broeder, *op. cit.,* p. 750.

[14] Schur, *op. cit.* p. 182.

[15] Fred L. Strodtbeck and Richard D. Mann, "Sex Role Differentiation in Jury Deliberations," 19 *Sociometry* 3 (1956); Fred L. Strodtbeck, Rita M. James and Charles H. Hawkins, "Social Status in Jury Deliberations," 22 *American Sociological Review* 713 (1957); Fred L. Strodtbeck and L. Harmon Hook, "The Social Dimensions of a Twelve-Man Jury Table," 24 *Sociometry* 397 (1961).

[16] William Bevan, Robert S. Albert, Pierre R. Loiseaux, Peter N. Mayfield and George Wright, "Jury Behavior as a Function of the Prestige of the Foreman and the Nature of His Leadership," 7 *Journal of Public Law* 419 (1958).

[17] Charles H. Hawkins, "Interaction Rates of Jurors Aligned in Factions," 27 *American Sociological Review* 5 (1962). See also Hawkins, *Interaction and Coalition Realignments in Consensus-Seeking Groups: A Study of Experimental Jury Deliberations,* (unpublished Ph.D. dissertation, University of Chicago, 1960); and Harry Kalven, Jr. and Fred L. Strodtbeck, *Social Process and the Law: A Study of the American Jury* (forthcoming).

[18] Hans Zeisel, "What Determines the Amount of Argument Per Juror?" 28 *American Sociological Review* 2 (1963).

[19] Rita M. James, "Status and Competence of Jurors," 64 *American Journal of Sociology* 563 (1959).

[20] W. S. Robinson, "Bias, Probability, and Trial by Jury," 15 *American Sociological Review* 73 (1950).

[21] Waldo Burchard, "Lawyers, Political Scientists, Sociologists—and Concealed Microphones," 23 *American Sociological Review* 686 (1958).

[22] *Rakes* v. *United States,* 169 F. 2d 739, 745-6 (2d Cir. 1948).

[23] *Fortner* v. *Koch,* 272 Mich. 273, 261 N.W. 762 (1935).

[24] Clarence G. Galston, "Civil Jury Trials and Tribulations," 29 *American Bar Association Journal* 195 (1943).

[25] Letter from Harry Kalven Jr. to Hon. Herbert F. Goodrich of the American Law Institute, Sept. 16, 1960 (with a copy to the author).

[26] F. Gerald Kline and Paul H. Jess, "The Effect of Prejudicial Publicity on Mock Juries at the University of Minnesota Law School," paper presented at the Association for Education in Journalism Convention, Syracuse, New York, August, 1965. A condensed version of this study appears in the Spring 1966 *Journalism Quarterly.*

[26a] Rita James Simon, *"The Effects of Newspapers on the Verdicts of Potential Jurors,"* (forthcoming).

[27] Robert F. Bales, *Interaction Process Analysis: A Method for Study of Small Groups* (Cambridge, Mass.: Addison-Wesley Publishing Company, 1950).

[28] T. W. Adorno, *et al., The Authoritarian Personality* (New York: Harper Press, 1950). For this study the authors used Verling C. Troldahl and Frederick A. Powell, *A Short-Form Dogmatism Scale for Use in Field Studies,* Mimeographed paper. See also Milton Rokeach, *The Open and Closed Mind* (New York: Basic Books, 1960).

[29] For a comprehensive discussion of survey findings as legal evidence see Robert C. Sorenson and Theodore C. Sorenson, "The Admissibility and Use of Opinion Research Evidence," 28 *New York University Law Review* 1213 (1953); and Hiram C. Barksdale, *The Use of Survey Research Findings as Legal Evidence* (Printers' Ink Books, Pleasantville, N.Y., 1957).

[30] Note "Contempt by Publication," 59 *Yale Law Journal* 534, 543 (1950).

[31] *Irvin* v. *State,* 66 S. 2d 288 (Fla. 1953), certiorari denied, 346 U.S. 927 (1954). For a discussion of this case see Jerome H. Spingarn, "Newspapers and the Pursuit of Justice," *Saturday Review,* April 3, 1954, p. 9, and Goldfarb, *op. cit.,* p. 837. All judges and lawyers do not react this way, see Note, "Public Opinion Surveys as Evidence: The Pollsters Go To Court," 66 *Harvard Law Review* 498 (1953); *Judicial Conference of the U.S. Courts, Handbook of Procedure for the Trial of Protracted Cases* (Minneapolis: West Publishing Company, 1960), and Sorenson and Sorenson, *op. cit.*

[32] Joseph T. Klapper and Charles Y. Glock, "Trial by Newspaper," 180 *Scientific American* 16-21 (February 1949).

[32a] *Editor & Publisher,* December 4, 1965.

[33] Joseph T. Klapper, *The Effects of Mass Communication* (Gencoe, Ill.: The Free Press, 1960), p. 8.

[34] Percy H. Tannenbaum, "Initial Attitude Toward Source and Concept as Factors in Attitude Change Through Communication," 20 *Public Opinion Quarterly* 413 (1956).

[35] Bernard Berelson, "Communications and Public Opinion," in *Communication in Modern Society,* Wilbur Schramm, ed., (Urbana, Ill.: University of Illinois Press, 1948), p. 496, and Klapper, *op. cit.,* p. 60.

[36] Klapper, *op. cit.,* p. 60.

[37] Irving L. Janis and S. Feshbach, "Effects of Fear-Arousing Communications," 48 *Journal of Abnormal and Social Psychology* 78 (1958).

[38] Paul Lazarsfeld and Robert K. Merton, "Mass Communications, Popular Taste and Organized Social Action," in *The Communication of Ideas,* Lyman Bryson, ed., (New York: Harper, 1948), p. 104.

[39] Douglas Waples, Bernard Berelson and Franklyn R. Bradshaw, *What Reading Does to People* (Chicago: University of Chicago Press, 1940).

[40] Klapper, *op. cit.,* p. 130. For a summary of psychological findings see Herbert J. Abelson, *Persuasion* (New York: Springer, 1959).

[41] Hadley Cantril, "The Invasion from Mars," in *Readings in Social Psychology,* Theodore Newcomb and Eugene Hartley, eds. (New York: Holt, 1947), p. 619, and Donald M. Johnson, "The 'Phantom Anesthetist' of Mattoon: A Field Study of Mass Hysteria," *id.,* p. 639.

[42] Wilbur Schramm, "The Effects of Mass Communication: A Review," 26 *Journalism Quarterly,* 407 (December 1949).

[43] David Riesman and Reuel Denney, "Do the Mass Media 'Escape' from Politics?" in *Reader in Public Opinion and Communication* 2d ed., Bernard Berelson and Morris Janowitz, eds. (Glencoe, Ill.: The Free Press, 1953), p. 327.

[44] Klapper, *op. cit.,* p. 130.

[45] Letter from Justice Bernard S. Meyer of the Supreme Court of the State of New York to Professor Maurice J. Rosenberg, Director of Columbia University's Project for Effective Justice, November 26, 1962.

[46] *The Effects of News Media on Jury Verdicts: An Examination of the Problem and a Proposal,* Bureau of Applied Social Research and the Graduate School of Journalism, Columbia University, May 4, 1964.

[47] *Mass Media Coverage of Governmental Processes: Project Proposal,* The Brookings Institution, Governmental Studies, September, 1964.

[48] *Editor & Publisher,* January 28, 1956.

[49] *Publisher's Auxiliary,* December 3, 1955.

[50] Sorenson and Sorenson, *op. cit.,* p. 1213.

[51] 165 F. 2d 152 (2d Cir. 1947).

[52] Frederick K. Beutel, "An Outline of the Nature and Methods of Experimental Jurisprudence," 51 *Columbia Law Review* 415 (1951).

CHAPTER 15

[1] *Present Status of the Philosophy of Law and of Rights* (New Haven: Yale University Press, 1926), p. 55.

[2] John Kaplan and Jon R. Waltz, *The Trial of Jack Ruby* (New York: The Macmillan Company, 1965), p. 291.

[3] *United States* v. *Bufalino,* 285 F. 2d 408 (1960).

[4] Zechariah Chafee, Jr., *Government and Mass Communications* Vol. II (Chicago: University of Chicago Press, 1947), pp. 643, 717.

Appendix 1

SUPREME COURT OF THE UNITED STATES

No. 490.—October Term, 1965.

Samuel H. Sheppard, Petitioner, *v.* E. L. Maxwell, Warden.	On Writ of Certiorari to the United States Court of Appeals for the Sixth Circuit.

[June 6, 1966.]

MR. JUSTICE CLARK delivered the opinion of the Court.

This federal habeas corpus application involves the question whether Sheppard was deprived of a fair trial in his state conviction for the second-degree murder of his wife because of the trial judge's failure to protect Sheppard sufficiently from the massive, pervasive and prejudicial publicity that attended his prosecution.[1] The United States District Court held that he was not afforded a fair trial and granted the writ subject to the State's right to put Sheppard to trial again, 231 F. Supp. 37 (D.C.S.D. Ohio 1964). The Court of Appeals for the Sixth Circuit reversed by a divided vote, 346 F. 2d 707 (1965). We granted certiorari, 382 U. S. 916 (1966). We have concluded that Sheppard did not receive a fair trial consistent with the Due Process Clause of the Fourteenth Amendment and, therefore, reverse the judgment. . . .

We now reach the conduct of the trial. While the intense publicity continued unabated, it is sufficient to relate only the more flagrant episodes. . . .

While the jury was being selected, a two-inch headline asked: "But Who Will Speak for Marilyn?" The front-page story spoke of the "perfect face" of the accused. "Study that face as long as you want. Never will you get from it a hint of what might be the answer . . . ." The two brothers of the accused were described as "Prosperous, poised. His two sisters-in law. Smart, chic, well-groomed. His elderly father. Courtly, reserved. A perfect type for the patriarch

---

[1] Sheppard was convicted in 1954 in the Court of Common Pleas of Cuyahoga County, Ohio. His conviction was affirmed by the Court of Appeals for Cuyahoga County, 100 Ohio App. 345, 128 N. E. 2d 471 (1955), and the Ohio Supreme Court, 165 Ohio St., 293, 135 N. E. 2d 340 (1956). We denied certiorari on the original appeal. 352 U. S. 910 (1956).

of a staunch clan." The author then noted Marilyn Sheppard was "still off stage," and that she was an only child whose mother died when she was very young and whose father had no interest in the case. But the author—through quotes from Detective Chief James McArthur—assured readers that the prosecution's exhibits would speak for Marilyn. "Her story," McArthur stated, "will come into this courtroom through our witnesses." The article ends:

> "Then you realize how what and who is missing from the perfect setting will be supplied.
> "How in the Big Case justice will be done.
> "Justice to Sam Sheppard.
> "And to Marilyn Sheppard."

. . . On Nov. 24, a story appeared under an eight-column headline: "Sam Called A 'Jekyll-Hyde' By Marilyn, Cousin To Testify." It related that Marilyn had recently told friends that Sheppard was a "Dr. Jekyll and Mr. Hyde" character. No such testimony was ever produced at the trial. The story went on to announce: "The prosecution has a 'bombshell witness' on tap who will testify to Dr. Sam's display of fiery temper—countering the defense claim that the defendant is a gentle physician with an even disposition." Defense counsel made motions for change of venue, continuance and mistrial, but they were denied. No action was taken by the court . . . .

On December 9, while Sheppard was on the witness stand he testified that he had been mistreated by Cleveland detectives after his arrest. Although he was not at the trial, Captain Kerr of the Homicide Bureau issued a press statement denying Sheppard's allegations which appeared under the headline: " 'Bare-faced Liar,' Kerr Says of Sam." Captain Kerr never appeared as a witness at the trial.

After the case was submitted to the jury, it was sequestered for its deliberations, which took five days and four nights. After the verdict, defense counsel ascertained that the jurors had been allowed to make telephone calls to their homes every day while they were sequestered at the hotel. Although the telephones had been removed from the jurors' rooms, the jurors were permitted to use the phones in the bailiff's rooms. The calls were placed by the jurors themselves; no record was kept of the jurors who made calls, the telephone numbers or the parties called. The bailiffs sat in the room where they could hear only the jurors' end of the conversation. The court had not instructed the bailiffs to prevent such calls. By a subsequent motion, defense counsel urged that this ground alone warranted a new trial, but the motion was overruled and no evidence was taken on the question. . . .

Unlike Estes, Sheppard was not granted a change of venue to a locale away from where the publicity originated; nor was his jury sequestered. The Estes jury saw none of the television broadcasts from the courtroom. On the contrary, the Sheppard jurors were subjected to newspaper, radio and television coverage of the trial while not taking part in the proceedings. They were allowed to go their separate ways outside of the courtroom, without adequate directions not to read or listen to anything concerning the case. The judge's "admonitions" at the beginning of the trial are representative:

> "I would suggest to you and caution you that you do not read any newspapers during the progress of this trial, that you do not listen to radio comments nor watch or listen to television comments, insofar as this case is concerned. You will feel very much better as the trial proceeds . . . . I am sure that we shall all feel very much better if we do not indulge in any newspaper reading or listening to any comments whatever about the matter while the case is in progress. After it is all over, you can read it all to your heart's content . . . ."

At intervals during the trial, the judge simply repeated his "suggestions" and "requests" that the jury not expose themselves to comment upon the case. Moreover, the jurors were thrust into the role of celebrities by the judge's failure to insulate them from reporters and photographers . . . . The numerous pictures of the jurors, with their addresses, which appeared in the newspapers before and during the trial itself exposed them to expressions of opinion from both cranks and friends. The fact that anonymous letters had been received by prospective jurors should have made the judge aware that this publicity seriously threatened the jurors' privacy.

The press coverage of the Estes trial was not nearly as massive and pervasive as the attention given by the Cleveland newspapers and broadcasting stations to Sheppard's prosecution. Sheppard stood indicted for the murder of his wife; the State was demanding the death penalty. For months the virulent publicity about Sheppard and the murder had made the case notorious. Charges and countercharges were aired in the news media besides those for which Sheppard was called to trial. In addition, only three months before the trial, Sheppard was examined for more than five hours without counsel during a three-day inquest which ended in a public brawl. The inquest was televised live from a high school gymnasium seating hundreds of people. Furthermore, the trial began two weeks before a hotly contested election at which both Chief Prosecutor Mahon and Judge Blythin were candidates for judgeships.

While we cannot say that Sheppard was denied due process by the judge's refusal to take precautions against the influence of pretrial publicity alone, the court's later ruling must be considered against the setting in which the trial was held. In light of this background, we believe that the arrangements made by the judge with the news media caused Sheppard to be deprived of that "judicial serenity and calm to which [he] was entitled." . . . . The fact is that bedlam reigned at the courthouse during the trial and newsmen took over practically the entire courtroom, hounding most of the participants in the trial, especially Sheppard. At a temporary table within a few feet of the jury box and counsel table sat some 20 reporters staring at Sheppard and taking notes. The erection of a press table for reporters inside the bar is unprecedented. The bar of the court is reserved for counsel, providing them a safe place in which to keep papers and exhibits, and to confer privately with client and co-counsel. It is designed to protect the witness and the jury from any distractions, intrusions or influences, and to permit bench discussions of the judge's rulings away from the hearing of the public and the jury. Having assigned almost all of the available seats in the courtroom to the news media the judge lost his ability to supervise that environment. The movement of the reporters in and out of the courtroom caused frequent confusion and disruption of the trial. And the record reveals constant commotion within the bar. Moreover, the judge gave the throng of newsmen gathered in the corridors of the courthouse absolute free rein. Participants in the trial, including the jury, were forced to run a gantlet of reporters and photographers each time they entered or left the courtroom. The total lack of consideration for the privacy of the jury was demonstrated by the assignment to a broadcasting station of space next to the jury room on the floor above the courtroom, as well as the fact that jurors were allowed to make telephone calls during their five-day deliberation.

There can be no question about the nature of the publicity which surrounded Sheppard's trial. We agree, as did the Court of Appeals, with the findings in Judge Bell's opinion for the Ohio Supreme Court:

> "Murder and mystery, society, sex and suspense were combined in this case in such a manner as to intrigue and captivate the public fancy to a degree perhaps unparalleled in recent annals. Throughout the preindictment investigation, the subsequent legal skirmishes and the nine-week trial, circulation-conscious editors catered to the insatiable interest of the American public in the bizarre. . . . In this atmosphere of a

'Roman holiday' for the news media, Sam Sheppard stood trial
for his life." 165 Ohio St., at 294.

Indeed every court that has considered this case, save the court that
tried it, has deplored the manner in which the news media inflamed
and prejudiced the public.

Much of the material printed or broadcast during the trial was
never heard from the witness stand, such as the charges that Sheppard
had purposely impeded the murder investigation and must be guilty
since he had hired a prominent criminal lawyer; that Sheppard was
a perjurer; that he had sexual relations with numerous women; that
his slain wife had characterized him as a "Jekyll-Hyde"; that he was
"a bare-faced liar" because of his testimony as to police treatment;
and, finally, that a woman convict claimed Sheppard to be the father
of her illegitimate child. As the trial progressed, the newspapers summarized and interpreted the evidence, devoting particular attention to
the material that incriminated Sheppard, and often drew unwar-
ranted inferences from testimony. At one point, a front-page picture
of Mrs. Sheppard's blood-stained pillow was published after being
"doctored" to show more clearly an alleged imprint of a surgical
instrument.

Nor is there doubt that this deluge of publicity reached at least
some of the jury. On the only occasion that the jury was queried,
two jurors admitted in open court to hearing the highly inflammatory
charge that a prison inmate claimed Sheppard as the father of her
illegitimate child. Despite the extent and nature of the publicity to
which the jury was exposed during the trial, the judge refused defense counsel's other requests that the jury be asked whether they
had read or heard specific prejudicial comment about the case, including the incidents we have previously summarized. In these circumstances, we can assume that some of this material reached members of the jury. . . .

The court's fundamental error is compounded by the holding that
it lacked power to control the publicity about the trial. From the
very inception of the proceedings the judge announced that neither
he nor anyone else could restrict prejudicial news accounts. And he
reiterated this view on numerous occasions. Since he viewed the news
media as his target, the judge never considered other means that are
often utilized to reduce the appearance of prejudicial material and
to protect the jury from outside influence. *We conclude that these
procedures would have been sufficient to guarantee Sheppard a fair
trial and so do not consider what sanctions might be available against*

a recalcitrant press nor the charges of bias now made against the
state trial judge. (Emphasis added).

The carnival atmosphere at trial could easily have been avoided since the courtroom and courthouse premises are subject to the control of the court. As we stressed in *Estes*, the presence of the press at judicial proceedings must be limited when it is apparent that the accused might otherwise be prejudiced or disadvantaged. Bearing in mind the massive pretrial publicity, the judge should have adopted stricter rules governing the use of the courtroom by newsmen, as Sheppard's counsel requested. The number of reporters in the courtroom itself could have been limited at the first sign that their presence would disrupt the trial. They certainly should not have been placed inside the bar. Furthermore, the judge should have more closely regulated the conduct of newsmen in the courtroom. For instance, the judge belatedly asked them not to handle and photograph trial exhibits laying on the counsel table during recesses.

Secondly, the court should have insulated the witnesses. All of the newspapers and radio stations apparently interviewed prospective witnesses at will, and in many instances disclosed their testimony. A typical example was the publication of numerous statements by Susan Hayes, before her appearance in court, regarding her love affair with Sheppard. Although the witnesses were barred from the courtroom during the trial the full *verbatim* testimony was available to them in the press. This completely nullified the judge's imposition of the rule. . . .

Thirdly, the court should have made some effort to control the release of leads, information, and gossip to the press by police officers, witnesses, and the counsel for both sides. Much of the information thus disclosed was inaccurate, leading to groundless rumors and confusion. That the judge was aware of his responsibility in this respect may be seen from his warning to Steve Sheppard, the accused's brother, who had apparently made public statements in an attempt to discredit testimony for the prosecution. The judge made this statement in the presence of the jury:

> "Now, the court wants to say a word. That he was told—he has not read anything about it at all—but he was informed that Dr. Steve Sheppard, who has been granted the privilege of remaining in the courtroom during the trial, has been trying the case in the newspapers and making rather uncomplimentary comments about the testimony of the witnesses for the State.

"Let it be now understood that if Dr. Steve Sheppard wishes to use the newspapers to try his case while we are trying it here, he will be barred from remaining in the courtroom during the progress of the trial if he is to be a witness in the case.

"The Court appreciates he cannot deny Steve Sheppard the right of free speech, but he can deny him the . . . privilege of being in the courtroom, if he wants to avail himself of that method during the progress of the trial."

Defense counsel immediately brought to the court's attention the tremendous amount of publicity in the Cleveland press that "misrepresented entirely the testimony" in the case. Under such circumstances, the judge should have at least warned the newspapers to check the accuracy of their accounts. And it is obvious that the judge should have further sought to alleviate this problem by imposing control over the statements made to the news media by counsel, witnesses, and especially the Coroner and police officers. The prosecution repeatedly made evidence available to the news media which was never offered in the trial. Much of the "evidence" disseminated in this fashion was clearly inadmissible. The exclusion of such evidence in court is rendered meaningless when a news media makes it available to the public. For example, the publicity about Sheppard's refusal to take a lie detector test came directly from police officers and the Coroner. The story that Sheppard had been called a "Jekyll-Hyde" personality by his wife was attributed to a prosecution witness. No such testimony was given. The further report that there was "a 'bombshell witness' on tap" who would testify as to Sheppard's "fiery temper" could only have emanated from the prosecution. Moreover, the newspapers described in detail clues that had been found by the police, but not put into the record.

The fact that many of the prejudicial news items can be traced to the prosecution, as well as the defense, aggravates the judge's failure to take action. . . . Effective control of these sources—concededly within the court's power—might well have prevented the divulgence of inaccurate information, rumors, and accusations that made up much of the inflammatory publicity, at least after Sheppard's indictment.

More specifically, the trial court might well have proscribed extrajudicial statements by any lawyer, party, witness, or court official which divulged prejudicial matters, such as the refusal of Sheppard to submit to interrogation or take any lie detector tests; any statement made by Sheppard to officials; the identity of prospective witnesses or their probable testimony; any belief in guilt or innocence; or like statements concerning merits of the case. . . . Being advised of the great public interest in the case, the mass coverage of the press, and the potential prejudicial impact of publicity, the court could also have requested the appropriate city and county officials to promulgate a regulation with respect to dissemination of information about the case by their employees. In addition, reporters who wrote or broadcasted prejudicial stories, could have been warned as to the impropriety of publishing material not introduced in the proceedings. The judge was put on notice of such events by defense counsel's complaint about the broadcast on the second day of trial. . . . In this manner, Sheppard's right to a trial free from outside interference would have been given added protection without corresponding curtailment of the news media. Had the judge, the other officers of the court, and the police placed the interest of justice first, the news media would have soon learned to be content with the task of reporting the case as it unfolded in the courtroom—not pieced together from extra-judicial statements.

From the cases coming here we note that unfair and prejudicial news comment on pending trials has become increasingly prevalent. Due process requires that the accused receive a trial by an impartial jury free from outside influences. Given the pervasiveness of modern communications and the difficulty of effacing prejudicial publicity from the minds of the jurors, the trial courts must take strong measures to ensure that the balance is never weighed against the accused. And appellate tribunals have the duty to make an independent evaluation of the circumstances. Of course, there is nothing that proscribes the press from reporting events that transpire in the courtroom. But where there is a reasonable likelihood that prejudicial news prior to trial will prevent a fair trial, the judge should continue the case until the threat abates, or transfer it to another county not so permeated with publicity. In addition, sequestration of the jury was something the judge should have raised sua sponte with counsel. If publicity during the proceedings threatens the fairness of the trial, a new trial should be ordered. But we must remember that reversals are but palliatives; the cure lies in those remedial measures that will prevent the prejudice at its inception. The courts must take such steps by rule and regulation that will protect their processes from prejudicial outside interferences. Neither prosecutors, counsel for defense, the accused, witnesses, court staff nor enforcement officers coming under the jurisdiction of the court should be permitted to frustrate its function. Collaboration between counsel and the press as to infor-

mation affecting the fairness of a criminal trial is not only subject to regulation, but is highly censurable and worthy of disciplinary measures. (Emphasis added).

Since the state trial judge did not fulfill his duty to protect Sheppard from the inherently prejudicial publicity which saturated the community and to control disruptive influences in the courtroom, we must reverse the denial of the habeas petition. The case is remanded to the District Court with instructions to issue the writ and order that Sheppard be released from custody unless the State puts him to its charges again within a reasonable time.

INDEX OF LEADING CASES

INDEX

*Cases discussed   †Trials discussed